BANKING THEORY 1870–1930

**Edited and with a new introduction by
Forrest Capie and Geoffrey E. Wood**

BANKING THEORY 1870–1930
Edited and with a new introduction by Forrest Capie and Geoffrey E. Wood

VOLUME 6

The Amalgamation Movement in English Banking 1825–1924

Joseph Sykes

London and New York

First published by P.S. King and Son, London in 1926
This edition published by Routledge 1999
Routledge
11 New Fetter Lane
London EC4P 4EE

Banking Theory 1870–1930
7 Volumes: ISBN 0–415–20159–4
Volume 6 ISBN 0–415–20165–9

Routledge is an imprint of the Taylor & Francis Group

This is a reprint of the 1926 edition
Typeset in Times by Routledge
Printed and bound in Great Britain by T.J.I. Digital, Padstow,
Cornwall

British Library Cataloguing in Publication Data
A CIP record of this set is available from the British Library

Library of Congress Cataloging in Publication Data
A catalog record for this book has been requested

THE AMALGAMATION MOVEMENT IN ENGLISH BANKING, 1825-1924

BY

JOSEPH SYKES,

B.A. (Leeds), M.Com. (Manchester),

ASSISTANT LECTURER IN ECONOMICS, UNIVERSITY COLLEGE, EXETER

LONDON
P. S. KING & SON, LTD.
ORCHARD HOUSE, 14 GREAT SMITH STREET
WESTMINSTER
1926

CONTENTS

PREFACE

THE movement towards consolidation in English banking has been a pronounced feature of its development since the first years of the present century. Like many other large movements exhibiting similar characteristics, however, it has been in progress over a long period of years in one or other of its somewhat diverse forms. In the latter part of the seventeenth century, for example, there are definite instances of amalgamation ; and there have since doubtless been many others. But not until the discovery in the 'twenties of the nineteenth century, that joint-stock banks might actually be set up, and until subsequent agitation had provoked the passing of the 1826 Act, was it possible for the concentration movement to assume its modern phase. Since this date saw the beginnings of the joint-stock movement, which gave a direct and powerful stimulus to amalgamation policy, it is from this time that the history is related.

The whole period has been divided into five sections. The first three are based on dates which were notable ones for banking history, each of which gave a special impetus to the banking current ; e.g. the 1844 Act had a definitely arresting influence on joint-stock growth, while it gave assistance to private firms, but the 1862 Act stimulated company enterprise to the detriment of the private bank, and the 1890 crisis was the last occasion of those when the banking structure was threatened with certain collapse. The period 1890–1924 saw so much activity in amalgamation moves that it was found necessary to divide it, and the date most suitable for doing this was 1902—the year which saw the final break up of the private system.

The method used throughout each chapter of the history has been to state the general causes of the events occurring during the period, then to quote illustrative instances, and lastly to refer to unusual and exceptional arrangements. The choice of this has been determined by the large number of individual amalgamations (well over five hundred) which have taken place, and by the great difficulty of extracting necessary information from over-secretive bankers. In one or two cases it has been found impossible to obtain full information, largely because sources do not now exist.

It may be pointed out, finally, that the subject has been found so large as to need a specialised attention throughout, so that many useful comparisons with other banking systems and other aspects of the general movement towards consolidation and expansion have necessarily been omitted.

It is here that acknowledgment should be made of the great assistance which has been given by many present-day bankers and others. In particular, Sir D. Drummond Fraser has assisted and advised on the work on many occasions, and has read through the whole of the MS. Sir Felix Schuster facilitated greatly an inquiry into the records of the National Provincial Bank and the Union Bank of London. Dr. Walter Leaf supplied records of the amalgamations of the Westminster Bank, while the executives of Lloyds Bank and Barclays Bank and the Bank of Liverpool and Martins, gave me many details respecting the growths of these concerns. Mr. F. E. Steele gave considerable assistance, mainly by indicating an extensive bibliography, while Sir Herbert Hambling, Sir Charles Addis, and Mr. Henry Bell provided helpful discussions of various points.

I am indebted to Mr. D. Spring-Rice for safeguarding my inquiries into Money Market developments, and reading passages relating thereto ; while Mr. E. Sykes and Mr. F. Gray have rendered many courtesies at the Institute of Bankers.

Mention should also be made of my gratitude to the surviving witnesses who appeared before the 1918 Bank Amalgamations Committee, all of whom allowed me to read their evidence. And lastly, Mr. T. S. Ashton, M.A., of the University of Manchester, was an inspiring guide and stimulating adviser throughout.

INTRODUCTORY HISTORICAL NOTE

SOME mention should be made of the condition of general banking prior to 1825—the year from which the history following is related.

The material available for this is scanty, but it seems clear that the Act of 1708, and subsequent confirming Acts, account for the utterly one-sided development of banking enterprise which obtained until the passing of the 1826 Act. The former Act definitely provided that (with the exception of the Bank of England) the number of partners in a banking firm was not to exceed six. This, therefore, set a limit to the size of banks, and in effect dictated that only small private firms, working over a delimited local area, should be formed. The absence of transport facilities, and the concentration of large wealth in the hands of a relatively small number of people, were also factors contributing to this eighteenth century type of growth. Most banks indeed did not possess more than one office.

It appears that developments in the first half of the century were slow and comparatively unimportant; and that not until the effects of the changes wrought by the Industrial Revolution in the latter half were being felt, and until the profitable nature of banking by issuing excessive and inconvertible notes was fully realised, did local country banking greatly extend. Even so late as 1797, according to the evidence of John Tritton to the Bullion Committee of 1810, there were only 230 private country banks in existence—although certainly failures were of such frequent occurrence as to detract from the significance of this figure. Nevertheless, the fact that the same witness mentioned that in 1808 and 1810 respectively the numbers were about 600 and 721, shows that greater progress was registered in later years. This statement receives support from the facts that the Post Office Directory of 1803 records 387 country private banks, and in 1814 so many as 940 licences were issued in the aggregate.

Figures, however, are not so clear a guide to banking developments during this early period (especially since many which are available are obviously not accurate), as the quality of the banking itself. From a MS. which indicates in great and accurate detail the nature of banking development in Yorkshire,[1] it is evident that the importance of banking, the necessity for safety, and for the provision of sufficiently varied facilities, were by no means recognised. For instance, it might be mentioned that a private bank was conducted in Whitby in the late eighteenth and early nineteenth century, by a lady of the name of Margaret Campion, who was also a general merchant, a sail-cloth maker and dealer, and a wine merchant. Little wonder that her bank failed! Another Whitby example of the same period is the firm of Clark Richardson and Hodgson, which carried on (in addition to banking) the business of drapers, wine merchants, and mercers. The following comment by the author of *Observations on Banks of Issue and the Currency* (1841)[2] contains a useful and apposite generalisation on this point :

" The country banks of England had been a source of great derangement, and it is a matter of astonishment that they had been suffered to continue so long possessed of such vast privileges and such vast power, without measure or control. A general dealer getting into good trade and credit in a country town would separate a window off from his store and write ' Bank ' upon it and then commence the issue of notes " (p. 15).

The unsafe and unscientific character of the local banking which was the outcome of the restrictive 1708 Act, and subsequent confirming Acts, is shown also by such facts as that in 1814–16, 240 country banks failed as a result of unwise lending of money on farm mortgages,[3] and that in the 1825–6 crisis, 104 banks, involving liabilities of £18,750,000, came to grief.[4]

---

[1] Backhouse MS. (Private Collection).   [2] D. Price.
[3] Vide p. 4 of the text.   [4] *British Losses by Banking Failures* (1858).

In view of the extremely undesirable state of affairs revealed by these disclosures, there can be little wonder that Joplin's agitation was successful in securing the passing of the 1826 Act authorising the formation of joint-stock banks; and sympathy will be felt with Lord Liverpool's declaration of 1826 that " If such a system can be formed there can be little doubt that it would ultimately extinguish and absorb all that is objectionable and dangerous in the present banking establishments." [1]

From this brief account it will be apparent that amalgamation developments in this period were necessarily confined to the union of one or more—usually the former—local banks with another, and these were generally restricted to alliances between families connected by blood relation or friendship. Largely, too, it was only resorted to for the purpose of supplying gaps in existing partnerships— even though partnerships were not so numerous as banks conducted by individual proprietors. These were not by any means of the same economic significance as the various types of amalgamation discussed in the following chapters, and for this reason, as well as the fact that they belong to another and distinct period, no further discussion of them is undertaken. But it is hoped, if only because of their attractive and romantic nature, that a study of them will not be long delayed.

[1] Quoted in *A View of the Banking Question* (Anon., 1832).

Part I

CHAPTER I.

HISTORICAL SURVEY, 1825–1843.

WITH the passing of the Act of 1826 banking in England began to undergo a change, inasmuch as joint-stock companies could then be formed to take a share in the general banking business of the country.   Movement was, however, neither sudden nor spectacular, for the difficulties attendant upon the commencement of a totally new type of company business were many.   The chief of these was obviously that of securing a sufficient number of persons possessing a satisfactory knowledge of banking practice to set up and staff the new banks.   Additionally, the Act of 1826 did not permit the formation of banks in London, and this was a severe handicap to progress.   The result was that only eleven companies were created in the first three years, compared with thirty-nine in the first seven years.[1]   Not until the passing of the Act of 1833, which authorised the establishment of joint-stock banks in the metropolis, did the movement make headway ; but by 1841 it is reported that 118 new joint-stock banks were in full working, while some had already disappeared.[2]

Such a development could not occur without affecting the position of the private houses.   And, indeed, their numbers were seriously reduced during the period, for in 1825 there were 554, and in 1841 only 311.[3]   Of this reduction there is

---

[1] Speech by Mr. Clay in Parliament, reported in *The Times* of May 13, 1836.

[2] The *Atlas*, January 27, 1844, says : " From 1841 to 1842 the number of the former was 311, and of the latter 118" (private and joint-stock banks respectively).

[3] Parliamentary Return No. 85, Session 1843.

more than one explanation, but, generally speaking, it may safely be ascribed to the progress of the newly created joint-stock firms, and to the number of failures occurring between the two dates mentioned. Closer investigation shows that there were from 1825–43 a number of disappearances due to the amalgamation of one bank with another, and, indeed, it seems as if this too were a separate and distinct reason for the fall in the number of private bankers. Actually, however, this supposition is not correct, for a detailed analysis which it is now proposed to attempt, shows that it is not a separate cause, but is the effect of the working, together or separate, of the two reasons mentioned above.

In beginning the analysis, it is necessary to observe that the materials available for such a study are not plentiful. With one or two notable exceptions, it appears that the early bankers, joint-stock as well as private, were not accustomed to keep records of their progress, beyond periodical statements of account. In the case of the private banks, which were usually conducted by members of one or two families at the most, it is not difficult to understand the reasons for this, as there was no necessity to inform a wide circle of people of the activities of the bank. Indeed, secrecy in affairs was obviously desirable for that type of business. In the case of the joint-stock banks, their modern descendants possess no records beyond the half-yearly statements of account, which were more often read to than circulated amongst the early shareholders. The idea underlying this practice was to prevent rival banks and also joint-stock competitors from obtaining information which might possibly assist them in the struggle to obtain business. In the case of some of the large joint-stock banks, indeed, e.g. the London and County, no mention is made (in reports) of some of the earlier absorptions in which they were concerned as principals. Again, it appears that some of the records and books which did survive have been consigned for the purpose of making pulp during the late war. For this period at least, therefore, it is necessary to turn to other sources for information.

The first source is a pamphlet by D. Hardcastle, Jr.,

written in 1842, entitled *Banks and Bankers*.   On page 257 he says :

" The most interesting fact, however, connected with the progress of these institutions, is the number of private banks that had by this time emerged into joint-stock establishments. There were computed to have been not fewer than 130 in 1839, during which year the old and respectable house of Sir M. W. Ridley and Co., of Newcastle, also resolved itself into a joint-stock company."

Another pamphlet,[1] written anonymously in 1846, referring to the downfall of the private banks, says :

" Of these we find one hundred and fifty-four, who, foreseeing the downfall of their own system, have become incorporated with various joint-stock banks.   The number of such changes was in—

1827	15	1836	55
1829	3	1842	3
1831	10	1843	4
1832	2	1844	1
1833	30	Unknown dates	11
1834	16		—
1835	4		154 "

Detailed examination of the individual amalgamations and other contemporary sources shows, however, that the table quoted in the anonymous pamphlet of 1844 is not accurate, for the total number of amalgamations has been arrived at by counting the absorption of each branch of the same bank as one complete amalgamation.   In doing this no allowance has been made for cases where all the branches of one bank were amalgamated with one joint-stock bank, but each has apparently been counted as a separate fusion. Again, where branches of the same bank each amalgamated with a separate outside bank, no allowance has been made ; and some of the dates are not accurate.

The explanation of the irregularity seems to be that in the early part of the century it was customary to regard each office of the same or another bank as a separate bank.   The new table, based on the other sources mentioned, is given below. It will be noted that whereas the previous table did not

---

[1] *A Contrast between the Rival Systems of Banking*, p. 3.

include the amalgamations in which joint-stock banks were concerned, these are now included for the sake of completeness.

Year.	Private with Private.	Joint absorbs Private.	Joint with Joint.	Private absorbs Joint.	Total.
1826	6	3	—	—	9
1828	—	1	—	—	1
1829	1	3	—	—	4
1831	1	1	—	—	2
1832	—	2	—	—	2
1833	—	2	—	—	2
1834	—	6	1	—	7
1835	3	5	—	—	8
1836	4	26	2	—	32
1837	—	3	1	—	4
1838	2	1	—	—	3
1839	1	2	—	—	3
1840	—	5	1	—	6
1841	3	3	—	—	6
1842	2	6	—	—	8
1843	—	7	1	—	8
Unknown dates .	—	17	—	—	17
	23	93	6	—	122

The arresting feature of this table is the large proportion of amalgamations of private by joint-stock banks. Almost equally notable is the smallness of the number of instances in which two private banks join.

Both these features demand explanation. At first glance it would seem as if special causes were at work to bring about the disappearance of private firms, and in view of the large numbers of amalgamations in 1833, 1834, and 1836, their speedy disappearance. And from what is known of the earlier history of private concerns, it is evident that periodically there were numerous failures. In a speech made by Sir Robert Peel in Parliament he said : " I go further, I go back to the years 1814, 1815, and 1816. In

those years over 240 country banks failed, and there were 89
commissions of bankruptcy issued." From a list prepared
by Hardcastle in his pamphlet it appears that as many as
170 private banks failed or suspended payment in the
period 1825-44.[1] In contemporary pamphlets many other
divergent figures are given, but this total corresponds with
detailed particulars given in an authoritative pamphlet
published in 1858, entitled *British Losses by Bank Failures
1820-1857* (Anon.), and its accuracy is therefore attested.
Evidently so many failures had some relation to the
numbers of banks amalgamating, and this conclusion is
supported by the unusually large numbers of banks taken
over in 1826 and 1836,—years in which there were financial
crises,—and the years subsequent to 1836 (in particular
1839-41 inclusive). An examination of the reasons governing a number of individual amalgamations also supports this
conclusion. In 1840, for instance, Messrs. Hammersley's
Bank was absorbed by the National Provincial Bank ;
Hardcastle points out that the private bank failed in that
year.[2] Again, the bank of Sparkes and Co. at Exeter failed
in 1829 and it was absorbed by the Devon and Cornwall
Banking Co.[3] The amalgamation made with the Sheffield
Union Bank in 1843 by Messrs. Shore's Bank, of Sheffield,
was also occasioned by the failure of the latter. *The Times*
of November 21, 1836, reports the failure of the private bank
of J. and J. Connell, of Carlisle. From the deed of settlement of the Carlisle District Bank, formed in the year following, it appears that the business was founded on that of the
private bank. And as a last instance might be quoted the
firm of Douglas Smalley and Co., of Holywell, who, after
failing in 1839, were absorbed by the North and South
Wales Bank.[4] The gist of the whole matter is put in a few
words in Sir C. H. Cave's *History of Banking in Bristol*, when
he says, "Several banking houses were materially weakened,
more than one relinquishing business, while other establish-

---

[1] *Banks and Banking* (2nd edition, 1843), pp. 423-57.
[2] P. 271.
[3] *British Losses by Bank Failures*, p. 19, and *Circular to Bankers*, October 5, 1838.
[4] *Chester Chronicle*, December 14, 1839.

ments, to strengthen themselves, resorted to amalgamation "
(p, 24)

It is clear that this reason does not account for the whole
of the large number of banks amalgamating, and that other
causes were at work.   Undoubtedly the passing of the Act
of 1833, which permitted the formation of joint-stock banks
within 65 miles of London, and affirmed the legality of the
issue of cheques by joint-stock firms, gave an impetus to the
creation of more joint-stock banks and to the development
of those already existing.   This is demonstrated by the comparative figures quoted on page 1.   It may safely be assumed
that this impetus affected the progress of the fusion movement.   For example, the National Provincial Bank of
England was set up as a result of the passing of the Act, and
it immediately set out on the policy which it afterwards
pursued with so much vigour as to cause the absorption of at
least twenty banks in ten years.   Additionally six other
joint-stock companies were established as a result of the
passing of this Act.

Again, the year 1836 was a " mania " year which saw the
creation of no fewer than 47 joint-stock banks.[1]   The movement became very fashionable, following, as it did, the crises
of 1835–6, when many private banks failed.   Even the
Chancellor of the Exchequer gave it his blessing, for he said,
" I look upon the principle of joint-stock companies as one
of the great discoveries of modern times."   And the Parliamentary Committee of that year, though apparently desiring
to criticise the conduct of joint-stock banks, was led to
declare, " A principle of competition exists, which leads to
the extinction of all Private Banks and to their conversion
into banking companies."   The reason for this extraordinary growth is not immediately apparent, but probably
a recognition of their superiority was filling the minds of the
public.   Joint-stock banks had then been in existence for
ten years, and during that short period, even, had made sub-

---

[1] Report presented to Parliament in 1837, which pointed out that by
that year 102 joint-stock banks had been formed, and 47 were formed in
1836 alone.   A pamphlet published in 1842, written by John Wade, entitled
Principles of Money, says : " And in the first ten months of 1836 there
was the large increase of 45 Joint-Stock Banks."

stantial progress. In the majority of cases dividends had been regularly declared and paid.[1] This progress permitted of the London and Westminster Bank issuing in 1836 9,333 shares at a premium of £4½ per share.[2] It was seen too that the arguments contained in the prospectuses of such banks as the Northamptonshire Banking Co., the North of England Joint Stock Banking Co., and the London and Westminster Bank, were not merely vain assertions, but were vindicated by results.[3]

It is interesting to observe as well, that about this time a surprising number of books, pamphlets, and periodicals are to be found setting forth the merits or demerits of each system, e.g. works by Gilbart, Joplin, Vincent Stuckey, Macardy, in favour of joint-stock; and by George Farren, Thomas Doubleday, Attwood, and anonymous writers, for private banks. The newspapers of the time, such as the *Banking Atlas*, the *Circular to Bankers*, *The Times*, and *The Globe*, all bear witness to the keen discussion prevailing. For the sake of illustration of the various views advanced, two which are representative are included here. Writing in 1833 Farren[4] refers to the banks of Messrs. Child, and Snow and Dean, of London, as examples of the solidity of private banks: arguing that both had functioned uninterruptedly

---

[1] E.g. The London and Westminster paid first 4 per cent., then 5 per cent., and later 6 per cent.

[2] Vide Reports. The 1839 report of Moore and Robinsons', Nottinghamshire, Joint Stock Bank, also points out that—" They had also the satisfaction of stating that the shares sold during the year had realised an advanced premium."

[3] An extract from the prospectus of the London and Westminster Bank will serve to illustrate the nature of these : " The capital cannot be diminished by either deaths or retirements; their numerous proprietors ensure to them confidence and credit, as well as ample business on deposits, loans, and discounts ; and their rigid exclusion of every kind of mercantile and special transaction affords a satisfactory guarantee to the community at large that their means are only employed in legitimate banking operations. They are under the management and control of men who are elected by the respective proprietors, who have no individual interest which can induce them to depart from an approved prudential course, and who are a safe and constant check upon every officer in the several establishments ; and their system of accounts is so accurate that there is little trouble in producing at any time a clear and full statement of their stock and business, however great the one or extensive the other."

[4] *Hints on the Legal, Practical, and Mercantile Difficulties attending the Foundation and Management of Joint-Stock Companies,"* Guildhall Library, London.

since 1650.   He affirms that partners were necessarily more confidential than ordinary directors ; and that there was a prevalent opinion that joint-stock banks were not so secret in their dealings as their rivals.   To people accustomed to personal dealings in every sphere of life, this was a consideration of weight.   Joint-stock companies, he says, were subject to many legal disabilities.   Additionally the Bank of England was hostile to them, as shown by the fact that during the railway boom of the 'thirties the Bank issued a statement that no bills would be discounted if they carried the endorsement of a joint-stock bank.   To this there was a reply by " Civis " in the same year.   He demonstrated that in 1810 there were 70 private bankers in London, whereas by 1833 no fewer than 22 had stopped payment, out of which 19 were really insolvent.   On the contrary, as evidence of joint-stock progress, he cited the third report of the Manchester and District Bank to show that it had secured over 700 customers, (none of whom were proprietors,) in Manchester.   This, in a stronghold of the private bankers, was no mean achievement.

It appears from such writings that it was easier to display the merits of the new system than to defend the old, and this, coupled with the aggressive tactics of the *Banking Atlas* and the success of the system, undoubtedly took effect on the public mind.

Lastly, the advantages of the system of branches, on which joint-stock banks from the first concentrated, were in course of realisation.   The National Provincial Bank had, by May 1836, at least 47 branches in different parts of the country ; the Commercial Bank of England had 18 ; and Stuckeys had 16 establishments in Somerset.   The contrast in this respect to the attitude of the private bankers is well shown by a quotation from the evidence given by Mr. Robert Paul to the 1826 committee on Small Note Currency.   He said :

" Bank branches were accompanied with so much hazard, require such constant watching and inspection, and involve us altogether in such a degree of superintendence, that, upon the whole, my general impression is that the branches are not the most advantageous part of our business.",

There are many examples of amalgamation carried out during this year of activity, e.g. Messrs. Chapman's business at Newcastle was sold to the Newcastle, Shields and Sunderland Union Joint Stock Bank.[1] The reasons cited were the purchase consideration of £20,000, the death of the senior partner, but especially the rage for joint-stock banks. Another excellent instance is the absorption of Sir William Chaytor and Co. by the Newcastle, Shields and Sunderland Union Bank, "partly " (as the circular put it) " because some of the partners were getting up in age, and partly because it was thought that the joint-stock banks, then very popular, would take away the business from the private banks."

One of the most interesting uses of amalgamation machinery is displayed in a number of arrangements recorded in 1836. This was for a joint-stock bank about to be or newly founded, to absorb a private business in order to get a definite hold on a considerable volume of business at one stroke. In some cases this took the shape of purchasing businesses which were not quite so prosperous or safe as they had been formerly, and in these cases the bargain was mutually advantageous. In others, from the point of view of the joint-stock firms, it was largely a question of expediency. As showing the general tendency towards this method of obtaining business it is interesting to read the following quotation from the prospectus of the London Joint Stock Bank which was issued in 1836 :

" With the view of effecting a consolidation with some London Private Banking firms, a power will be contained in the Deed of Settlement of admitting members of such firms into the directorship ; and shares will be reserved for the purpose of facilitating arrangements of that nature."

A somewhat unusual but very complete example of this process is shown by the following quotation taken from the *Circular to Bankers* of 1836 (p. 331) :

" Four of the private country banks of Shropshire, viz. the Shiffnal, the Newport, the Wellington and the Coalbrookdale, have advertised their intention of forming a joint-stock bank, entitled the Shropshire Banking Co., upon the foundation of their respective businesses and connexions."

[1] This business, together with that of Sir William Chaytor & Co., formed the real basis of the joint-stock bank.

In this case, indeed, the four private banks coalesced in order to form a company, but the same idea of using their private established businesses as a basis for the new departure is the guiding motive. The more common form is exemplified by the setting up of the businesses of the Halifax Commercial Bank on that of Messrs. Briggs and Co., and the Huddersfield and Halifax Union Banking Co. on that of Messrs. Rawson and Co.[1]   Again, Messrs. Aspinall and Co.'s business formed the basis of the Liverpool Central Bank ; Messrs. Hope and Co., of the Liverpool Boro' Bank ; [2] Pares and Co., of the Leicester Joint Stock Bank ; [3] Bywater and Co., of the Leeds Commercial Bank.[4]   Lastly, the case of the formation of the Swaledale and Wensleydale Joint Stock Bank by means of the purchase of the business of Hutton Other and Co., may be cited.[5]

It must be mentioned, for the sake of clearness, that the reasons governing the numerous absorptions of 1836 do not apply specifically to that year alone, but also to other amalgamations which occurred both in earlier and later years. The amalgamation of Sir W. M. Ridley's business with the Northumberland and Durham District Bank in 1839 may be cited as an example, for the circular mentions :

" Having long observed an increasing preference on the part of the public for the proprietary system of banking, as affording, under proper management, both the most unquestionable

---

[1] Records of these banks in the possession of the local offices. The circular announcing the conversion of Messrs. Briggs Bank mentioned that they had foreseen the necessity of converting their business into a joint-stock establishment, but were practically not quite ready when the unexpected issue of their neighbour's circular forced their hand. It is dated April 1836, and the neighbour referred to is the Halifax and Huddersfield Union Bank mentioned above.

It is interesting to note that Messrs. Briggs received £12,500 for their goodwill. In connection with this the following comment, taken from *The Times* of July 8, 1836, anent the conversion of the businesses of Messrs. Hope and Aspinall of Liverpool, is interesting : " This practice seems to have been borrowed from the West of England, where several instances of the kind have taken place, and it is pretty notorious that the parties have contrived to make a very good market for their property out of the arrangement."

[2] *The Times*, July 8, 1836.
[3] *Circular to Bankers*, 1836, p. 325.
[4] *British Losses by Bank Failures* (pamphlet, 1858), p. 43.
[5] *Backhouse Collection and Deed of Settlement*, p. 3.

security, and at the same time a very advantageous investment of capital for the proprietors, we were not indisposed to entertain that proposition." [1]

Again, the business of this joint-stock bank was founded in 1836 by making an alliance with the old-established business of Messrs. Backhouse and Co., of Darlington.[2] Similarly the business of the Dudley and West Bromwich Bank was set up on the business of Messrs. Hordern Molineux and Co., in 1834.[3]

Yet another instance is the formation in 1832 of the Mirfield and Huddersfield Joint Stock Banking Co. With respect to this a Huddersfield newspaper says that:

" Some of the principal business men of Mirfield and neighbourhood, being of opinion that it was desirable to establish a joint-stock banking company, applied to Messrs. Wilson for the conversion of their bank into an establishment of that nature. The request was agreed to, and accordingly a joint-stock bank was formed."

From these citations it is evident, then, that similar reasons governed amalgamations before and after 1836, but the importance of this year as an outstanding landmark is in no way diminished as a result.

The remaining reason for the wholesale amalgamations of the private by the joint-stock houses is to be found in the natural desire of the latter to expand and consolidate their businesses.   This has already been hinted at above, and it is not necessary to go into detail.   It is expedient to point out, however, that there is little if any trace of the movement towards securing a definite expansion governed simply by geographical considerations, by means of amalgamation. This is perhaps due to the comparative newness of the companies, the slow development of transport, and the lack of efficient and trained bankers.   The only conscious expression of such a policy is to be seen in the agreements made by Messrs. Stuckey's Bank.   By the absorptions of Messrs. Whitmarsh and White, Kingslake and Co., Phelps and Co.,

---

[1] Quoted *Atlas*, March 30, 1839.
[2] Backhouse Collection.
[3] *Dudley Banks, Bankers, and Banking Notes* (Perkin), p. 152.

Reeves and Porch, Woodlands and Co., Tufnell Falkner and Co., and Rickets Thorne and Wait, they were able to extend from their base, at Langport, to towns such as Yeovil, Taunton, Crewkerne, Wells, Bridgwater, Bath, and Bristol. All these places are within easy reach of each other, and form a ring of local connections. The policy of the National Provincial was to secure branches in different parts of the country, and in due time to use these as local centres from which to make further developments [1]—an example of this is mentioned in the report of 1841. Referring to the junction made with a bank previously owned by Messrs. Fryer Andrew and Co., the report says :

" The junction had two recommendations. Firstly, that the fields which it embraced had hitherto been comparatively unoccupied by joint-stock banks ; and, secondly, that a link was supplied in the chain of connection between the company's branches in Devonshire and Hampshire."

The amalgamations made by one private bank with another may next be mentioned. Of these there were only three, and they occurred towards the end of the period. All are somewhat special groupings, and represent the strengthening of the businesses of already strong private banks. Particularly is this the case in the absorptions made by Messrs. Glyn and Co. of Messrs. Dorriens and Co., and by Messrs. Currie and Co. of Messrs. Ladbroke and Co.—for these were both London banks of higher status by far than their country brethren. This is shown, if by nothing else, by the fact that these banks survived the amalgamation process until late in the century.

It remains to discuss the amalgamations of the joint-stock concerns with others of the same type. The numbers of these are comparatively few, as may be expected from the fact that banking companies were not extensively set up until the middle 'thirties. And in most cases the absorbed bank had either failed already or was entangled in difficulties from which it could only be extricated by a stronger among its fellows. The Southern District Banking Co., for

[1] *Vide* the earlier reports.

instance, was set up in 1837, but by 1840 it had ceased business, and was taken over by the Hampshire Banking Co.[1] Similarly, the Gloucester City and County Bank failed in 1836 and was absorbed by its former rival—the Gloucester County Bank.[2]

Another notable example is afforded by the ill-starred Northern and Central Bank, which also only survived two years, after commencing business in 1834. Its business was taken by the National Provincial Bank. Perhaps this concern exhibited the most flagrant case of mismanagement and fraud of all others which failed in the period. It issued shares and therefore secured its capital by the method of allowing to each of its shareholders a cash credit to the extent of half the amount paid up on its shares. The directors as well as shareholders consistently overdrew their accounts, and eventually one director owed £23,903, for which the only security held by the bank was the shares he possessed in the bank—for which he had not paid![3] Another bank which found itself in difficulties was the Rugely Tamworth and Lichfield Joint Stock Bank.[4] It was a local concern of small size which was finally taken over by the Isle of Wight Joint Stock Bank. This failed in that year, and again the National Provincial Bank bought the goodwill.

While dealing with this part of the subject it is interesting to note what an able pamphleteer says of the reasons for the many discrepancies and failures among the joint-stock companies in these early years. In his *Principles of Money* (1842), page 17, John Wade refers to

" The discrepancies between the nominal and real capital paid

---

[1] The sixth report of this bank reads : " The Southern District Banking Co. having, in the month of April last, considered it advisable to discontinue their business, their directors commenced a negotiation for the disposal of their several establishments to the Hampshire Banking Co."

[2] "Originated, like the preceding, more in individual fancy than public demand, and notwithstanding the breadth of its title and assumption, succumbed in less than two years to well-established rivals, and became a branch of the County of Gloucester Bank." *British Losses by Bank Failures* (pamphlet, 1858, p. 26).

[3] *Reports, Secret Committee*, 1837, Appendix D, and *Banks, Banking and Currency*, Jos. Macardy (1840), pp. 15–20.

[4] *Reports, National Provincial Bank.*

up—between the regulation number of partners and those actually liable by having signed the deed of settlement—in the concealment by the directors of the liabilities and assets of the bank from the shareholders—in not limiting sales and purchases and speculative traffic—and allowing factitious dividends to be made up and paid without the allowance of losses, and out of other sources than clear banking profits."

The Times of November 26, 1836, also pointed to the evils of the practice of re-discounting. It said :

" Their more immediate danger seems to lie in the practice universally followed by the weak ones among them of endorsing and re-discounting the bills presented to them, the greater part of which liabilities might, by any disastrous turn in commercial affairs, come suddenly into play, and absorb much more than the limited capital they possess."

It remains to discuss the question of the motives causing the large number of amalgamations which have been traced in this period.   Some of these will be evident from the details already given.   The chief one undoubtedly was that the private bankers—and especially the weaker houses—were unable to compete with the new organisation.   The evidence for this is supplied by the number of failures which occurred among private banks, which were certainly not less than 170 for the period 1825–44.   Mismanagement was undoubtedly the main cause of this doleful record, and instances in support could be multiplied.   It will suffice, perhaps, to quote from a speech of Sir Robert Peel (May 20, 1844) :

" The Dover Bank, the latest failure, held balances amounting to £88,600, and the nett profits for twelve years were £16,300, or about £1,350 per annum.   So far from anything being laid aside from this source, we find the partners drawing out about £2,500 per annum, or nearly double the profits ; and yet this bank stood as high as most, and higher than many in the country."

Other causes are to be found in the differences of the methods on which the two systems were managed.   These are excellently described by Gilbart in his book *The Elements of Banking* (2nd edition, 1854).   On page 9, for example, he says :

" The fact that the Private Bankers are generally engaged in some other trade, greatly increases the dangers of this temptation to speculation because it renders it more easy to do so without detection ; thus a Brewer might speculate in hops, a Miller in corn, a Merchant in anything (!) ; and yet no suspicion be excited that they were carrying on illegitimate business with the bank's funds."

Further light on their methods is cast by the statement that :

" Private Banks had copied the methods of the Bank of England and only encouraged large, ' steady ' accounts. It was a point of honour not to accept small and ' unsteady ' accounts. Further, it was not the practice of the private banks to allow interest on balances lodged with them, while the joint-stock banks allowed interest on all sums, whether merely deposited for a long or short time.[1] Lastly, the reserves of the private bankers were often insufficient or not liquid ; [2] the fact that they did not publish any form of account operated to cause this, and generally to encourage unsafe transactions."

All these statements point to the differences existing between the two systems, which had the effect of causing some of the amalgamations described earlier.

A few agreements, however, were due to certain specific causes not already mentioned, e.g. some were due to the intermarriage of two or more families. Others, again, were made simply because the private banker profited by the transaction. It has already been mentioned that Messrs. Chapman's business at Newcastle was sold to a joint-stock bank on payment of £20,000 for the goodwill. It was indicated that the partners were quite satisfied with such a good price. Again, Messrs. Briggs' business at Halifax was

---

[1] Speaking of joint-stock accounts, the writer of an anonymous pamphlet lodged in the Goldsmiths' Library, entitled *The Banker's Clerk* (1843), says : " The rate of interest varies from 2 per cent. or 3 per cent. to 4 per cent. . . . The interest he receives from the parties to whom he lends it is perhaps 5 per cent. or 6 per cent. (p. 40). On p. 43 he says, referring to private bankers : " And they allow no interest on the money lodged, however long it may remain in their hands." . . . " The joint-stock banks allow interest on the sums deposited with them."

[2] The author of the *Circular to Bankers*, a protagonist of private banking, stated to the 1832 Committee (Q. 5557) that private bankers' reserves varied exceedingly—the most usual proportion seemed to be one-quarter of the amount of notes issued. They were held in specie and Bank of England notes, but the proportions of these were not known.

sold for £12,500. For that of the Rawsons at Huddersfield the sum of £25,000 was received—in this instance two branches were open. In other cases it was obviously better to accept the offer of the joint-stock firm at the time it was made than to suffer later from the enhanced competition and greater efficiency of companies. Consequently, there is no doubt that financial reasons governed many of the agreements, as they did in all the years of the period 1825–1924.

The end of the year 1843 found the numbers of the private bankers much reduced, while those of the joint-stock rivals had greatly increased, in comparison with the totals of the earlier years. Yet the struggle was by no means over, since there were still remaining many private houses, e.g. Jones Loyd, Glyn, Bosanquet, Hanbury Lloyd, who were not only stronger and larger than their fallen comrades, but were almost as strong as some of the joint-stock banks. How they fared in following years will be discussed in subsequent chapters.

Gathering together the various reasons for the disappearance of so many private bankers and so few joint-stock we may summarise by saying that the failure of individual private bankers was one important cause, and many such banks were absorbed by the more comprehensive companies. Probably the most important reason, however, was that after the 1833 Act was passed, joint-stock companies made steady, if irregular progress, and secured a notable share of public favour. Especially is this true of years when company promotion became very fashionable, when the private concerns, bowing to public opinion, took refuge in amalgamation. Many joint-stock companies realised the great advantage of founding their businesses on those of private banks already established, and this was a strong cause of amalgamation—especially in 1836. Again, some private bankers foresaw that companies would gradually wrest business from them, and were disposed to take advantage of the good terms offered them at boom periods. Once established, the companies at first found business difficult to procure, if only because the movement was at times overdone. Additionally, those companies which had been in existence a few years often found that growth was not so rapid as they desired.   In both cases it was found that amalgamation with a private bank in the same areas provided a speedy and certain growth of business, with the result that there are numerous examples of this type of alliance.   Linked to this is the effect of the adoption of the branch policy by the companies.   From the first few years this was so successful that private bankers, finding themselves unable to compete, resorted to amalgamation.

Those alliances made between one private bank and another were relatively few.   They were arranged in order to resist joint-stock progress, and usually because of family ties such as marriage and intermarriage.

Also few in number were the absorptions of one joint-stock bank of the businesses of others, and these were mainly due, as may be expected, to the failure of small and badly administered concerns.

CHAPTER II.

HISTORICAL SURVEY, 1844-1861.

THE period now to be surveyed is nearly the same length as that which preceded it. But in this respect alone, perhaps, are the two periods alike. Compared with 1825–43, which was a time of activity in the amalgamation world, when the total number of alliances averaged over six yearly, this period is seemingly uneventful, for the yearly average is under three, and the full total is 44, compared with 122.

As the natural conditions governing amalgamations were not suddenly changed, and as there were still many private banks in existence, a large number of which were by no means so well established as the banking companies, it is only to be expected that amalgamations would be registered nearly, if not quite so fast as in the earlier period. Evidently some strong cause or causes of an artificial character were responsible for the check. Largely these are to be found in the passing of the Bank Charter Act, and the Joint Stock Banks Act of 1844. For some time previous the condition of the Bank of England's note issues had given rise to considerable dissatisfaction. There had been crises in 1835–6–7, 1839, and a period of unsettled trading accompanied by unstable financial conditions from 1840 to 1842. A Parliamentary Committee was set up to investigate the position, and this led to the passing of the Bank Charter Act.

Closely linked with the discussion as to the note issues was the relative position of the private and joint-stock banks respectively : and it was part of the task of the committee to decide how these should be regulated in order that the proposed legislation should fully achieve its end. How these types of banking concerns were affected is best seen by considering the main provisions relating to them. Stated briefly these were :

(1) If any country bank were to cease from any reason to issue notes, the Bank of England was empowered to issue its own notes to the extent of two-thirds of such lapsed issue.

(2) If any bank failed, its right of issue expired automatically.

(3) A maximum issue was prescribed for country bankers, based on their circulation prior to the passing of the Act.

(4) No new banks were to have the power of issuing notes.

(5) If any private bank increased its partners to more than six, it was to lose the right of issue. If the number of partners were maintained at six or less, the note issue was not affected.

(6) Two country banks, one of which did, and the other of which did not, possess the right of issue, might unite without losing the one note issue. But

(7) If two joint-stock country banks, each of which possessed a note issue, were to unite, only the issue of the absorbing bank was in future to be permitted.

(8) In the case of two joint-stock banks amalgamating one of which had an office in London or within 65 miles of London, or that of a joint-stock bank having a note issue uniting with a private bank situate in London or within the radius, then the Act of 1833 applied, and the right to issue was forfeited. Incidentally it might be noted that

(9) A similar result occurred if a country joint-stock bank with a right to issue opened a London office.

These numerous provisions were elaborated with the view of protecting the rights of those banks which formerly possessed a note issue, but additionally they were so designed as to give the eventual monopoly of the note issues to the Bank of England, and to prevent the growing joint-stock banks from acquiring, through amalgamation, excess issues.[1] It remains to discuss the effect which they had on the movement towards amalgamation. In the first place private banks were definitely permitted to ally themselves, so long as they took the precaution to maintain only the statutory number of partners. As this was a matter of arrangement only, a new lease of life was therefore offered to these concerns, since had amalgamation pursued its normal course, there is no doubt that many of them would have been taken over. Again, the natural current of amalgamations which flowed so strongly after 1833 was diverted.

Secondly, the larger country banks—whether private or joint-stock—were stimulated to join with banks which did not possess a note issue. , Here again (though perhaps it was relatively unimportant) the current was diverted. Thirdly, the alliance of joint-stock banks, or a joint-stock with a private bank—in the cases where the bank which it was proposed to take over had no right of issue—were not encouraged. Lastly, the fusion of country banks with London concerns was decisively negatived, and ambitious country banks were deterred from making advances in the London area so long as these institutions possessed a note issue.

Nor was this the whole effect, for if a bank were driven to liquidate, the law offered no encouragement to other banks to rescue it by the process of absorption. In view of the number of such cases in the earlier years, and also bearing in mind that banking was as yet neither safe nor scientific, this was an important provision tending to take away one of the few banking safeguards. It should be mentioned additionally that Section 2 of the Act required all shares to be of a denomination not less than £100. This naturally tended to restrict greatly the number of shareholders, and operated as an effective check to the formation of new banking companies. If it is remembered that there

---

[1] One reason given in a speech by Sir Robert Peel for the restrictive legislation of 1844 is (quoted by the *Atlas*): " In fact, he was resolved to restrain joint-stock banks under any circumstances from increasing their present amount of issue . . . that is, he would not allow joint-stock banks to absorb private banks and buy up their issues " (1844, p. 339).

are numerous instances in the first period of new banks absorbing private businesses in order to provide an adequate foundation for the new venture, it will be recognised that here was another check on the joining of private to joint-stock firms. Lastly, the Act prevented the union of strong banks, while it artificially stimulated the joining of banks which were inherently weak. This was a development which must be deprecated, for two joint-stock banks, with 1,000 partners and a circulation of £100,000 each, could not join without losing, say, £2,000 per year. On the other hand, two private banks each possessing six partners and a circulation of £100,000, might amalgamate and retain a circulation of £200,000.

To summarise, then, the tendency of the Act was undoubtedly a reactionary one, inasmuch as it clearly struck various blows at a customary and valuable method of joint-stock expansion, and deferred the development, on evolutionary lines, of the system best equipped to serve the growing financial needs of the country. The result is seen in the low number of agreements registered, and the fact that only one new joint-stock bank was set up between 1846 and 1860.[1]

To some extent the effects of the Act were offset by developments during the period. For example, the gold discoveries of the years 1851 and following years naturally operated to stimulate banking. Similarly the development of the facilities of penny postage, first instituted in 1840, and the use of the railways for carrying mails, contributed to the more effective linking of the districts. This had the effect of assisting the growth and spread of banking opera-

---

[1] The view advanced by Geo. Rae, the well-known country banker to the 1875 committee, is of interest. Replying to Q. 5576, he said : " I think there are restrictions placed by the Act of 1844 as to the transference of the circulation from one bank to another bank, which have been uncertain in their working. . . . If they had been allowed the privileges of amalgamation on the same principles as the Scotch Banks, I take it that we should find the English circulation far closer to its authorised limit than it is at the present moment."

The *Economist* of February 13, 1858, has it that : " The reason why no new banks have been established since 1844 must undoubtedly be referred to the provisions of the two Acts passed in that year, the Joint Stock Bank Act and the Bank Charter Act."

tions. More important still was the effect of the admission of joint-stock banks to the London Clearing House in 1854. Previously the Private Bankers had very jealously guarded the privileges resulting from membership of the Clearing House, and membership was limited to a few select concerns. The admission of the joint-stock banks is a landmark in the history of their development, since it simplified and cheapened, and therefore assisted the process of cheque clearing. Lastly, it is necessary to point to the growth of the use of cheque currency. In 1840 a pamphleteer declared that there had been a distinct increase in the use of cheques, and that two-thirds of the total business was transacted by the use of this instrument.[1] By 1855, in which year it was proposed to put a penny stamp on cheques for revenue purposes, they had become so extensively used that the bankers united to oppose such a step, which they regarded with much seriousness.

All these developments assisted the quicker growth of company banking, and in particular the increased use of cheques rendered the note issues of less importance, so that with the progress of the years the loss of the note issue, consequent on amalgamating, became a less serious matter. The natural result was to revive this handy method of obtaining progress, although it can hardly be said to occur in the present period.[2]

Of the 44 amalgamations recorded it is noteworthy that an analysis shows that the largest number of absorptions were those of private by joint-stock banks, viz. :

Private with Private.	Joint Stock absorbs Private.	Joint Stock with Joint Stock.	Total.
11	23	10	44

[1] " The circulation of notes has of late years undergone, and is still undergoing, considerable changes by the general introduction of cheques . . . so that in the exchanges constantly had among Bankers two-thirds of the amount are now in cheques, the remainder only in notes, whereas a few years ago the proportions would have been just the contrary." *Sketch of Country Bank Practice*, by a Country Bank Manager (Rylands Collection).

[2] In support of this it may be mentioned that, although the National Provincial Bank had possessed its premises in Bishopsgate since 1838 (as shown in the report for that year), it was not deemed advisable to forfeit the note issue until 1866, in order to establish the much desired London branch.

This leads to the assumption that there were still many private bankers who felt the strain of competing against the more advantageous system of their rivals, and who were driven to seek safety in fusion. A quotation taken from an impartially written pamphlet before mentioned [1] points to the accuracy of this assumption. The writer says :

" Several other conversions have since occurred " [i.e. since 1844], " and it is known that many more would gladly have thrown themselves into the arms of their provincial rivals if they could have exhibited a clear balance sheet—or in common parlance, if they could have found the means of paying their liabilities in full—a necessary part of any such arrangement."

The absorption of the business of Messrs. Dixon Dalton and Co. of Birmingham, in 1849, by the first Birmingham Joint Stock Banking Co., is an excellent instance. In 1849, too, the London and County Bank took over the business of Messrs. Trapp Halfhead and Co., which had apparently fallen into a very weak condition. Ten years later, the same bank acquired the firm of Messrs. Robt. Davies and Co. on its failure.[2] Speaking of this aspect of the London banks' business, Mr. Jas. Knight read a paper to the British Association in 1854 in which he said : " This institution is remarkable for the number of its branches, and the influence which, since the accession of the present general manager, Mr. Luard, the bank has acquired by the judicious absorption of weak private banks in country towns." The failure of Messrs. Ledgard and Co. in 1860 was the means of adding to the well-established business of the National Provincial Bank yet another private concern.[3] Another London bank, the London and Westminster, purchased in 1856 the goodwill of the business of Messrs. Strahan Paul and Co. after that house had made a disastrous failure in the preceding year.[4]

It will be obvious that not all the agreements coming

[1] *A Contrast between the Rival Systems of Banking*, A Country Manager (1846), p. 4.

[2] Reports—London and County Bank, and *British Losses by Bank Failures* (1858), p. 51.

[3] Reports—National Provincial Bank.

[4] Report of proceedings of meeting, 1857.

under this head are of the same type. For instance, the purchase of the business of Messrs. Dixon and Co. by the Union Bank of London in 1859 hardly seems to belong to this category, as the cause cited in the circular was ill-health. In *A Monetary Manual* (Anon., 1861) there is the following comment : "The extensive business of Messrs. Dixon, Private Bankers, was some time ago transferred to the Union Bank, with, it is understood, considerable advantage to the latter " (page 87). It would therefore seem to be a case where illness caused the necessity for disposing of the business. In 1858 the National Provincial Bank bought the business of Mr. Moore's bank, the reason cited being that the owner desired to retire after being in business over fifty years. In cases like these, however, it is difficult to discover exactly what were the deciding reasons to cause amalgamation. It must always be remembered that the joint-stock banks were both able to and desirous of securing a business already established, because they were able to offer advantageous terms for it. How far the financial reason prevailed it is impossible to say, but the views of modern bankers who have had experience in this type of amalgamation are that price was always a great consideration with the private bankers. When, in 1853, the National Provincial[1] acquired the business of Messrs. Kinnersley and Sons, there were the somewhat exceptional circumstances that all the partners had died, and the business had not been sold. The executors therefore took steps to dispose of it without delay to the joint-stock bank. Lastly, the amalgamation which caused, perhaps, the greatest stir in the ranks of the private banks, should be noticed. This resulted from the absorption, by the London and Westminster Bank in 1849, of the London private house of Messrs. Young and Sons,[2] and is explained by the fact that a London private bank had never before been absorbed by a joint-stock bank, since all the private concerns which had been acquired by the banking companies had been situate in the provinces. Actually this was the first of a series of similar absorptions.

[1] Report, 1854.
[2] Records of Amalgamations, Westminster Bank.

Turning to inquire what were the reasons for the increase in the number of alliances of private banks among themselves, it is necessary to remember that this aspect of amalgamation was scarcely in evidence in the earlier period, whereas now 22 private banks coalesced. The main reason is to be found in the provisions of the Act of 1844, since it has been shown that they had the specific effect of stimulating this type of fusion. An excellent example is the alliance of Messrs. Barnard and Co. with Messrs. Dimsdale and Co. in 1852. They were London banks which took advantage of the Act to preserve in the new bank the issues of both the old concerns. Coupled to this reason is the desire to strengthen themselves against the rival organisation. This reason is especially apparent after the admission of the joint-stock banks to the Clearing House in 1854, e.g. in 1859 Messrs. Fuller and Co. joined interests with Messrs. Sapte Muspratt Banbury and Co.[1] Again, in 1860 Messrs. Lubbock and Co. joined with Messrs. Robarts Curtis and Co. All these banks were members of the Clearing group, and found amalgamation to be the best means of strengthening their positions.[2]

Another reason, of a different type, is supplied by the taking over in 1847 by Sir W. B. Cooke and Co. of the Doncaster business of Messrs. Leatham Tew and Co., of Wakefield, for it appears that the difficulty of maintaining communication between the two towns rendered its sale desirable.[3] This throws an interesting sidelight on the state of transport at that time, and explains why the private bankers did not stray very far from the locality in which they mainly functioned. It also explains the practice of the joint-stock banks linking branches closely together into a chain.

. Somewhat different again from any of the reasons previously cited is that explaining the fusing of two banks

---

[1] *The Times*, 1859, June 15.
[2] The admission to the Clearing of joint-stock banks aroused the enmity of some of the old private bankers. This is illustrated by the story that Lord Overstone, formerly S. J. Loyd, a renowned private banker, remarked after the 1857 crisis that he wished the Treasury suspending letter had arrived twenty-four hours later, for if so the joint-stock banks would have " tumbled to pieces."
[3] Records of Leatham Tew and Co.

functioning in Banbury. The circular to the customers took the following form :

" SIR,—

The recent alterations in the law affecting the business of Banks of Issue have determined us to anticipate the period when a great part of the country's banking business will probably be conducted by companies, chartered under the Act of Parliament passed in 1844 (7 and 8 Vic. 113). Requesting your attention to this Act, we beg to apprise you that a Chartered Banking Co., in conformity with the provisions of the new law, shall commence business here on the 6th April, 1846. . . ." [1]

It is believed that the bankers concerned were Messrs. T. R. and E. Cobb and Messrs. Gillett, Tawney and Co., and that they amalgamated in 1845. They point to the growing character of joint-stock business, and realise that it is their best policy to anticipate the probable trend of events. The alliance is inspired by motives similar to those which inspired the 122 amalgamations in the first period, but possesses the unusual feature that the private bankers still retain their full hold on the business by arranging between themselves to make the necessary conversion.

The third type of amalgamation—namely, the purchase by joint-stock concerns of rival companies—now calls for notice. As was the case in the earlier period, most of these agreements are due to the failures of the absorbed concerns, which are generally the smaller banks. In 1856 the Western Bank of London was apparently on the verge of failure when it was taken under the protecting arm of the old London and County Bank.[2] A small bank, known as the Nantwich and South Cheshire Joint Stock Bank, failed in 1845 and was absorbed into the Manchester and Liverpool District Bank,[3] while in the year 1848 the Sheffield and Retford Bank liquidated and fell to one of its former rivals— The Sheffield Joint Stock Banking Co.[4] The following year

[1] Quoted by A Country Manager in *A Contrast between the Rival Systems of Banking* (1846).

[2] " And would soon have floundered had not its directors transferred its business to the London and County, which must have tended greatly to increase its West End connection." *A Monetary Manual* (Anon., 1861), p. 81.

[3] Pamphlet, *British Losses by Bank Failures* (Anon., 1858), p. 42.

[4] Reports—National Provincial Bank, and *Banking Almanack*, 1846.

the business of the Stockton and Durham Joint Stock Bank was amalgamated with that of the National Provincial—again after the failure of the amalgamated bank.

The latter bank also acquired in 1844 the "very respectable business" of the Isle of Wight Joint Stock Bank.[1] In connection with this amalgamation it is interesting to observe the comment which the writer of *British Losses by Bank Failures* (1858) made as to the failure of this firm. He says (page 42) : "Losses occasioned by the nursing of bad debts and loan accounts purchased from the private bank on which the association was founded." A similar case is that of the Sheffield and Retford Bank, just mentioned, for it was founded on the business of Rimington's of the same town, just over four years before it failed. These are two instances out of others which point to the fact that banking in those days was not conducted in a scientific manner ; otherwise the weaknesses of the private houses would have been more fully realised and allowed for at the time of amalgamation. They demonstrate, additionally, the danger of adopting a bank which was already too far involved to be rescued.

The last example of this type of agreement to be noted is the absorption by the London and Westminster Bank of the Commercial Bank of London in 1860.[2] There then remains but one example of the amalgamation of joint-stock banks in this period, and it appears to be the only one which is not due to the failure of the bank taken over. Actually it seems to have been due to the desire of the County of Gloucester Bank to expand its activities on a local basis, for it took over the Cheltenham and Gloucester Bank in 1856.[3]

---

[1] Report, 1844.
[2] Reports of Proceedings of Meetings, 1860. This amalgamation supplies a good example of the utility of the amalgamation process, as the following extract from *The Times* of February 19, 1861, shows : " A resolution was almost immediately arrived at that it would be better to prevent all anxiety and alarm by transferring the business to the London and Westminster, and thus assuring the depositors of their perfect safety." Its beneficial effect in such a case is apparent, and provided that due allowance was made for the bad debts of the absorbed bank, the danger was not great.
[3] *Bankers' Almanack*, 1857.

The mention of this leads to a consideration as to how the geographical expansion of banking, which (as described in the last chapter) had definitely commenced, progressed during these years.   In the cases of most banks the movement went ahead but slowly, and only in concerns such as the National Provincial was there a change to a policy of wider expansion.   This bank, as has been shown, absorbed concerns so far apart as Durham and the Isle of Wight, and did not hesitate to take a business at Newcastle-under-Lyme, but there is no indication that a conscious policy of preconceived design was being pursued.   Rather was it a policy of opportunism, in seizing the benefits resulting from the failures of competitors.   It is true that the establishments obtained were used as bases from which to open other branches, but the underlying idea of such development is obviously effect rather than cause.   Indeed, most of the amalgamations are still confined to extension into the district immediately surrounding, as is evidenced by such alliances as the North Wilts Bank with Messrs. Everett, Ravenhill and Co.   The latter bank had premises at Warminster, a town immediately outside the area occupied by the joint-stock firm.   Again, the York City and County Bank took over the business of Messrs. Frankland and Wilkinson, of Whitby,[1] and Clark Richardson and Hodgson, of the same town.   Similarly, the Stamford and Spalding Joint Stock Bank obtained the business of Simpson and White at Peterborough.[2]   Lastly, the absorption of Messrs. Craddock and Bull, of Nuneaton, was made by the Coventry Union Joint Stock Bank.[3]

The end of the period is reached, consequently, with no great changes to be recorded.   The effects of the 1844 Act are visible throughout, so that the opportunity is given to the private bankers to strengthen their position, either by seeking increased business or by allying among themselves.   Many such alliances are due to this specific reason, and excellent instances are supplied by the joining of

[1] Backhouse Collection.
[2] *Bankers' Magazine*, 1849.
[3] Circular issued by Craddock and Bell, *Bankers' Magazine* (1861).

private concerns who were members of the Clearing House.
At least one arrangement, however, was due to the necessity
for closing branches which were too distant to be worked
with ease and safety. The general explanation of the
absorptions of private banks by the companies seems to
be identical with one which operated in the earlier period,
i.e. the increasing strength and growth which on the whole
was secured by the majority of joint-stock concerns, tending
to destroy the business of the older bankers, amalgamation
became necessary. In some cases the private firms were
on the verge of failure or had already collapsed, before
being taken over, and some few of these failures were
occasioned by the mismanagement of business, of which the
pamphlet *British Losses by Bank Failures* gives ample
evidence. In other cases the illness, death, or desire to
withdraw from business, of the private partners, was a
sufficient cause of amalgamation. In examples like these,
the gain to be secured from selling the goodwill at so many
years' purchase was always a strong inducement to take
the measures necessary for fusion. The few alliances
between joint-stock concerns solely were again occasioned
by failure, mainly through mismanagement and lack of
banking knowledge, of concerns floated in the " mania "
years referred to in Chapter I. Of geographical extension,
as such, little is to be seen except in the case of individual
progressive concerns such as the National Provincial Bank.

CHAPTER III.

HISTORICAL SURVEY, 1862-1889.

THIS period saw many changes of importance to the commercial world as a whole, and to the banking world in particular. It is a long period which opens with the passing of the Companies Act of 1862, which sees the severe crisis of 1866 and the pressure of 1875, and which closes immediately before the Baring crisis of 1890. Actually, then, it is ten years longer than either of the two periods preceding. Because of this alone, it is to be expected that there will be a record of greater total activity in the amalgamation movement than occurred previously. This expectation is realised, for the number of agreements traced is 138, giving an average of over four each year. This compares with an average of over two for the years 1844-61, and over six for 1825-43. On the one hand it is not greatly desirable to stress the results accruing from such a rude arithmetical measure, but on the other it is necessary to add that the amalgamations of this period are of greater importance than those which have already been discussed. The following is an analysis of the various types :

Private with Private.	Joint Stock absorbs Private.	Joint Stock with Joint Stock.	Private absorbs Joint Stock.	Total.
31	66	40	1	138

Again it is the joint-stock banks which are the largest amalgamators by far, and these figures testify to the progress effected by them throughout the medium of amalgamation. The fact that 64 private concerns lost their identity compared with 21 joint-stock also points to the success which the companies experienced. With this in mind it will be interesting to glance first at the course of events which effected the absorptions of private by joint-stock banks.

It was not until 1858 that banks could be formed on the principle of limited liability, except by Special Act, Royal Charter, or Letters Patent. Even then limited liability was not extended to the note issues, and the lowest nominal share was still £100. The non-removal of these important disabilities and the presence of other troublesome and qualifying provisions prevented banks generally from taking advantage of the Act. It was not till four years later, with the Act of 1862, that the various statutes affecting joint-stock companies were consolidated and elucidated. The most important provision of this Act, so far as banking companies were concerned, was that which permitted liability on shares to be limited. Another clause set the minimum of partners in a banking company at ten. The natural result of these enabling clauses was that there was a considerable and speedy growth in the number of companies formed. This, in turn, provided a stimulant for amalgamation—as is shown by the figures for the separate years 1863–6, which were 8, 10, 8 and 7 respectively. All these are above the average stated on the previous page.

Since the joint-stock companies were so favourably assisted, they made several absorptions in these years. In 1863 and 1864, for example, the private banks lost two of their most distinguished representatives in Messrs. Jones Loyd and Co. and Heywood Kennard and Co. Both these were London banks which possessed a high-class clientèle. Both decided to amalgamate because their best business was drifting from them in consequence of the success of joint-stock rivals.[1] The latter bank was taken by the Bank of Manchester in 1863, and the former by the London and Westminster in 1864. The value of such businesses may be realised from the amount paid for Messrs. Jones Loyd's goodwill, for this was £187,500. As showing the

---

[1] *Bankers' Magazine*, 1864, and *Money Market Review*, April 9, 1864. It is mentioned in *The Lloyds of Birmingham* (by S. Lloyd) that " One of the partners told me that there had been in the last few years a perceptible tendency towards losing the larger accounts and being left with a multitude of small accounts. This was a general experience with private bankers, and has proved a great factor in that rapid conversion of private into Joint Stock banks in which Lloyds, since its incorporation, has taken a leading part" (p. 74).

extent of the changes wrought by the amalgamation process it is interesting to find that the head of Messrs. Jones Loyd and Co. (afterwards Lord Overstone) had declared to the 1840 Committee that " Joint Stock banks are deficient in everything requisite for the conduct of banking business except extended responsibility."

So serious did the event seem to the private banking community at the time that one of their number declared in 1865 that:

" The absorption of Jones Loyd and Co. by the London and Westminster, in 1864, marks an era in the history of joint-stock banking. Private banking has now ceased to be of any importance, and the amalgamation of the still existing houses with great Joint Stock banks has become a mere question of time." [1]

Again, one of the outstanding events of this period, the formation of the modern Lloyds Bank, is apparently largely due to the enhanced position of joint-stock companies, resulting from the Act of 1862. This bank was set up in 1865 and the prospectus announcing it reads:

" The recent alterations in the law affecting banking partnerships and the growing requirements of the trade of the district have determined Messrs. Lloyd and Co. and Messrs. Moilliet and Sons to extend the basis of their present partnerships by converting them into a joint-stock company, with limited liability." [2]

In connection with this alliance, it is interesting to note that the agreement " 12,500 shares ($£12\frac{1}{2}$ paid), to be issued to Lloyd and Co. and Moilliet and Sons " ; 12,500 shares in addition were issued to the public, " and this it is estimated will raise a sum equal to the amount required to be paid for the purchase of the goodwill, so that the whole amount to be received for deposits and subsequent calls may be available for the purposes of the bank." The price paid

---

[1] *Banks and Bankers*, F. Martin, 1865, p. 186.
[2] Lloyds Bank dates back so far as 1765, when it functioned as Taylor and Lloyds Bank. Mr. Taylor was a manufacturer of japanned goods and snuff boxes. Ten years later he committed suicide for some unascertained reason, so that the business passed to S. Lloyd, an ironmaster. From him it passed to the third Sampson Lloyd. Messrs. Moilliet's business represented an amalgamation between Coates Woolley and Gordon, and Moilliet Smith and Pearson.

for the goodwill of these banks was therefore £156,250 nominal, or £218,750 actual.

There are other examples serving to illustrate the well-marked effect of the Act of 1862 on the prosperity of companies, as opposed to private banking concerns. In 1864 the West Surrey bank of Messrs. Mangles was taken over by the South-Eastern Joint Stock Banking Co., and an extract from the circular shows that public opinion was sensible of the benefits accruing from the Act. In the same year the business of the newly constituted Albion Bank was set up on that of the private firm of Messrs. Challis and Son.[1] Again, in the early part of 1863, the Midland Counties Bank was formed in response to the surge of popular feeling, on the basis of a private business.[2]

Another factor influencing the movement now is to be found in the effects of the failure of the old-established house of Overend Gurney and Co. in 1866. It was a heavy one, and it was taken seriously by the financial world, if only because since 1826 the firm had been styled the "Bankers' Bank," on account of its reputation for dispensing help freely at times of crisis. Private banking was adversely affected, especially since the only other important failure was that of Barned's Banking Co., which, although pursuing the methods of a joint-stock company, was also a private concern. This is seen in the record of the 12 amalgamations registered in 1866–8, of which no fewer than 11 concerned private Banks. As an instance may be given the in 1866 purchase of the house of Rogers Olding and Co., of Norwich, by the English Joint Stock Bank. From an unusual source it is learnt that the purchase price was £210,000, for in *The Life of Charles Bradlaugh*, by the Rt. Hon. J. M. Robertson, it is mentioned that : " In 1867 he (i.e. Bradlaugh) brought an action against the English Joint Stock Bank, then being wound up, for £12,000 agreed to be

---

[1] *The Times*, March 7, 1864, and *Bankers' Magazine*, 1864. The *Times* article said : " Public opinion has of late been most decidedly pronounced in favour of joint stock banks. Most men seem to prefer the distinctly ascertained security of a definite published capital and depositors choose to share in the profit arising from the transaction of their business."
[2] *Money Market Review*, October 29, 1864.

paid to him by the general manager for negotiating the purchase of a Norwich banking business for £210,000." Another instance shows the indirect effect of the failure. In 1866 it was announced that Lloyds' newly-formed joint-stock company would take over the business of Messrs. Stephenson, Salt and Co.   The prime cause of amalgamation was death, but it is evident from the tone of the circular that the actual time of amalgamating was dictated by the events of 1866.   This assumption is strengthened by the fact that the private bank appears to have asked to be absorbed.

Another explanation of the taking over of the private by joint-stock concerns is that the private bankers, for a long period after it was first suggested by Peel, refused to publish accounts showing their financial positions.   Some of the joint-stock firms, on the contrary, had published some form of account (if it was only given to the shareholders at annual meetings) from the date of commencing business ; and the majority of the new firms set up in the 'sixties followed their examples.   By degrees, and especially after crises such as those of 1857, 1866, and 1875, the value of accounts became increasingly recognised, and customers began to transfer their business from private to joint-stock firms in consequence.[1]   At one time, when joint-stock balance sheets were showing the favourable results of increased business, the movement almost became a fashion, so strongly was it in evidence.   The result was to cause amalgamation.   Moreover the additional particulars furnished in the joint-stock balance sheets at this time facilitated the course of amalgamation, because a private banker who realised the necessity of selling his business was the better able to choose the bank with whom he deemed it wisest to deal.   It is especially true of the stronger private banks, and when later they began the publishing of accounts this worked in a reciprocal manner.

Again, the joint-stock banks developed strongly and rapidly during this period, and this was a potent cause of amalgamation.   The numerous restrictions of earlier years, and the

---

[1] The 1879 Companies Act provided that there should be a compulsory independent audit of bank accounts and an annual election of auditors. This safeguard naturally assisted the process of transfer.

1844 Act in especial, operated to defer the development of which the later years of the 'thirties had given promise. It has been shown in connection with this point that only one new joint-stock bank was formed from 1846 to 1860 ; on the other hand, from 1860 to 1875 no less than 24 such concerns were set up, all of which are mentioned in Mr. J. Dun's *Banking Statistics*, published in 1875. As showing that this growth did not extend to the rival organisation, it may be pointed out that the *Bankers' Almanack* gives particulars of only one new private concern in the whole period of twenty-eight years. This was set up in 1885, but succumbed nine years later.[1] Evidence of an increased prestige accruing to the companies is given by the fact that, although not admitted to the Clearing House until 1854, by 1867 there were only 13 private firms included, compared with 11 joint-stock. The following accounts of net profit and total working resources also indicate the progress made :

TOTAL RESOURCES OF JOINT-STOCK BANKS.
(Six o's omitted.)

	1850 (Newmarch).[2]	1871 (Palgrave).[2]	1874 (Dun).[3]
London Banks .	64	174	234
Country Banks in England and Wales	97	210	256
	161	384	490

NET PROFITS OF ALL LONDON JOINT-STOCK BANKS.[4]

No. of Banks.	1858.	1863.	1868.	1873.
6.	£262,906	—	—	—
9.	—	£571,764	—	—
10.	—	—	£472,218	—
13.	—	—	—	£783,596
Average per Bank	£45,484	£63,529	£47,222 [5]	£60,274

[1] This was the London and Lancashire Bank of Southport—a local concern—which was taken over by the Mercantile Bank of Lancashire in 1894.

[2] Quoted Palgrave, *Notes on Banking*, p. 5.

[3] Dun, *Journal of Institute of Bankers*, 1877 and 1897.

[4] Abstracted from the balance sheets quoted in the *Bankers' Magazine* of these years.

[5] The depression consequent on the 1866 crisis affected the results for this year.

Lastly, joint-stock banking developed extensively from the policy of opening branches. This is shown in the table following :

TOTAL NUMBER OF BRANCHES IN ENGLAND AND WALES.
(Private and Joint-Stock.)

Year.	Number.
1858 (Palgrave)	1,195
1872[1]	1,779
1881[1]	2,413
1886[1]	2,716

The private bankers did not compete with the joint-stock banks in this respect, for in the *Bankers' Almanack* of 1870, 255 private firms are designated possessing a total of only 517 offices ; 113 joint-stock firms are indicated and these possess 970 offices. The averages per bank are therefore about 2 and nearly 9 respectively. Again, an examination of the individual places at which joint-stock and private banks were established reveals the fact that there was (ignoring large towns) surprisingly little overlapping of areas. From this the inference may be drawn that the companies were utilising the branch system as a means of tapping the resources not previously worked by private concerns, and especially the recently established manufacturing areas such as the Yorkshire West Riding, Lancashire, the Midlands, and South Wales, and the area immediately outside London.

All these points refer to the speedier progress and increased size of the joint-stock companies—more noticeable in the older banks. As mentioned earlier, this was the means of bringing about many amalgamations and absorptions of private banks. As an illustration, mention may be made of the taking over of the well-known Merionethshire Bank of Messrs. Wills by the North and South Wales Bank in 1873. The reason given in the circular, according to the *Bankers' Magazine,* was the recognition of the superiority of company banking, and the desire to share in the advantages of such a system.

So fast was this progress that some developments occurred

---

[1] *Bankers' Almanack.*

which in those days were regarded as little short of revolutionary. For example, in 1884 Lloyds Bank took over two private firms at one and the same step—Messrs. Barnet Hoare Hanbury and Lloyd, and Messrs. Bosanquet Salt and Co. The importance of the move is due to the fact that both these were London banks of standing, which possessed seats in the Clearing House. Lloyds Bank—the joint-stock company had been formed less than nineteen years before—was thus the first country bank to displace a London concern from its status of a clearing bank. Testimony to the progress of company banking, and Lloyds Bank in particular, is afforded if it is recollected that the bank now amalgamated was formed as a result of the fusion of the two Clearing banks which amalgamated in order to safeguard the position now captured. While discussing the agreement it is of interest to quote from the reasons given for it. Messrs. Bosanquet's circular said : " Our partner, Mr. Thos. Salt, M.P., has long been a director of Lloyds Banking Co., and we have been one of their agents in London." . . . " Messrs. Barnet were their other agents in London." Lloyds' circular ran :

" The two banks and the partnerships from which they have been constituted have been connected in origin and business relations for upwards of a century, and the Directors are much gratified with this result of their long association. . . . The large and increasing business of the company has for some time past rendered direct representation in London desirable."

The *Daily Gazette* of March 11, 1884, amplifies the last reason by pointing out that : " There is a prestige about a London bank doing business in the country which an agency cannot supply."

The amalgamation is clearly due to a combination of reasons ; yet it would certainly not have come to pass had not joint-stock concerns made considerable progress in business. To no small extent it was generated by the fact that Lloyds thereby secured London representation. And how highly a London office was valued is apparent from the fact that in 1866 the National Provincial Bank sacrificed the profits on a note issue amounting to £442,371, in order to

D

secure the right to open the London premises possessed since 1838. Other advantages accruing were mentioned by the chairman of Lloyds at the annual meeting. He said :

" We could employ our spare funds to better advantage and more economically and profitably on the spot than from Birmingham. Besides being able to economise on certain expenses we should get a considerable increase of business of a safe character by the change, and we should afford additional convenience to our customers."

Hence the usefulness of amalgamation in obtaining a business in London by the minimum of trouble is emphasised. Other examples might be cited to show the effect on amalgamation progress of the speedy growth of the joint-stock movement, but enough has been said to serve as illustration.

Another outstanding event of the period which contributed to further development was the notorious failure of the City of Glasgow Bank in 1878. This concern failed for £12,500,000. Other banks were dragged down, including the West of England and South Wales Joint Stock Bank. The shareholders were called on to pay so much as £2,750 as call money on each £100 share. The consequence was that joint-stock banking received a set-back, although the failure of four private banks offset this somewhat ; but the real effect was to cause the English banks to give immediate attention to the question of registering under the Limited Liability Act, to which, previously, some banks had not paid much heed. Even now strong opposition was shown by some bank directors and members of the public, but in spite of this, in the years 1880–3 the principle was widely adopted.

The result is seen in the increased average number of agreements registered in the years 1883–91 [1]—the reason being that limitation of liability was a means of adding to the magnitude of joint-stock operations. Doubtless to some extent this was accounted for by the fact that a new and a wealthier type of shareholder was thereby encouraged to

---

[1] The total of agreements registered in these years was 66.

invest in bank shares.   This tended to bring more business, since it was then a cardinal axiom of banking practice that shareholders were expected to become customers of the banks in which they took interests.   Again, as long as unlimited liability existed, the executor of a testator who held shares in a bank was forced to wait three years before he could distribute any part of the estate.   The removal of this restriction naturally made a wider market in bank shares, and so promoted interest in joint-stock banks.

The last explanation of the large number of absorptions of private by joint-stock firms is concerned with the motive of seeking geographical expansion.   It has been mentioned that this was a reason for earlier amalgamations, although the element of deliberate planning scarcely entered into the arrangements made.   In this period the idea undoubtedly served as a basis for geographical expansion on a wider scale than before, but even yet (except in one or two cases like Lloyds and the Midland Bank) it is difficult to trace evidences of a definitely planned movement on an extended basis.   An example of a local extension is afforded by the absorption in 1864 of Messrs. Seymour and Co. (who were domiciled at Basingstoke) by the Hampshire Banking Co. More deliberate, perhaps, were the amalgamations of Messrs. Lock Hulme and Co. and Messrs. McLean and Co. with the Bank of Wales in 1864, because the last-named bank was set up in 1863 with the idea of forming a company to purchase several Welsh businesses.[1]   A similar local extension was made by the Manchester and Liverpool District Bank, for it absorbed Messrs. Alcock and Co., of Burslem, in 1865.[2]   Similarly again, the Manchester and County Bank secured the joint-stock banks trading as the Saddleworth Banking Co (1866) and the Bank of Stockport (1871).   Stuckeys, whose activity in this direction has been already noticed, obtained a stronger grip on the whole business and note issues of Somerset and Devon by taking over Messrs. Badcock and Co., of

---

[1] " A prospectus has been issued by the Bank of Wales . . . The company propose to purchase several of the existing banking establishments in Wales. . . ."   *The Times*, January 22, 1863.

[2] *Bankers' Magazine*, 1865.

Taunton, and Messrs. Dunsford and Co., of Tiverton, in 1873 and 1883 respectively.

Another of the pioneers of geographical expansion, the National Provincial Bank, was comparatively inactive during this period, and it is Lloyds Bank which provides the best instances. In 1872, for example, the business of Messrs. Fryer was absorbed. This was intended to secure expansion and consolidation in home districts, for the report of the chairman's speech as rendered by the *Birmingham Daily Gazette* of May 23, 1872, runs : " They had been on all sides of the town of Wolverhampton—north, south, east, and west— with their branches, and there were many reasons which made it desirable why they should have a basis in that safe and thriving town."   Again, in 1874 Lloyds acquired the Shropshire Banking Co.   Referring to this move the chairman of Lloyds is reported as saying : " The district in which this bank was situate was one peculiarly advantageous for .banking.   It was the southern part of Shropshire, and Shropshire, as they knew, was a wealthy county . . . and the district was one which was peculiarly capable of being developed into a much larger business by a strong bank."   Again, the Birmingham and Midland Bank, as it was then, made extensions by taking over in 1862 the private house of Messrs. Nicholls Baker and Crane, whose business was situate at Bewdley.   In 1883 it secured the adjacent business of the Union Bank of Birmingham. In each of these amalgamations, therefore, geographical considerations were dominant.

In mentioning the development of this process several amalgamations of joint-stock with joint-stock banks have been cited, and it is desirable now to give attention to this aspect of the movement.

It will be apparent that some of the agreements of this type were the result of the working of the causes described in the earlier pages of this chapter.   The impetus given to joint stock banking, for instance, brought into being a number of new companies, hastily formed, possessing neither the experience nor the prestige which resulted from thirty and forty years of sound banking.   The movement was overdone, and inevitably the weaker banks went to the wall, or were driven to seek an alliance with their stronger competitors. Such a bank was the London and Northern. It was founded in 1862, started business under prosperous auspices, but engaged in unsound banking operations which caused its amalgamation with the Midland Banking Co. in 1864.[1] In the same year the Provincial Bank, a concern which, like the Bank of Wales, had been floated to buy up small businesses, took over the business of the South Hants Joint Stock Bank, which had failed.[2] The Staffordshire Joint Stock Bank, founded in 1864, was able to survive for some years, but it, too, was compelled to seek absorption at the hands of the Birmingham Banking Co. in 1889.[3]

Other alliances may be traced to a more important cause, which is seen operating strongly in this period—the desire of the efficient and strong joint-stock concerns to secure progress and size. It is in the joining of Lloyds with the Warwick and Leamington Bank in 1869 that mention of this is first found ; for the chairman of Lloyds said :

" He thought he might, without exceeding the truth, say that the business was now the largest of any local country bank in the Midland counties, and he believed that there were not more than five or six country banks in England which had a larger business." [4]

Reading this carefully, it is possible to detect the first faint writing on the wall as to what the future holds in store. It will be noticed that not only size, but comparative size, is mentioned. Twenty years later Lloyds supplies another good instance of this type of agreement, when the Worcester City and County Bank and the Birmingham Joint Stock Bank were absorbed—after competition with another concern. Lloyds therefore acquired two banks at one stroke, and this agreement provided the first example

---

[1] *Money Market Review*, October 29, 1864. This disclosure resulted from the evidence given during the hearing of an action against the bank by a dissatisfied shareholder of the name of Simon, reported in the *Bankers' Magazine*.

[2] *Bankers' Magazine*, 1865.

[3] *Bankers' Almanack*, 1890.

[4] As reported by the *Birmingham Gazette* of February 12, 1869.

it has been possible to discover of one or more banks entering into competition for the purpose of absorbing another.
For this reason it is important as marking a new stage in the
general process.

The nature of the terms offered to the Birmingham Bank
may be quoted to demonstrate the state of competition
prevailing. In exchange for 30,000 shares of £10 paid,
Lloyds gave 50,000 shares of £8 paid, together with a bonus
of £7 per share. In each case the previous rates of dividend
had been identical. Since, then, £400,000 Lloyds nominal
capital with a market value of £1,275,000 and £210,000 cash
were given for 30,000 Birmingham shares, the latter acquired
a value of £49½. It was pointed out at the confirmatory
meeting that the bonus was to be given from the reserve of
the amalgamated bank; even if this is omitted, however,
the shares were given a value of £42½. This compares with
a price of £25½ for Lloyds shares, which, it should be remembered, yielded an equivalent dividend, and in addition
possessed the prestige of a London bank compared with that
attaching to a local concern.

The discussion of these agreements points to another
reason for amalgamation, which, however, is not peculiar to
joint-stock banks alone—it was in the power of the strong
joint-stock concerns to pay a price for the businesses
absorbed which was such as to provide a powerful inducement to amalgamate. The argument usually advanced in
support of this by ambitious bank chairmen mentioned the
expense and slowness of the ordinary method of opening new
branches, and asserted that it was cheaper to give a good
price for an existing business than to seek expansion on these
lines. To banks such as Lloyds, the Midland, and, later,
Parrs, which aimed at securing speedy expansion, amalgamation was therefore preferred before normal methods of
extending. Obviously the justification for this policy lies
in the relative expenses of the two methods.[1] In the chairman's speech, made on March 18, 1889, he gave an indication
of the policy which had been followed in this case and pointed
to the ideas governing future amalgamations when he said :

[1] This question is surveyed in Chapter VII.

" Lloyds Bank will then become the greatest banking institution in the Midland Counties." This is the second reference
of its kind. A similar amalgamation occurred when the
Midland Bank took over the Leamington Priors and War-
wickshire Bank in 1889, the circular mentioned that : " This
arrangement will assure to the Leamington Priors and War-
wickshire Bank the same amount of dividend as is now paid
on the capital of that bank, in addition to the cash payment
of £1 10s. per share."

Other alliances among joint-stock banks are due to special
causes, such as fraud. The Birmingham and Midland Bank,
as it was in 1883, took over one of its former colleagues—
the Union Bank of Birmingham. The latter was defrauded
of a considerable amount of money by a manager of the
name of Burgan. The deception was discovered on the
Monday, but by Wednesday an amalgamation had been
arranged with the Midland Bank. The terms originally
provided that 7 Union shares on which previously a dividend
of 10 per cent. had been paid, and which were quoted at
£4¾, were to be given for one Midland share quoted at £32½.
Market values of £33¼ and £32½ were therefore to be exchanged. But finally the absorbed bank had to give 8
instead of 7 shares—making a difference of £5½ between the
respective market values.[1] Again, the Darlington Joint
Stock Bank was taken over by the York City and County
Bank in 1884. It appears that the former bank was
defrauded by a manager in the Bedale district of Yorkshire,
and was hardly hit in resources as well as prestige. The
York bank made an offer of £20 for £12 capital, which was
gladly accepted.[2]

The joining together of private banks yet calls for discussion. Here again, some of the causes mentioned at the
beginning of the chapter were operative in provoking this
type of combination. The speedy growth of companies
naturally caused the association of those private firms which
were not disposed to yield place. For this reason Messrs.

[1] Details cited in the *Bankers' Magazine*, 1882.
[2] Maberly Phillips, *Banks, Bankers and Banking in Northumberland,
Durham and North Yorkshire*, p. 238.

Glyn and Co. took the business of Messrs. Currie and Co., in 1864.[1] Another cause prevailed in this instance, for Messrs. Currie's business had been falling off for a period, and consequently it was deemed wise to amalgamate. But the important point is that the partners chose to combine with another private bank instead of a joint-stock. Similarly, Bosanquet and Co. joined with Stephenson Salt and Sons in 1867, in order to strengthen both partnerships.[2]

In the case of Messrs. Beckett and Co.'s absorption of Messrs. Swann and Clough in 1879 the reason was different, for the latter bank, which carried on business at York, had failed.[3] The purchase allowed Beckett's to extend from Leeds to York, and this created a sort of district geographical expansion for them. This is not the only instance of its kind, for in 1888 Messrs. Gurney and Co., of Norwich, bought the failed business of Messrs. Jarvis, of Kings Lynn.[4]

It must be mentioned, too, that those of the private bankers who were able to do so began to copy the methods of their joint-stock competitors, and particularly they emulated them towards the end of the period in the matter of opening branches. In 1870, as mentioned earlier, there were 255 private bankers possessing only 517 branches ; but from 1876–85, 94 new branches were opened by private houses.[5] In 1885, too, the first private firm adopted joint-stock organisation by registering as a limited company—Glyn Mills Currie and Co. Again, some private concerns began to see the wisdom of publishing a balance sheet, and the custom, though slowly adopted at first, became a regular feature of private as well as joint-stock practice. In the matter of interest rates, though it is not possible to present evidence on the point, it is understood that private firms introduced greater elasticity into their methods of dealing with customers. These changes naturally brought about

---

[1] *Money Market Review*, June 25, 1864.
[2] Circular quoted in *Money Market Review*, May 25, 1867.
[3] Backhouse Collection.
[4] *Annals of an East Anglian Bank*, Bidwell, p. 346.
[5] According to the regular enumerations given in the *Bankers' Magazine*.

greater equality between the two organisations, with the result that the lives of some of the private firms were prolonged, and there were incentives to amalgamate to coordinate these measures. An example of amalgamations of this type was that of Fox Fowler and Co. with Gill Morshead and Co. (1866)—who were neighbouring firms. Again, Barclay Bevan and Co. joined with Ransome Bouverie and Co. (1888)—although in this case relationship existed between the parties concerned.

So strong indeed was one of the private concerns that it absorbed a joint-stock bank. This was in 1878, when the local bank of Messrs. Crompton and Evans took over the Chesterfield and North Derbyshire Bank. Unfortunately this was not done before the latter had failed badly, and created a great amount of distress in the district.[1] Nevertheless, the fact that the private firm was afterwards able to purchase the goodwill, etc., shows the unusual comparative strength of its business, since there are only three examples of this type of amalgamation from 1825–1924.

It will be evident, from a reading of the reasons cited, that there were many causes of amalgamation at work during this active period, and to summarise them compactly is difficult. One main point is that the growth of cheque currency, the consequent decline in the use of notes, and the fresh legislation of this period, tended effectively to counteract the effects of the 1844 Act. To the direct and indirect effects of the 1862 Act many absorptions can be traced, for joint-stock banking received a decided impetus. The Gurney failure strengthened and widened this current, and the failure of private banks to publish accounts and to lose their former austerity and conservativeness assisted its progress. The 1879 Act respecting limited liability was also a powerful aid to joint-stock growth, and the slow-moving and weak private banks were therefore swept into the amalgamation net. The notable increase in branches strongly assisted company growth, especially as it was not challenged by

---

[1] " After futile attempts to transfer the concern to Crompton and Evans Union Bank, Ltd., the company failed so irretrievably as to cause widespread suffering throughout the District."—*History of Sheffield Banking Co., Ltd.*, written for the directors by R. E. Leader, p. 50.

imitation until very late in the period. The desire of joint-stock firms to secure geographical extension easily and inexpensively also provoked several absorptions, while their keenness to secure London representation and increased comparative size (the latter being first noticeable in these years) were also factors of importance. Lastly, nothing occurred to assist to prolong the system of private working, but some of the strongest firms gave up the struggle and surrendered their businesses for good prices. On the other hand, a few of the metropolitan houses joined for mutual protection and aggressive defence, while some of the failed private firms were even taken over by others more stable. (This latter is a new and non-permanent type of alliance.) Relationships and other direct connections account for a few other alliances, while when some of the more energetic firms saw that possible preservation was dependent on their success in imitating features of joint-stock organisation which had assisted its success, amalgamation was resorted to as a means of carrying it out, e.g. the opening of branches, increased size of resources, the adoption of limited liability, and joint-stock form.

The amalgamations of one joint-stock bank with another were mainly occasioned by the desire to secure increased size, branch growth, and speedy development. The energy of one or two individuals who managed large concerns was partly responsible, as well as the notion that a larger bank would secure greater proportionate profits owing to reduced expenses. Many other alliances were occasioned by the fraud and mismanagement which prevailed in some of the banks formed during the " boom " years after 1860. Inexperience of commercial banking also occasioned reverses and drove some concerns to seek safety in absorption, while in other cases the comparatively large clientèle and the strong organisation possessed by banks established thirty years earlier proved too strong an obstacle for new banks to overcome.

CHAPTER IV.

HISTORICAL SURVEY, 1890–1902.

It is convenient to divide what may be conceived to be the modern period of amalgamations into two parts—the earlier ending with the stoppage of amalgamations between private banks in their endeavour to resist the joint-stock encroachment, and the latter dealing with the twentieth-century aspect of the movement.

Compared with former periods the early part is both a busy and an important one, for there were so many as 153 [1] amalgamations. True, this is only 15 more than the previous period, but the time involved is only 13 as compared with 28 years. Additionally the number of banks which might carry out agreements was fewer than ever before (273), because of the difficulty of creating new joint-stock concerns in face of the certain opposition of the old, and because of the reduction in numbers effected by previous amalgamations. Moreover, the size of those making alliances is larger than in earlier years, mainly because, as described earlier, the tendency has been for the larger to absorb the smaller concerns, but also because joint-stock banking made large strides in the later years of the century.

The opening year is marked by the Baring crisis, ascribed to the speculative dealings of the two years immediately preceding, and the bad state of the finances in Argentina. Unlike earlier crises, it was met by firm measures and a decisive policy. The Governor of the Bank of England took

[1] The analysis into types is as follows :

Private with Private.	Joint Stock absorbs Private.	Joint Stock with Joint Stock.	Private absorbs Joint Stock.	Total
37	64	51	1	153

Again the preponderating type is the absorption of Private by Joint-Stock concerns.

immediate steps to open a Guarantee Fund in which the leading joint-stock banks were asked to participate. The response was both full and speedy. The Government, too, lent support, and the situation was eased by the action of the Bank of France, which sent a supply of gold. Undoubtedly much turned on the capacity as well as the willingness of the large joint-stock banks to subscribe liberally to the guarantee fund, and in later years Sir Edward Holden was always ready to point out that this, the first occasion on which the large joint-stock banks took concerted action, was due to the policy of amalgamation which had made them strong enough to do so. The crisis undoubtedly had its effect on amalgamation policy, and paved the way for the absorption of private banks. The numbers of agreements made admirably reflect this, for in the years 1891, 1892, 1893, and 1894, they were respectively 26, 8, 9, and 11 ; and of these 31 concerned private banks. Yet these figures are so large as to suggest that other causes were at work : e.g. the years 1892–5 were years of excessively low money rates—on occasion as low as 1 per cent. for weeks together. The fact that they endured for some years caused those bankers mainly engaged in London business to seek alternative fields of employment for their constantly growing deposits, chiefly because London banks of standing now made it a point of business to secure successful results regularly so that they might stabilise dividend rates : e.g. Lloyds paid a steady 15 per cent. for 1886 and the two succeeding years ; the London City and Midland paid from 1888 to 1895, inclusive, 15 per cent., with only one year's exception ; while the London and Westminster Bank paid 20 per cent. from 1885–90. Since money rates in the provinces were not only more remunerative but also more stable, it was natural for the London banks to seek alliances with banks having a preponderance of such business. The number of such alliances during the five years was 18,[1] and typical instances are : Lloyds Bank with Beechings Hodkin and Co., Tunbridge Wells ; Cobb and Co., Margate ; Curteis Pomfret and Co., Rye ; Bromage and Co., Monmouth ; London and

[1] Chronological Table—Appendix I.

County with Hove Banking Co. ; London and Midland with Bank of Westmorland ; Preston Banking Co., with Carlisle and District Bank.

A third cause of the increased amalgamations is not so apparent, but is of undoubted importance. In 1890, Viscount Goschen made a strong complaint about the condition of the joint-stock banks following on the disclosures at the crisis of 1890. According to the *Economist* of 1879 the liabilities of 11 large banks were £126,000,000, while their cash holdings were £16,200,000 ; in 1889 the *Economist* gave these as £170,000,000 and £17,500,000 respectively. Cash in proportion to liabilities had therefore fallen from 12·9 per cent. to 10·3 per cent. This reduction caused him to declare :

" I must give utterance to a strong conviction that the present scale of cash reserves of Private Banks and of other financial institutions is inadequate to the necessities of the country, too small as compared with the gigantic liabilities which are incurred. . . . I wish to insist on the point that, in times of crisis, reserves are essential, and that it is of supreme importance that all the great banks of the country at the moment when a crisis comes, should be able to afford relief to their customers rather than that they should feel at that very moment bound to curtail facilities which they ordinarily give." [1]

Definite mention was made of the weakness of private banks, and doubtless this was due mainly to the fact that few were yet willing to follow the example of the joint-stock concerns in displaying balance sheets, as well as to their inherent weakness. Such destructive criticism made by a high financial authority and repeatedly expressed paved the way for the absorption of weaker banks.

A fourth reason is that, as a result of the lead given by Lloyds, several of the larger banks had now definitely entered into competition with each other in the matter of size. If by nothing else, this is shown by the occasional militant and proud speeches of bank chairmen at the annual meetings, and especially at meetings called to sanction the amalgamations. It is also shown by the large proportions

---

[1] *Essays and Addresses*, p. 106.

which these banks made ; for during the period Barclays took over 21 banks, Lloyds a like number, the London and Midland 18, the Capital and Counties 15, while Parrs took 9. As a cause of amalgamation it had far-reaching effects, as will be evident from the discussion, in later pages, of individual agreements.

These are the four main reasons operating to produce the numerous amalgamations of the period. The discussion following reveals that it was the indirect, as well as the direct, effects of them which provoked some of the agreements : e.g. it is shown that some schemes were based on the notion of alliance as a safeguard against *possible* encroachment by large metropolitan concerns. The likelihood of such alliances occurring was a remote one so long as there was no great activity among leading banks. But the fear of suffering loss of identity generated by the unusual and unprecedented competition of the leaders produced a crop of amalgamations which, while not directly occasioned by this one and only cause, were yet precipitated by it. Additionally, mention must be made of the fact that leading joint-stock banks were extending their functions (as instanced by the assaults made on the monopoly of accepting which was held by West End private bankers), and were widening the scope of those which already they exercised. And further, throughout these years, there was a definite tendency for industrial and commercial concerns to enlarge their sizes by horizontal and vertical integration, inspired by the examples set in Germany and America. This slowly reacted on the size of the banking structure,[1] and, coupled with the general increase in the volume of trading operations, assisted the growth of that competition between the large banks which had its origin in constantly developing rivalry. Finally, the discredit of private banking which is to be found earlier, increased markedly, for out of 153 amalgamations 64[2]

---

[1] Not only did individual banks grow bigger, but the number of their branches also increased quickly during the period ; for in the eleven years 1891–1901, inclusive, the number of bank branches increased from 3,383 to 4,762—a gain of 1,379, or over 130 a year.

[2] Thirty-one of these occurred before 1894, thus showing how private banking was discredited as a result of the relations following the Baring crisis.

were absorptions of private by joint-stock firms, and 37 others were mainly inspired by the necessity for combining in order to maintain previous positions. Referring to these latter types of agreement the speech made by the President of the Institute of Bankers in 1891 is of interest. He said :

" There are two incentives to Private Bankers to form combinations among themselves, or to become absorbed with large undertakings. Either they are too rich, or they are too poor. In the first case they are glad to have escaped the cares of a business that has greatly changed its old, easy, comfortable character. In the second case they feel themselves unable to meet the extended requirements of modern times. To these may be added other causes of recent growth. The public criticism of all institutions has become much more intense. Competition has now developed in a manner hitherto unknown. With some notable exceptions that will, I trust, long continue, the Private Banker has the feeling that his day is past. His great joint-stock neighbour overshadows and disturbs him . . . and lastly, the desire created in the public mind for large reserves and published balance sheets will drive some to adopt the habits of joint-stock banks, and others with less courage into the haven of amalgamation." [1]

Instances of such amalgamations are supplied by that of the banks which joined to form Prescott's Bank, the unique fusion of the " Barclay " group of banks, and also the amalgamation of Lloyds with Grant and Maddison's Union Bank—discussed later.

Certain of them it will be profitable to discuss separately and in detail. The Prescott amalgamation matured in 1891—the year following the Baring scare—when as many as seven private bankers fused themselves into one new large private concern, which immediately afterwards began the publishing of balance sheets. Two of these were located in London, but the remainder were situate in the neighbourhood of Bath and Winchester. The main cause was the fact that the London houses were clearing-house representatives for the other firms ; but also (and this was of equal importance as a reason) the partners of the bank were related. An extract from the circular announcing the first grouping runs :

[1] *Journal of the Institute of Bankers*, November 1891.

" The intimate and pleasurable relations which have always existed between the four banks have led us to take this step. We believe at the same time that the increased facilities thereby afforded for transacting the business of our customers will be to their own advantage, and will strengthen our connexions generally."

There is a hint here that they had deemed it necessary to combine to maintain effective competition with joint-stock rivals.   This was an unprecedented step for private bankers to take, but, nevertheless, the new firm only lived a dozen years longer !   The amalgamation supplies a good illustration of the copying of joint-stock methods by private companies, for the new organisation had London offices and branches, clearing-house representation, and it published a balance sheet.   It therefore points unmistakably to the success of those joint-stock methods which private bankers were once accustomed to decry.   It also shows that the only sure resource for the remaining private bankers who desired to escape the tentacles of the rapidly growing octopus (provided that they did not possess an exceptional business such as that of Messrs. Glyn and Co.) was to arrange not one but a series of alliances among suitable banks, in order that the combined resources should permit of their being able to deal with customers of large means, and to offer facilities equal to those given by joint-stock firms.   Lastly, such an arrangement permitted of branches being opened, and this in turn allowed of the collecting of surplus funds from the various districts.

While the Prescott amalgamations were the first of this type, they are by no means so important as those arranged in 1896 by Barclays and other banks.   This combination included as many as fifteen different firms—all private. It was accepted by the financial world as a distinct innovation, though clearly it was not such.   The names of the firms involved were :

Barclay Bevan Tritton Ransome Bouverie and Co., of
    London and Brighton.
Goslings and Sharpe, of London.

Gurney and Co., of Norwich, Fakenham, Halesworth,
    Kings Lynn, Wisbech, and Great Yarmouth.
Gurneys Alexanders and Co., of Ipswich.
Gurneys Round and Co., of Colchester.
J. Backhouse and Co., of Darlington.
Bassett Sons and Harris, of Leighton Buzzard.
Fordham Gibson and Co., of Royston.
Gibson Tuke and Gibson, of Saffron Walden.
Molineux Whitfield and Co., of Lewes.
J. Mortlock and Co., of Cambridge.
Sharples Tuke, Lucas and Seebohm, of Hitchin.
Sparrow Tufnell and Co., Essex.
Veasey Desboro Bevan Tillard and Co., of Huntingdon.
Woodall Hebden and Co., of Scarborough.

The mere citation of their names shows how intimately
the firms were connected in relationship, for one name is
common to several firms, e.g. Gurney. Many others are
descendants of the Gurney family which originally,
by the efforts of one Bartlet Gurney, a century before,
established a banking house at Norwich. This was in the
days when that town was an important port serving as a
centre for the collection of goods made for the Indian woollen
trade and for their export. Members of Bartlet Gurney's
family intermarried with that of the Backhouses at
Darlington, who, like the Gurneys, were well-known members
of the Quaker sect. Again, the only daughter of the
renowned David Barclay who died in 1809 was married to
Richard Gurney, of Norwich. Samuel Gurney, the first head
of the firm of Overend Gurney and Co., left no fewer than
9 children and 40 grandchildren, and the intermarriage of
these with families of other bankers accounts for the wide
relationships existing between so many of the above groups.[1]

Religion, marriage, and friendship, therefore point to the
immediate reason for fusion, but it will be noted that most
of the banks cited were located in country areas where
previously the penetration of the joint-stock banks had not

---

[1] *The Records of the House of Gournay*, by Gournay (British Museum)
and *The Gurneys of Earlham*, by A. J. C. Hare.

E

been felt. It is apparent that the stress of extended competition was now being experienced and this probably
explains why the invitation issued by Messrs. Barclay and
Co. was so readily accepted. An interesting point about the
arrangement is that it provided for the creation, not of one
large private concern, but for a joint-stock concern with
limited liability. This is excellent testimony to the decline
of private banking in the period. Again, the branches
numbered no fewer than 180, while the total of deposits was
over £26,000,000.

The last example of this type of amalgamation was that
which occurred in 1902, when the Union Bank of London
absorbed at one and the same time the private banks of
Messrs. Smith Payne and Smith, London ; S. Smith and Co.,
Nottingham ; Smith Ellis and Co., Lincoln ; Sam Smith
Bros. and Co., Hull ; S. Smith and Co., Derby ; S. Smith
and Co., Newark. By way of contrast this was not a combination of private bankers simply, as in the case of Barclays.
It involved the absorption by a joint-stock firm, itself of
high standing, of the businesses controlled by the noted
Smith family of bankers. Of this there are two aspects
which call for notice. In the first place, Messrs. Smith and
Co. decided that in spite of the unusually good businesses,
highly select in character, which they possessed, the day of
the private banker was passed. In the second place the
Union Bank of London took the step—an uncommon one at
the time—of obtaining not only a supplement to their
existing business, but a group of country businesses possessing 25 branches, by the method of purchase. At the meeting
called to sanction the arrangement it was pointed out that
this was the second amalgamation in which the joint-stock
bank had been engaged during the period of 67 years of
independent existence.

The progress made by Lloyds Bank during this busy period
now calls for attention. The bank appears to have secured
most of its new business by a continual process of absorptions, since it made no fewer than 24, and most of them were
concerned with banks of substantial size. In view of the
importance and variety of its amalgamations, special atten-

tion will be given to them.   The first one was made in 1890,
when Messrs. Wilkins and Co., the proprietors of the Brecon
Old Bank, agreed to dispose of their old-established business.
It was a strong bank with a reputation for being well
managed, and additionally, it was one of the largest of the
remaining private banks.[1]   The main reason for seeking
amalgamation appears to have been that the partners desired
to adopt joint-stock form, and the news that it was accomplished brought forth many comments from the newspapers
of the day, but none so tersely descriptive as that appearing
in the *South Wales Daily News* of July 1, 1890, which ran :
" The history of Lloyds Banking Co., like that of a dipso-
maniac, may be comprised in the one word—' Swallow.' "
As if in answer to these comments the chairman declared at
the following meeting : " The fact is, we refuse quite as
many as we take."

In the next year the businesses of Cobb and Co., of
Margate, Praeds and Co., of London, Hart Fellows and Co.,[2]
of Nottingham, and Beechings and Co., of Tonbridge, were
absorbed.   Such a rate of progress astonished and con-
founded competitor banks, and caused the *Financial Times*
of May 14, 1892, to make the following satirical comment :
" Bankers are asking how long this conquering career of
Lloyds will go on, and whether, and if so when, they
propose to absorb the Bank of England."   The amalgamation
with Praeds' old banking house gave to Lloyds a distinguished
business in the West End of London.   When in the following
year (1892) the famous business of Messrs. Twining and Co.
(who had always been dealers in tea as well as bankers, and
who yet carry on the former business) was obtained, a hand-
some office in the Strand was added.   Both cases are excellent

---

[1] " The Brecon Old Bank being one of the largest of the remaining
private banks in the country."—*Birmingham Daily Post*, June 30, 1890.

[2] Relationship played no small part here, as the following quotation
from the *Nottingham Daily Guardian*, August 5, 1891, shows : " Close
relationships because Mr. Hart married a Miss Lloyd, and their only child
became the wife of the late Sir Chas. Fellows, whose only son, Mr. C.
Fellows, was a partner in the firm in Nottingham for a short period some
15 years ago, when he went to reside in London."

Speaking at the extraordinary meeting on August 31, 1891, Lloyds
chairman said : " Many of our old customers come to us and say : ' Will
you buy us ? If you will not, we will go to somebody else.' "

instances of a new process—the acquisition of select London businesses—but what was more important, of buildings the sites of which afterwards became of greater value as banking centres.   Especially in the West End, the best positions had long been possessed by the great private banks, and to purchase these was the only way to secure them.   Hence the value of amalgamation in securing the extension of joint-stock banks in the Metropolis.

In comparison it may be observed that Parrs Bank, in the year 1891, amalgamated with Messrs. Fuller Banbury and Co., who also were established in London.   Prior to 1883 Parrs was a provincial bank having its bases at Warrington and St. Helens.   It had shown steady progress both in normal business expansion and in amalgamation.   In 1883 it secured the business of the National Bank of Liverpool, which had previously strengthened itself by taking over the Liverpool office of the Alliance Bank.   This stride to one of the foremost ports gave Parrs a new type of business, and also provided an outlet for the always increasing deposits drawn from provincial traders.   But when it acquired the business of Messrs. Fuller, not only was a compact little office secured in London (giving the advantages of representation there), but it also succeeded to their seat in the Bankers' Clearing House—thus copying the example set by Lloyds but seven years earlier.   Again, in the same eventful year, the announcement was made that the Birmingham and Midland Bank, which was a concern representing the united forces of several strong provincial banks, had similarly obtained a London office and a seat in the Clearing House, by its absorption of the Central Bank of London.   All this activity was, notwithstanding, but the prelude to that of subsequent years.

An interesting feature of the events of this period is the curious manner in which each of the banks afterwards destined to become large and important, was copying the methods of the other : e.g. the absorption by Lloyds in 1893 of the business of Messrs. Herries Farquhar and Co., who were located in the West End, and who had an additional office in St. James' Street, may be cited.   In 1894 Parrs responded by taking the business of Sir Samuel Scott and Co. This latter was a particularly distinctive business, since the firm acted as bankers to the Queen. Their premises were noted for splendour and magnificence above that of the ordinary London private banker.

Another two extensions made during 1893 afford a contrast to this concentration of banks in the London area. The London and Midland Bank (as it had now become) secured a northerly connection by amalgamating with the Bank of Westmorland, while the Metropolitan Bank (of England and Wales) obtained a good geographical extension by absorbing the National Bank of Wales. These agreements indicate the consolidation secured by two banks, which, as it happened, were afterwards linked together. But in the year following the contrast is more complete, inasmuch as then the greatest number of absorptions represent the amalgamation of provincial joint-stock banks with others of the same type. This feature is new and yet old, for at least three of the growing London banks began their careers by making similar amalgamations. Perhaps the most significant aspect of the present agreements is that the growing competition among the larger banks was evidently affecting the hitherto snugly esconced strong country banks, and this assumption is borne out by the speeches of their chairmen made at the time of the amalgamations. Examples are the alliances between the York Union Bank and Messrs. Pease, the Lancashire and Yorkshire Bank and the Preston Union Bank, the Mercantile Bank of Lancashire and the London and Lancashire Bank, and the York City and County Bank with the Hull Banking Co. It will be observed that neighbouring provincial banks were absorbed, so preventing the large London banks making immediate attacks in the country.

A continuance of the policy is especially in evidence in 1897, of which the following are examples : Wilts and Dorset Bank with Pinckney Bros. ; York City and County with the Barnsley Banking Co. ; and the Manchester and County Bank with the Bank of Bolton. Again all are with banks in the same area as the amalgamating banks, and, therefore, while geographical expansion was a result of such moves, they were also designed to remove out of the grasp of London banks concerns which might have become dangerous rivals if they had been taken over by them.

Reverting to the history of Lloyds, in 1897 this concern made two important captures in the County of Gloucester Bank, and Messrs. Williams and Co., of Chester. The terms of the former agreement reflect the keen competition mentioned earlier. They were that one Gloucester share £25 paid (quoted at £71) should exchange for two and three-quarters shares of Lloyds, £8 paid (quoted £27). As it is pointed out by the *Cheltenham Examiner* of March 16: " The terms of the amalgamation are decidedly advantageous to the shareholders in the County of Gloucester Bank. . . . The amalgamation is equivalent to a gift of about £5 15s." (per share). Another side of the amalgamation is shown by another quotation from the same paper : " For very many years the Cheltenham Corporation's banking account had been at the County of Gloucester Bank. A few months ago the corporation wished to borrow a large sum, and Lloyds bank offered better terms than could be offered by the County Bank "—testimony that larger banks with their larger resources and their varied fields of employment for money were able to grant better terms than the purely provincial bankers whose funds were influenced by all affairs influencing the locality in which they functioned. It is the first time that mere size as an argument in favour of amalgamations has been met, and this is interesting since an extensive use of it is made in later years. Indeed it appears in the next amalgamation arranged by Lloyds—in 1898 with the Burton Union Bank. The *Burton Gazette*, in discussing the reasons for it, makes much of " the recent heavy business necessitating a transfer to a larger bank."

Lloyds' next step was delayed until 1900. In that year it took over the Liverpool Union, a bank for whom it had acted as London agents for a considerable period. The chairman of the absorbed bank pointed out that " it is almost equally well known that the growth of our deposits has not kept anything like pace with these first-class lending opportunities." Evidently then, it required branches to feed it with deposits. Located mostly in manufacturing districts which produced surplus deposits, Lloyds' offer to absorb came as a welcome one. It was the easiest way out of the difficulty, for the trouble and expense of opening branches were saved (all of which would take time), and the fact that the terms gave a present of about £4 10s. per share to the Liverpool shareholders came as a sufficient inducement for consent ; nor must it be over-looked that the total dividend was increased from £75,000 to £82,000.[1] From the point of view of Lloyds it was urged that good offices in Liverpool were being sought, and this was a cheap method of securing suitable positions.

This year (1900) was a red-letter one in the history of Lloyds, for in addition to this amalgamation four private concerns were induced to throw in their lot with this bank. One of these—Messrs. Brooks and Co.—was the last private house remaining in Lombard Street, where in 1884 there were twelve separate firms. The result of this collection of amalgamations was to give to Lloyds first place among all the banks in the United Kingdom in point of size of deposits. Its branches, too, reached the number of over 300.

There is another amalgamation made by Lloyds in the period which should be discussed. This occurred in 1901, when the Bucks and Oxon Union Bank was absorbed. The chairman of the smaller bank said, in explanation of this, that " Lloyds have more than once made overtures to us. . . . As a small bank we frequently found ourselves out-distanced—particularly near London—and we have had to refuse business which was too much for our limit." The words are full of significance for the history since they show that a small bank was now definitely unable to compete for the more remunerative large business on terms of

---

[1] For particulars of terms, see *Bankers' Magazine*, 1900. Mr. Henry Bell, a late general manager of Lloyds Bank, was engaged in this agreement on behalf of the Liverpool Union Bank. He pointed out in an interview that the growth of large transactions for the purpose of financing imports of cotton and wheat was so great that one individual firm asked his bank for a very large overdraft. And resort to amalgamation with a large bank became necessary if the business was to be adequately financed.

equality with London joint-stock concerns. Taken along with utterances from different sources, previously quoted, they show how greatly competition had grown. An exceptional part of the amalgamation is that the shareholders' meeting was a stormy one, for shareholders lost approximately £6 per share. Hitherto this is the only example where proprietors lost from amalgamating—except in the case of failed banks.

To return to the general movement.

In 1897 the London and Midland Bank became suddenly active. Its absorptions numbered three joint-stock banks, two situate so far apart as Huddersfield and the Channel Islands. With those referred to before, effected by Lloyds, these amalgamations with banks at great distances from each other and differing greatly in character, point to the modern aspect of amalgamations ; for they are an evidence of the increased and increasing ambitions of general managers and of the strong competition discussed in previous paragraphs. Nevertheless it must not be thought that they were all made haphazardly and without systematic planning. Undoubtedly there were instances where this did happen ; but, generally, the banks were seeking to strengthen themselves in places where already they had only a weak or moderately strong representation. It is in this connection that the influence of Mr. E. H. Holden [1] should be noticed. He was appointed to the position of general manager of the London and Midland Bank in 1897. His policy was, from the first, to develop the size and capacity of the bank by all possible means. For many years, as is evident later, he was not only personally responsible for many amalgamations, but he set the pace, and therefore the fashion, in all developments of policy. The absorption of the Huddersfield Union Bank is an excellent instance of his liberal methods and reflects the keenness of the desire of the large banks to secure expansion over the heads of insistent competitors. Otherwise such tempting terms as the

[1] "Sir Edward Holden, then Mr. Holden, joined the bank in 1881, and was no doubt largely responsible for the commencement of the amalgamation movement " (p. 12, of the history of the Midland Bank, contained in the book *A Great Bank*).

following would not have been offered : For a paid-up capital
and reserve of £636,575, the Midland Bank gave 22,581
shares of £12½ paid (quoted £46), and £22,581 in cash.
The shares of the Huddersfield Bank were quoted at about
£58, so that the Midland gave actual value of £1,061,307
for an actual value of £942,354—a bonus of £118,773.

Another fusion which must be noticed because of its
significance was also made by him—with the City Bank,
in 1898. By this a purely metropolitan bank of more than
average size was linked to a growing London and provincial concern. When the news became known City
financiers were much surprised,[1] since the City Bank had
always set its face expressly against any kind of expansion
either by amalgamation or by opening new branches. At
the Midland Bank's meeting the chairman remarked that
many criticisms as well as comments had been made, but
his reply to them was that the agreement had given the
Midland Bank what it most needed—a large, suitable head
office. Again, the directors had long desired to make the
capital equal in amount to the reserve, and this now became
possible. Lastly, the City Bank possessed a London business of unusual value, with a good Stock Exchange clientèle,
as well as a foreign connection. The terms provided a bonus
of £7 on each five City shares, while, additionally, the City
shareholders gained £3 in dividend on each five shares.
This bonus was made possible by the fact that while the
shares of the City Bank stood at the respectable premium
of 140 per cent., those of the Midland Bank commanded a
premium of 320 per cent. By a later fusion in the same
year (with the Oldham Joint Stock Bank), the Midland Bank
joined the ranks of the largest joint-stock concerns, since it
possessed nearly 300 branches. In passing it may be
mentioned that the then Mr. Holden had attempted to buy
the City Bank ten years earlier, but his bank was then considered too small. He assured the directors that he would
nevertheless call again, with the result described above.

To sum up; this, the period which sees the beginning of
the modern movement in amalgamation, was influenced at

[1] *Vide The Times*, October 19, 1898.

the outset by the Baring difficulties. The acute shock
given to commerce after twenty-four years of comparative
calm directed public attention to banking, and the resulting
criticism added to the strong utterances of Viscount Goschen
influenced some, and caused other banks, to seek amalgamation. The very tangible benefits given by joint-stock
organisation stimulated the process, especially because it
was an easy step to join a company already well established.
Occasionally difficulties proved too heavy for the private
bankers, and release from them was sought ; and these,
coupled with such ties as that of relationship and friendship,
often caused alliances. Although one instance only has
been cited, there were not a few cases where small local
banks found themselves unable to meet enlarged and still
growing needs caused by industrial or commercial development, and, further, competition with larger banks accentu-
ated the embarrassments of such a position. Especially
and particularly, however, the growth of strong competition among joint-stock banks themselves, arising first
from the insistent endeavours of London banks to seek
both to maintain and increase the profits which were
seriously curtailed by a period of low rates in the London
Money Market, and second from the keen desire of progressive provincial concerns to secure London representation (and later, extended representation), was the provoking
cause of amalgamations. This competition later extended
to other areas of the country, being instigated by the
necessity for obtaining branches in the business centres of
the country and in areas contiguous to those where large
banks were already established. The effect of this extension
of both London and large provincial institutions was to
produce a series of defensive groupings among provincial
companies which had the foresight to see the danger to
their own positions, and the initiative to take the steps
necessary for alliance. The precarious condition of ordinary
private banking is well illustrated by the new type of
grouped amalgamations which was originated as a last
measure of defence. What success they had is shown by
the events related in the next chapter.

CHAPTER V.

HISTORICAL SURVEY, 1903-1924.

THIS, the last period, covers twenty-two years, compared with the thirteen years occupied by that preceding. The numbers of amalgamations occurring are respectively 95[1] and 153, giving averages of over 4 and over 12 per year. The explanation of so great a difference is that whereas in 1890 there were 273 banks, in 1903 there were but 157— of which a small number only were private banks. Nevertheless in this period, especially, it is necessary to remember that the amalgamations which did occur were more important and larger than in previous years : not only because the banks were swollen by the absorptions they had already made, but also because banking in the twentieth century has been very progressive.

Agreements are registered in every year of the period, and the numbers are fairly well distributed, showing that the movement was both steady and regular. Actually the greatest number—10—is reached in 1919. This is not large compared with, say, 26 in 1890, but the number gives no idea of the size of the figures involved, of the huge interests which were transferred, or of the immense changes in banking structure which resulted.

During these twenty-two years there are no specially exciting causes at work to produce specific agreements, similar to those at work in earlier years. One reason for this is that the once powerful and numerous private bankers

[1]
Private with Private.	Joint Stock absorbs Private.	Joint Stock with Joint Stock.	Private absorbs Joint Stock.	Total.
1	36	58	0	95

From this it is clear that the absorption of joint-stock by joint-stock banks is the most prominent feature of this last period.

have been deprived of their ability either to compete or to hold their own with the joint-stock firms owing to the regular progress of the latter. Another is that the strength of the competing firms, whether London or provincial, is now more equal than at any other time in history, so that banks are not driven to seek amalgamation on account of their intrinsic weakness to the same extent as before. A third is that there is a notable absence of crises similar to and so severe as those which troubled our banking fathers. From the point of view of banking competition the issue lay then between the large and very large banks on the one hand, and the smaller provincial companies on the other. And it is not until after the first decade has passed that the extra resources of the very large banks begins to tell distinctly in their favour in the trial of strength.

The years of war (1914-18) were productive of special causes—even though these were somewhat artificial in character—which had the effect of hastening the progress of the movement. Consequently it would seem advisable, even at this early stage, to make a division between pre-war and war years. Again, the conditions after the war were so patently affected by banking changes caused by war-time measures that a third division of the complete period should be made. To begin, then, with a discussion of events during 1903-14.

1903-14.

These years witnessed a steady process of amalgamations. The dominant reasons for it were those provided by the competition of banks for leadership, or their desire merely to make regular progress. As evidence of the first the speeches of chairmen at the annual meetings and the discussions following may be cited. Comparisons with rival banks were often made. The fundamental idea underlying the second reason is that of making geographical expansion. In the case of the large banks this is to secure an equal distribution of branches over the whole area of the country, and to link the various elements in the chain. Especial strength is sought in important entrepôt and market centres like Manchester, Leeds, and Birmingham, as well as at the principal ports. The smaller banks seek to consolidate their positions in the areas which they already serve, and to extend into districts not far removed. For example, the amalgamations of the Lancashire and Yorkshire Bank are confined to banks like the Mercantile Bank of Lancashire ; the District Bank to the Lancaster Banking Co. ; the Bank of Liverpool to the Carlisle and Cumberland Bank, and the North Eastern Bank, as well as to the Craven Bank of Skipton. Many of these moves were made purely for the sake of protection. The third reason—thought by many modern bankers to be a strong one—is that it was necessary to keep pace with the concentration movement in industry and commerce, which, bankers assert, preceded the integration of banking.

It is proposed now to glance at some of the amalgamations in detail, since this will serve to illustrate the general points just enumerated. The first to claim attention is that of the Union of London and Smiths Bank with the Prescott group. In the previous chapter it was mentioned that Prescott's was the first grouping of private bankers in one firm designed to resist the joint stock progress. Now, in 1903, they follow the Smith group in going over to the side of the Union Bank. It is curious to observe that of the three large groups of private bankers two of them thus find their way to the same joint-stock firm. The step was an important and valuable one for the Union Bank, since its country representation was not only poor, but the branches were not co-ordinated. This agreement considerably extended the branch area occupied by the London bank, as most of the Prescott branches were located in the south-west of England.

Other amalgamations registered in the early years of this period occur between Lancashire banks, and since this group is now the largest independent group outside the London banks there is especial interest in noting the various changes which they underwent. The first agreement is that made in 1904 by the Lancashire and Yorkshire Bank with the Mercantile Bank of Lancashire. The circular issued by the former runs :

" Your directors have satisfied themselves that this arrangement will be to the advantage of both institutions, and will give us a valuable connection in our sphere of influence. At the same time, it will be a satisfaction to the public to observe that local interests are secured by the bank remaining under the entire control of directors who possess a personal knowledge of the requirements of the trades and industries of Lancashire and Yorkshire."

It demonstrates that the self-containedness of the two banks is not to be interfered with. More especially it points to the peculiar conditions attendant on the specialised occupations of Lancashire and some parts of Yorkshire, e.g. the cotton and woollen trades—which create a special type of banking business—and the fact that it is not intended to change the methods of dealing with this which have been successful previously. Those methods involve the holding of directors' seats by men who are not merely financiers but are conversant with the technicalities of the trades, and who therefore understand their particular banking needs, e.g. in financing the purchase of the raw cotton, and in providing effective backing for the initiative necessary in trading in foreign markets.

The same year was witness to an unusual development in amalgamation procedure. In an unexpected move another Manchester bank—the Manchester and Liverpool District—sought to join forces with Lloyds.[1] Lloyds welcomed the proposal, as such an alliance offered them a strong hold of Lancashire business, and a liaison with a strong bank. Eventually the terms were announced. These showed that the proposed new bank was to be considerably larger than any existing joint-stock bank, with a capital and reserve of nearly £10,000,000, and nearly £70,000,000 in deposits, together with 485 branches. On the point of size

[1] Speaking on January 29, 1904, as to the numerous amalgamations which Lloyds had made, the chairman, Mr. J. S. Phillips, said that for every bank that had been taken, three had been refused, and that with the exception of one private bank, no institution had ever been asked to amalgamate with Lloyds (Report of chairman's speech, 1904).

alone, however, the scheme aroused the opposition of Manchester shareholders and business men, and the general public.
But it was especially criticised by Manchester people because
it provided for the transference to a London bank of Manchester's leading bank, whose identity would then be lost.
So strong was the opposition that the project was dropped
very quickly. This failure to carry through a projected
amalgamation is the first of which a record can be found.
Undoubtedly, as shown earlier, there had previously been
many fruitless negotiations, mainly as a result of the competition for one bank by several rivals. But the public
had never before succeeded in preventing amalgamation
merely by demonstrating its opposition.

It is worthy of note that the only other recorded example
of opposition and the consequent failure of the scheme
should also concern a Lancashire bank and occur in this
same period. In 1910 Parrs made an attempt to capture
the Lancashire and Yorkshire Bank. Again the negotiations
progressed up to the announcement of terms, but although
these provided for the continuance of the local directors,
and they were based on a generous valuation of the Lancashire Bank's shares, the scheme was perhaps more violently
opposed than that mooted in 1904. The result was that
it was dropped within a fortnight! Since then only the
Union Bank of Manchester has succumbed to advances
of a London bank. One of the effects of the display of
local sentiment has been to maintain the individual and
collective positions of the Lancashire banks so that now this
is the largest group outside London banks. Clearly such
a position could not have been obtained without some sort
of expansion, and this has been effected by ordinary business
growth, and by imitating the large London banks in their
concentration on amalgamation procedure. For instance,
the Manchester and Liverpool District Bank, saved from
amalgamation with Lloyds, proceeded in 1907 to acquire
the Lancaster Banking Co., which was purely a local concern.
Like the District, it was engaged in the specialised work of
financing Lancashire industry, particularly chemicals and
cotton. Its 57 branches were not widely spread and so did

not overlap at more than three places with those of the Manchester Bank. From this point of view, then, the amalgamation was a useful one. Again, the façt that the District was strongly represented in the manufacturing areas, while the Lancaster Bank was strongest in the agricultural districts, made the amalgamation an excellent one from the point of view of geographical extension in the county area. It will be seen later that almost all the alliances carried out by the District Bank partake of this nature. Again, all the directors were possessed of a knowledge of the special requirements of Lancashire trade. Another Lancashire bank, the Bank of Liverpool, following the example set by its neighbours, took over in 1906 the business of the Craven Bank—a private concern which was established in both Lancashire and Yorkshire, with the main office at Skipton. It was an instance of a type of agreement which then was comparatively rare, for, as mentioned before, there were not many private banks which were disposed to amalgamate. It represented the joining of two provincial banks, solely for the purpose of securing the geographical extension of the larger. Again, it is similar to the amalgamation just described inasmuch as the Bank of Liverpool was mainly established in towns, and the Craven Bank served rural areas, and market towns. But particularly it is a good instance of a defensive alliance as the following extract taken from the *Bankers' Magazine* of September, 1906, shows :

" . . . yet its general purport is descriptive of the banking world at present. Perhaps the position is best likened to a number of anglers fishing in the same stream, each endeavouring to secure a fine trout which is known to exist there. So in banking. The large banks are angling for the small ones, and that one which offers the best terms, other things being equal, secures the prize. So persistent are they, and so strong is the current, that few have been able, even if they so desired, to resist."

Allowing something for the personal bias, the quotation is interesting as showing the tendency of the times.

To these another amalgamation concerning the activities

of provincial northern banks offers a contrast because it was unorthodox in type. It was made between the Bradford Commercial and the Bradford District Banks. The former had been placed in a difficult position on account of advancing excessively to one firm, which afterwards defaulted. Owing to the weakened bargaining power of the Commercial, the neighbouring bank was able to exact favourable terms. Actually for an outlay of about £60,000[1] on extra premises and goodwill, it received an accretion of £1,200,000 to its deposits, but of this sum only £34,000 was paid for goodwill, so that the absorbing bank profited much from the transaction. On the other hand, a failure was avoided, and this resulted in a saving to the community. Similar agreements are more common in the earlier periods, but now they are relatively rare. This is a witness to the increased safety of banking to which reference has been made in former chapters, and the incident well serves to show the uses of amalgamation procedure, and the gain resulting from the absence of restrictive checks on such absorptions similar to those imposed in an earlier period by the Act of 1844. There is one other example only in the whole period. It occurred in 1911, when the Stamford Spalding and Boston Bank was taken over by Barclays. Again, apparently, through successive advances to a single firm, but also on account of the difficult position caused by the severe depreciation of gilt-edged securities over a long period (1897–1911), the local bank found itself in difficulties, from which it was saved by amalgamation.[2]

In view of the fact that the amalgamations carried out by Lloyds bank in these years are comparatively few and are not greatly different in type or in importance from those illustrated at length in the previous period, it will suffice if mention is made of their main aspects. One of the more interesting agreements was that made with the Devon and Cornwall Bank, in 1906. This bank was itself of moderately large size, and had a compact group of 59 main branches in the south-west of England. In giving an

---

[1] From details given in the *Banker's Magazine*, 1904, p. 238.
[2] *Bankers' Magazine*, 1911, p. 376.

explanation of the motives governing this amalgamation the chairman of the Devon and Cornwall Bank said : " We have to go to London in order to transact our business, and for that purpose to employ an agency, and that agency is a very costly item in our financial arrangements." Again, " Ourselves and London banking being in that position, we were approached by Lloyds Bank." Heavy agency expenses are therefore quoted as the main reason for this absorption.

Of the amalgamation in early 1914 made by Lloyds with the Wilts and Dorset Bank, the chairman, speaking at a complimentary dinner, said they had been approached by more than one London bank to amalgamate. It appears from the same speech that this absorption had been arranged two years earlier, but the time was not deemed suitable for making the disclosure ! And the actual moment was decided upon because competition had then just taken on a new phase of severity. This arrangement would therefore seem to point to the fact that competition was progressively increasing up to the first war year.

Two other amalgamations of these years may be described because they serve as a guide to the tendency then prevailing —that of consolidation on a growing scale. One is the union of the London City and Midland with the North and South Wales Bank (1908) ; the other is that of the York City and County with the London Joint Stock Bank (1909). Both these represent the incursion of large London concerns into areas hitherto quite unknown to them. Both also represent the absorption of strong country banks whose sphere of work was confined to local counties, and both the absorbed banks cited reasons for the amalgamation which are similar in essence. Again (but in different ways) they both testify to the advantages possessed by large banks. The circular of the York bank gives an impression that the amalgamation process was inevitable because of the difficulty experienced by provincial banks of competing with London concerns, resulting from the absence of London representation. It may be pointed out that the provincial banks could open offices in London, but the difficulties of doing this were greater than would appear at first sight. It was not that it was difficult to secure suitable premises as that when this had been done, it was still necessary to obtain representation in the Clearing House and the Money Market, to take the risk of obtaining sufficient business to justify the expense of opening in the metropolis, and, lastly, to overcome the antagonism of the great banks. The reasons against taking this step seemed to be strong, for it appears that no country bank came to London, even by the method of amalgamation, after 1891. On the other hand, to amalgamate with another bank already in practice there was not only much easier but generally more desirable on the ground of the certain financial gain which accrued. It must be observed, however, that full confession of the inevitableness of amalgamation has never before been indicated in the explanations given for fusion. The change is striking, and the more so because it comes from a provincial bank of strong reputation.

Lastly, it should be noted that the London Joint was the last metropolitan bank to realise the benefits accruing from the juxtaposition of London and provincial business. Similar to the Union Bank of London this bank had many large customers in the metropolis. Their extensive transactions necessitated the keeping of considerable sums of money at call, and in periods of low rates this obviously curtailed profits. Hence it was constrained to seek a provincial business. Special mention should now be made of the year 1909, since for the purposes of amalgamation history it was a year of more than ordinary significance. The event which warrants this description was the amalgamation between the London and County Bank and the London and Westminster Bank. This agreement was important because it represented the combination of two London joint-stock banks : both banks had previously engaged in amalgamation ; they were banks of the first magnitude ; and, lastly, the terms provided not for the allying of one bank with the other, but for the complete absorption of the London and Westminster Bank. Both concerns had been formed in the 'thirties of the nineteenth century, but while one had strayed a distance away from the metropolis the other had been content to stay at home —as evidenced by their names. The business of the Westminster Bank had been for some years at a standstill, while that of the County was constantly growing, if only by reason of smaller absorptions. One reason for this had been the inability of the Westminster Bank to amalgamate of recent years. The cause is rather curious, for it was that that bank possessed too much capital! And the reason for this was that it was the first bank to take advantage of the Companies' Acts in the early 'eighties, the mistake then being made of creating too large a paid-up capital. In seeking to amalgamate with a smaller concern it would have been necessary to add to this already large figure, when the reverse process was not only desirable (from the bank's point of view), but was the one which usually occurred. This explains why it was absorbed by and not amalgamated with the County Bank.

Adducing other reasons for the amalgamation the chairman of the Westminster Bank pointed out that they had long been desirous of securing a country connection, similar to that possessed by other London banks. Again, it is in this amalgamation that there is a first mention of the value of mere size, considered as such.

Among the reasons given by the chairman of the London and County was that his bank had ceased to grow, competition had increased, particularly over the last few years, and that amalgamation would doubtless increase profits. At the same time it was mentioned that one of the ways of increasing profits was to be the reduction of expenses effected by the fusion. This notwithstanding, he pointed out that " there is no doubt that many of these amalgamations in the past had not been successful."

The carrying out of the agreement, which involved the total disappearance of the Westminster Bank's capital, resulted in the curious fact that the new reserve was over 121 per cent. of the new capital. In only one other amalgamation is a similar effect produced. The new deposits totalled over seventy millions, so that the new bank was in every way qualified for its designation as a " great " bank.

An interesting feature was that the directorate was increased to 27, since no arrangements were made for retirements or withdrawals. The shareholders made lively comments as to the heavy expenses of maintaining a superabundant number of directors, and it illustrates a new phase of the difficulties attendant on the amalgamation process. These difficulties increase with the increase in size and importance of the amalgamations, and they are a source of much trouble in later years.

Lastly, it should be pointed out that this large step was not taken with the approval of City opinion. Unlike the amalgamations which were given up in face of the protests of Lancashire people, this opinion was not strong enough, however, to prevent the making of the agreement.

The next important year—1913—saw two of the alliances in which the Midland Bank was concerned in this period, and two which are entirely typical ; for on June 6 it was announced that the Sheffield and Hallamshire Bank had been acquired, and a fortnight later the Lincoln and Lindsey Bank (in the same locality) had also been absorbed. They are typical of the methods of Sir Edward Holden, inasmuch as they illustrate the speed and decision with which he invariably acted. It is interesting to note also the development of a new aspect of the movement by the amalgamation with Messrs. Armstrong and Co., of Paris and Havre, of Lloyds Bank. This step was not accepted in the City without much comment, of which the following, taken from the *Economist*, is typical (p. 552, 1913) : " The balance of advantage is nevertheless against the new enterprise."

1914-20.

To pass now to the period 1914–20.

It is convenient to date this period from the beginning of the war and to extend it into 1920.

For many months the banks were so beset by the task of meeting the normal requirements of customers with depleted staffs, so occupied with the problem of meeting the ever-increasing exigencies of war finance, and generally so much overworked, that it was not practicable to arrange amalgamations of one bank with another.   For a long time it was found necessary to compromise on the position already attained, and to co-operate in order to solve problems which demand concentration from a solely national standpoint.   This is reflected in the agreements made between the large banks to withhold from opening new branches and to close surplus competitive branches when it was found practicable.   Hence in 1915 there were only three agreements, none of which represented serious attempts at expansion, and two of which were very small movements. Again, in 1916 there was only one agreement, and this, between the Manchester and Liverpool District and the Bank of Whitehaven, was purely a geographical movement. But when it was realised that the war was apparently to endure for an indefinitely longer period, and that in any case the banks should not be caught unprepared for the task of rehabilitation, discerning general managers and chairmen made plans for consolidation of interests.   In late 1917, therefore, the London City and Midland Bank decided to extend to Ireland.   This step was at once copied by the London County and Westminster Bank, and the tide of activity having been set in motion, aided by specious reconstruction arguments, it flowed strongly and quickly throughout 1918 and the succeeding year.   In these two years 19 amalgamations, involving 38 large banks, were made at a very quick speed.   Even in 1920, after the wave was receding, it did not do so without another final surge, which resulted in the making of another 7 agreements of diverse sorts.   The reasons generally advanced were those of the necessity of keeping pace with banking developments abroad and of preparing for that magic period of " reconstruction." The public, usually complaisant, early took alarm, and called for the setting up of a commission of inquiry.   In April, 1918, therefore, a Treasury Committee was set up, to which reference will be made later.

The one large alliance made in 1915 represented the extension by Barclays into the midland counties, and was designed to fill the gaps in its area there.   On those grounds, then, it may be classed as a geographical amalgamation. It was made in early 1915, because Barclays had felt the gain which would result from a more compact organisation in view of the special conditions created by the war. The other bank concerned was the United Counties bank, which had evolved from Birmingham and Dudley as centres. The reasons advanced for the move by Barclays' chairman were that banks should combine in order to meet the demands for extra accommodation made by manufacturers and contractors, who were obtaining Government contracts for war materials, which were beyond their ordinary capacity to carry. Again, banks should prepare by amalgamation for the trial of strength with German banks which would occur after the war—which in those days was expected to be completed in a few months time. And, lastly: " Barclays would secure a large field, hitherto untouched upon, to us (at present there are only seven places where both banks have branches)." Whatever the disadvantages or advantages of the scheme, however, the Treasury, without giving any reason to the banks for so doing, refused to agree to the change being made. Indeed, consent was delayed for some months, and then (again without explanation) it gave permission to amalgamate. In the meantime it was necessary to resort to a working agreement.

Obviously the most interesting feature of this development was that for the first time two of the reasons cited in its support arose from war conditions, and these pre-dispose to the assumption that it was caused by those conditions.

The agreement of 1916 was also based on the principle of securing a rapid extension and consolidation of area, although in this case both banks operated in Lancashire and Cumberland only.

It is not till 1917 that there were extensions abroad on a large scale. In the early part of that year important moves were made both in Sweden and Germany, which were both explained in the newspapers of those countries as being due to the necessity of making ready for post-war conditions,[1]

[1] *Vide* reports in *Bankers' Magazine*, 1917,

By such moves the Deutsche Bank increased its deposits
to the equivalent of £176 millions. The London City and
Midland Bank had then £174 millions in deposits, so that
the German concern had taken the lead—by means of amalgamation. There is no wonder, therefore, that since all eyes
were on Germany, and since Sir Edward Holden for several
years compared. the German banking system favourably
with our own in the speeches he made at the Midland Bank
meetings, that the amalgamations occurring there should
influence to some extent amalgamation policy at home.
It is not surprising to find, then, that shortly afterwards
the London City and Midland Bank made an alliance with
the Belfast Banking Co. The alliance took the form of an
agreement for the exchange of shares. Over 90 per cent.
of the shares were obtained, and so a controlling interest was
acquired, which gave to the Midland Bank a command over
49 branches and 33 sub-branches. Not long afterwards
the London County and Westminster Bank arranged a
similar step by obtaining share control of the Ulster
Bank. In this case a very liberal price had to be paid
for a move which was apparently due to the fear of
being left behind in the banking race. And it points to the
resumption of that competition which had reached great
keenness in 1914, and this assumption is justified by the
events of the following year. The move was not well
received by the Irish bankers, as is shown by a quotation
from the work of Mr. R. J. Eaton, whose article on the
amalgamations appeared in the *Journal of the Institute of
Bankers in Ireland* (October, 1919). He said :

" The operations were effected in both cases by a purchase
of shares on terms very advantageous to the Irish shareholders.
Banking opinion in Ireland is on the whole inclined to resent
the invasion, as it seems to imply an accusation that the Irish
banks do not give sufficient support to the industries in this
country. A good deal of public criticism has been aroused to
the effect that Irish banks do not treat their customers as
generously as the English banks, or employ so large a proportion
of their resources in loans and advances. . . ."

Summing up on page 235 he says :

" The Irish banks will, nevertheless, be justified in resenting any further penetration from across the channel, as there is no reason to suppose them incapable of giving to Irish industry all the assistance their future development is likely to require."

Coincident with this extension to the sister isle, extensions were made in countries abroad. The National Provincial Bank joined with Lloyds, for instance, to form a separate private company to function in France ; while the London City and Midland Bank opened an advisory office in Russia, and the London County and Westminster Bank opened in Spain and increased its representation in France from two to four branches. All these developments testify to the working of the motive of expansion at this time and in following years.[1]

Turning now to 1918, even in the first month a surprise was sprung upon the financial world, for two amalgamations between joint-stock banks of moderately large size were announced. One involved the coalescing of the London and Provincial Bank and the London and South Western Bank, while the other involved the National Provincial Bank and the Union Bank of London and Smiths. The former was a good example of a " natural " amalgamation, while the latter was an amalgamation designed for strength and consolidation. Both were large amalgamations, and with them it may be said that the war movement proper began.

In his speech to the shareholders of the South Western Bank Sir Herbert Hambling, after mentioning that their previous policy had been to " set their faces against absorption which has as its sole object the aggregation of huge balances," pointed out that their banking business was mostly localised to London and immediate environs. The increase of foreign business and the extension of the branch system, which had caused customers to urge the need for

---

[1] Though it bears no direct relation to the amalgamation movement in banking, we may note that the fever for increased size was also in evidence in the insurance world, since in this year at least 10 prominent insurance companies were absorbed. Rather curiously, each of the purchasing companies was engaged in insurance business of a composite and miscellaneous type, while the companies absorbed were specialists— a move which is somewhat akin to that noticed earlier in the banking world, viz. that of distributing risks over a wide area.

additional facilities in the provinces, constrained them to seek amalgamation with a suitable bank. Such a bank was undoubtedly the London and Provincial, with whom, in 1912, negotiations had been in progress but had not fructified because no mutually satisfactory terms could be arranged. He went on to show that the latter bank had most of its branches in Wales, the seaports and industrial centres, and to argue that the joining of this country connection to the valuable London business of his own bank would make a perfect marriage. Evidently, then, the dominant reason for this alliance was that of securing a strong bank with a compact series of branches. Altogether these numbered 560, the deposits totalled about £70 millions, and the paid up capital £2,125,000. Compared with other large banks of that time, the totals were not of great size since the London City and Midland Bank, for example, had deposits totalling over £200 millions.

Its area, too, was confined to the midlands and the south of England. It is interesting to learn that the amalgamation would have been made earlier if agreement had been reached, for the fact that it was accomplished in the middle of the war years shows how war conditions were responsible for speeding up the process of fusion.

The second agreement referred to was more important in the matter of size, for the new deposit total was about £170 millions, and the effect of the scheme was therefore to create a " great " bank, which was not only a rival to others, but an effective competitor. In explanation of the motives governing it, the chairman of the Union Bank of London (Sir Felix Schuster) said : " It is highly important to be represented in all the industrial centres all over the country. . . . We have not been actuated by a desire to present big figures." The chairman of the National Provincial Bank said : " The amalgamation of their business with the National Provincial will prove to the material advantage of the trade of the country, not only at home, but abroad."

On account of its size and importance it is accurate to take this as being the first amalgamation arranged with a desire to create a large bank.   The date is not decided by accidental causes, but more probably is due to a conjunction of the special reasons governing the 1918 amalgamations. Clearly these included the fact that it was believed about this time that the war would shortly be concluded, the movements towards larger banking institutions in evidence in Germany, insistent demands from large combinations of manufacturing firms who were engaged in the production of war materials, generated to a large extent by the prevalent inflation, and the general recognition that there should be preparation for post-war trading needs.   Speaking of this agreement *The Times* (December 17, 1917) said :

" Not the least interesting aspect of the National Provincial's absorption of the Union of London and Smith's Bank is its indication of a widening acceptance of the new economic policy which the war has shown to be desirable.   Both banks have the reputation of being conservative, and the fact that they have decided to amalgamate at this particular period therefore shows that some of the most thoughtful of our leading bankers are prepared to participate in the movement for consolidating industrial, commercial, and financial organisations in this country.   The advantages of large-scale working have been amply demonstrated in the manufacturing industries under the stress of war.   And it was found that the handling of the banking situation at the beginning of the war was facilitated by the existence of a few large amalgamated institutions. . . .   In financing the war the great banks have been able to do much more than they would have done had they been split up into a number of small unrelated units."

This is the argument of size stated in full.

A few pages back it was mentioned that the London and County and the London and Westminster Banks, by their bold policy of 1909, had in that year created what was known as the first " large " bank.   On February 8 of this year an amalgamation with Parrs Bank was announced. This was therefore only a fortnight after the amalgamation just discussed.   By reason alone of the fact that negotiations necessarily occupied a certain period of time, it is evident that this scheme was being planned at the same time as the earlier amalgamations, and that the various directors were not ignorant of the steps in progress and in contemplation

by the other banks.   Keen rivalry was therefore displayed.
Again the reconstruction argument was used—if so it can
be called—while the other main argument cited 'was that of
linking with the London County and Westminster the
business of a bank which was strongly entrenched in
the midlands and north of England.   At the subsequent
confirmatory meetings, Mr. Cecil F. Parr pointed out
the clear gain which Parrs' shareholders obtained from
the agreement, which included £46,000 per annum in
increased dividends, an increase of 10 per cent. in the
total of paid-up capital, reduced liability on shares, and
a gain in capital value.   He further stressed the fact
that the banks were surprisingly complementary from
the geographical point of view, as evidenced by the fact
that overlapping only occurred in 13 towns out of 560.
Reference was made, too, to the strikingly keen competition existing between the banks—particularly in small
loans.

Dr. Leaf stressed the coalescing of the large banks of
Germany, and pointed out that there was a possibility of the
three large banks there working together under the supervision of the Government.[1]

From this and other speeches made by bank chairmen,
and in especial Sir Edward Holden, it is apparent that the
influence of banking developments abroad was now strongly
felt in England, and it was undoubtedly one of the minor
forces operating to set the pace during this eventful
year.

Ten days after the announcing of this alliance, a response
was made by the Midland Bank by its capture of the important old-established London Joint Stock Bank.   In this case
also the absorbed bank received very favourable terms,

---

[1] A particularly notable part of his long speech referred to the public
aspect of amalgamations.   He said, for instance : " The problem before
us is to see if we cannot attain the advantages of economy by extension,
without the dangers of monopoly. . . .   Consolidation must come ; the
public interest is that it should come in a way which should lead to a
group of banks of approximately equal power, stimulated by a competition which will keep them alert as well as strong, and ever on the
look-out for their own interests, which in these circumstances will be
intimately bound up with those of the State."

due in no small measure to the keen competition of the large banks for suitable connections in this new phase of amalgamation—the building up of businesses which should cover the entire country. Indeed, bearing in mind that both were joint-stock companies of premier position and large capitals (and therefore concerned a large number of shareholders), the size of the bonus offered was unusually large. It is perhaps the best reflex of the keenness of the competition just at this time, and was probably intended to prevent criticism from the absorbed shareholders. There certainly was none, for the amalgamation was agreed to unanimously.

The striking feature of this amalgamation is that not only did it ensure that the London Joint City and Midland was to continue as the largest English bank, but it gave a lead of about £70 millions in deposits over the next competitor. Incidentally it displaced the Deutsche Bank from its position as the world's largest bank. The effectiveness of Sir Edward Holden's rejoinder to the new move by other banks is displayed in this agreement, since the number of branches acquired was no fewer than 308. Immediately prior to the notification of the terms it had been announced that the Bank Amalgamations Committee was to be set up, and the carrying out of the agreement was therefore delayed until September. Sir Edward Holden then made a very full speech in statement of the reasons for its adoption. He mentioned that he sought to absorb this bank in 1913—when there were many amalgamations—but terms were not agreed on. Doubtless the terms now offered were substantially better than those to which the Midland Bank then found it unable to agree. The main reasons given for the fusion were that no less than £300 millions would be required for the reconstruction for industrial enterprises, and large banks were indispensable for creating this sum ; secondly, all efforts should be made to maintain London as the financial centre of the world ; thirdly, " amalgamations are taking place in other parts of the world, notably in Germany, Sweden, Canada, and Australia " ; while lastly, Sir Edward stated his firm conviction that amalgamations did not weaken competition.

In connection with the third part of the argument the fact that the Deutsche Bank controlled a group of 25 banks was emphasised, on the ground that this would make Germany a strong competitor for post-war markets.

Referring to the proposed alliance, he said that they admitted the charge of treating the shareholders of the London Joint Stock Bank in a liberal manner, e.g. they would be the gainers by an extra £41,000 in dividend alone. Yet to meet this a new issue of shares was about to be made to Midland shareholders which would give them an ample margin of profit, by reason of the amount received as premiums.

One aspect of this amalgamation requires comment. It appears that many of the branches of the two banks overlapped. Contrary to the usual custom, however, they were not to be closed, but maintained as though amalgamation had not occurred.[1] The reason as cited in the quotation below is not strong, especially if it is recollected that the war was still raging and consequently staffs were weakened by the absence of many trained bank men on service. The fear of losing business seems to be the only explanation.

Hitherto Lloyds has had no share in the war-time movement, but it is concerned in the next amalgamation, which is striking because of the unusual number of branches acquired at one swoop. The number was so high as 473. This total had been acquired by the Capital and Counties Bank in a series of 26 amalgamations accomplished in about thirty years. The Capital and Counties had confined its attention almost exclusively to the absorption of country banks, most of which were private houses, and it had therefore little representation in industrial areas. Lloyds was essentially a bank having its main connections in the midland and northern industrial towns, with certain extensions to Wales. This notwithstanding, overlapping occurred at no fewer than 114 branches. Again, the terms were productive of a substantial bonus to the absorbed shareholders, for the quotations in July were £26 for each Capital and Counties

---

[1] The explanation was: " The customers of each bank have become accustomed to their managers, and experience teaches that the proper policy to pursue in such circumstances is not to close offices, but to continue them as they exist at the present time " (Speech, Sir Edward Holden).

share (£10 paid) and £25½ for each Lloyds share (£8 paid). They provided that one Lloyds share should exchange for one Capital and Counties share, but in addition a bonus of £2 per share was given.   On 175,000 shares the bonus was therefore £350,000.

But this was not the whole of Lloyds' contribution to the new movement.   In addition it was proposed to acquire controlling interests in the National Bank of Scotland, the London and River Plate Bank, and a bank in India.   The last proposal was rejected by the Treasury.   The terms offered in each of these cases were so liberal (more so than in the case of the English bank) that the *Bankers' Magazine* (August, 1918) was moved to express the following comment : " Quite apart from the general wisdom or otherwise of this great departure on the part of one of the Clearing Banks, we cannot help thinking that it would be expressing it moderately to say that the terms paid by Lloyds Bank are ample."   The chief feature of interest is that the amalgamation marked an entirely new departure in amalgamation practice.   It involved, for example, the invasion of Scotland by an English bank ; and it meant that control was secured over a bank which operated abroad—mostly in Argentina—in territory hitherto entirely unknown to English banks.   The importance of these steps is apparent.   For the River Plate Bank £1,920,000 nominal paid-up capital was given, worth £6,120,000 in market values.   In exchange Lloyds received £1,800,000 paid-up capital and a reserve of £2,293,000. For this some idea of the size of the transaction will be gathered.   A total of £355½ was given for each share of £100 paid of the National Bank of Scotland.

An unusual development accompanied the arrangements for these large moves.   It was recognised that the problem of administering so many branches and banks was likely to become difficult.   Accordingly, in addition to the creation of new general managers, it was

" decided to appoint a General Council composed of representatives of Lloyds Bank and the associated banks, to whom will be added a Secretary with special qualifications for the post. The duties of the Council will comprise the gathering and recording of intelligence and keeping in the closest possible touch with the changing financial and commercial conditions both at home and abroad, so that they may be in a position to advise the Board in regard thereto."

Following very closely on this announcement came the news that the London Provincial and South Western Bank, which had only been created as the result of the amalgamation in January, was to be taken over by Barclays—in the month of August. Allowing for the delay of about three months involved by the sitting of the Bank Amalgamations Committee, it will be seen that hardly had the new bank been constituted than arrangements were being entered into for a new absorption involving its disappearance. It is, perhaps, this excessive speed which is the most striking characteristic of the 1918 movement. The resultant belief that the two independent gentlemen appointed by the 1918 committee were not using their powers effectively brought many complaints from the City. These apparently induced Sir Herbert Hambling to give full replies thereto in the editions of *The Times* newspaper.[1]

Among other things he mentioned that out of 550 branches owned by the absorbed bank no fewer than 250 were in London and suburbs. Barclays had 800 branches, but these were mostly located in the great provincial industrial and agricultural areas ; nevertheless much overlapping occurred. Doubtless the possession of so many branches in London was a strong incentive to the arranging of terms, for Barclays, compared with its other competitors, was here at a distinct disadvantage. Again, it was pointed out that : " This bank

---

[1] In a letter appearing on July 24, he said that German banks were previously firmly established in England and had secured a great deal of Britain's business by working with very small profits. Their being wound up was England's opportunity, though not if the banks were small. Therefore consolidation was necessary to obtain the necessary foreign representation for British trade. There was a necessity for ' a phenomenal increase in production,' and ' a policy of amalgamation provides the best all-round solution of a very complex and far-reaching problem.' Further, ' The provision of the facilities for the importation of raw meat and for the export trade of this country should give other large manufacturers and traders the help they will require, and the final result should be to provide more opposition for the smaller man and an increase in the amount of work available for the country.'

also acquires from the London Provincial and South Western Bank, Ltd., their own interests in Cox and Co. (France), Ltd., and also the benefits of their arrangements with other foreign institutions." In view of the fact that Barclays was not well supplied with foreign representation, this was a valuable accretion.

The terms provided that £2,125,000 capital in £5 shares (fully paid), with a market quotation of £20, were to be exchanged for £2,620,833 in £1 shares (fully paid) quoted at £3½. This meant that the market value of the absorbed bank's capital was £8,500,000, and that of Barclays was £9,172,915, so that a bonus of about £673,000 was given— about £1 10s. per share. Additionally the dividend was increased—a typical instance of the gain accruing to shareholders through amalgamation.

The last agreement of importance to be made this year necessitated the removal of a very old-established private bank. This was Martins, believed to be engaged in business in 1563. For many years it had been established in the middle of Lombard Street, trading under the sign of the " Grasshopper," and its removal by the modern process of amalgamation came as a shock. It appears that the expediency of amalgamating had become manifest, and it was deemed wisest to link with a provincial bank having a good hold on that especial kind of business. The circular issued by the absorbing bank to clients (the Bank of Liverpool) stated that two courses were available to them, i.e. (1) to join one of the large banking combinations ; (2) to remain independent and acquire an opening in London. The first alternative was not entertained because the directors felt that the disappearance of a bank of the importance of the Bank of Liverpool was contrary to public interest. With regard to the second they thought that there was room for a provincial bank which nevertheless would be able to offer London facilities.[1]

The move, therefore, represents a sort of retaliatory step to the sweeping moves of the great London banks, and it is noteworthy for demonstrating that the submission of

[1] Circular issued to shareholders, December, 1918.

G

smaller banks to an apparently inevitable process was not really dictated by such imperious necessity as most of the chairmen of smaller banks seemed anxious to explain.

The directors of Martins Bank stated that, as a result of the creation of great banks and the disappearance of many small banks, it was desirable to become associated with a bank having provincial connections, in order to provide complete banking facilities. Doubtless the more important reason is that they received a high offer for their business which the holding of a seat in the Clearing House justified. Since this is the last example of the capture of a seat in the Clearing House by means of amalgamation, there is interest in noticing it, and that this reason persisted from the early 'seventies until now as a cause of amalgamation moves.

With 1919 the year which saw most amalgamations in this busy period is reached. In scanning the list, however, it is apparent that these differ essentially from those just discussed since they do not record drastic changes in banking organisation of a spectacular sort. They rather represent consolidation and shaping of positions gained. True, the large London banks still make absorptions, and therefore grow bigger, but the guiding idea seems to be that of remedying defects in the new area, by means of special amalgamations. The agreements first announced in 1919 illustrate the point. These were between the National Provincial and Bradford District on the one hand, and the London County Westminster and Parrs with the Nottingham Joint Stock on the other. In the latter case the London bank had only a very weak representation around Nottingham.[1] Similarly the National Provincial was able to increase its representation in a woollen area where hitherto its branches had been few and scattered. Almost similar again are the absorptions made of the West Yorkshire Bank by Lloyds, and of the

---

[1] The 1919 Report said : " For our own business it is of great importance that we should have an established footing in Nottingham and the neighbourhood, where we are at the present without branches, though the district joins up well with that which we have gained in Derbyshire by Parrs' amalgamation with Crompton and Evan's Bank." Also, " It is necessary for us to recognise that we are not as well spread over England as are our four great competitors, and this inequality we are setting ourselves to make good."

Sheffield Banking Co. by the National Provincial. In this latter case, the reason assigned by the Sheffield Bank's circular mentions, additionally, that "they recognised that the war had materially altered the economic conditions of the world, and they anticipate that demands will be made for greatly increased banking accommodation when general trading is resumed." The alliance of the Westminster with the Notts Bank was also governed by this secondary reason.[1]

Later amalgamations were those made by the newly constituted Bank of Liverpool and Martins with the Palatine Bank, the Halifax Commercial Banking Co., and Cocks Biddulph and Co., in quick succession. They form a continuance of the policy mentioned at the time of their alliance with Martins.

But the outstanding event of the year was the coup effected by Barclays, which, it has been shown, was endeavouring to bring up the extent of its area, and to strengthen it. In this year it launched a scheme designed to give control of the Union Bank of Manchester, and the British Linen Bank. The important feature of the scheme was that amalgamation was not sought, but only "affiliation." This was to be effected, as in the case of Lloyds Bank in the previous year, by an attempt to secure control of the share capital of both banks. The reasons for this step seem to be not merely the desire to avoid giving the idea of too great an extent of area, but to avoid the clash with local feeling in Lancashire such as had been witnessed in 1904 and 1910, and to preserve the note issue of the Scottish Bank. Evidently Barclays had profited by the lessons of the two attempts at amalgamation referred to, and were disposed to risk nothing in the execution of a

---

[1] June 30, speech by Dr. Leaf. The 1919 Report said : " The Nottingham and Notts Bank has been a valued client of ours for many years past, and we have frequently discussed the possibility of a union with them. It is an apt illustration of the influence of the impending reconstruction period in bringing about such amalgamations, that our agreement was actually brought to a point by the prospects of large requirements in the near future and for the Nottingham trade, requirements which would be beyond the resources of a comparatively small local bank, but which are well within the compass of a bank such as our own with its exceptional liquidity and large deposits."

bold scheme. A notable part of the arrangement related to the terms proposed ; for it was decided to increase the capital of Barclays from £8,820,356 to £14,210,359, and to cancel all future liability on account of uncalled capital. Such a step had no precedent in banking history, and caused much discussion in the newspapers and journals such as the *Economist* and *Bankers' Magazine*. The total of the new resources was £360 millions and 1,880 branches. The reasons were stated as the desire to complete representation where Barclays were hitherto without it, and to give reciprocal accommodation to foreign banks.

It is interesting to note that in so far as the Union Bank of Manchester was a member of the Lancashire group it was the first to yield to the persuasion of a London firm.

The scheme was not many days old, when a rival one was announced by the largest bank—the London Joint City and Midland Bank. There is little reason to doubt that it was instigated by Barclays' move, since it followed on similar lines. The method of fusion was similar, i.e. exchange of shares instead of amalgamation proper; unusually good terms were offered—determined probably by the desire to make the agreement a successful one, so that the Midland might protect its interests against those of the four great banks who were now its competitors. How ambitious the scheme was may be gleaned from a glance at the figures. The total deposits then to be controlled were £417,257,000 ; the number of branches 1,646 ; and the total of advances £143,565,000. The reasons for the fusion were stated in the Midland Bank's circular as

" The growth of our interests in Scotland has compelled us for some time past to consider the opening of branches in that country, and we had already taken steps towards opening an office in Glasgow. We believe, however, that we shall be able through the proposed arrangement to develop our Scottish business far more rapidly and effectively than would be possible by means of new branches."

The bank concerned was the Clydesdale Bank of Scotland.

The last amalgamation to which reference should be made is that of the National Provincial Bank with Messrs. Coutts

and Co.   This also took the form of affiliation, for the reason
in this case that it was deemed best to preserve Coutts'
individuality on account of the select nature of its business.
Originally established in Scotland by Thomas Coutts, a
London branch was opened early in the eighteenth century,
and subsequently a very high-class remunerative business
was established.[1]   Doubtless good terms had to be offered
before this business was secured.

1920-1924.

The effect of the amalgamations of the war period was to
cause the emergence of five large banks which were so much
greater in size of resources and operations than other remaining concerns as to become popularly termed the " Big
Five."   Since 1920 moves have necessarily been somewhat
infrequent, and the order of priority has not been affected
by them.   The smaller banks have clung to their individual
positions, and if profits are a sufficient criterion, they have
worked successfully in spite of the prevalence of acute
competition.   They alone have not been implicated in
further amalgamations.

Altogether sixteen amalgamations and affiliations have
occurred in four years, and the yearly average of four only,
points to the reduced activity of these years, and since
most of these were absorptions of small concerns the relative
unimportance of 1920-4 is emphasised.

The most important move was that made by the Midland
Bank when in 1924 it secured additional expansion in
Scotland by affiliating with the North of Scotland Bank.
Most of the branches of this moderately sized concern are
to be found in the northerly parts of Scotland, so that they
helped to lengthen the chain which before only stretched
as far as the most northerly branch of the Clydesdale Bank—
acquired in 1919.   The terms offered were reminiscent of
the extraordinarily high terms given during the 1918–19
" boom " years, for to quote from the *Bankers' Magazine*
(of January, 1924) :

[1] Sir Wm. Forbes, *Memoirs of a Banking House.*

" The terms offered by the Midland appear highly favourable to the shareholders of the North of Scotland, whose share of £20 each, having £4 paid, commanded a price of about £15 prior to the announcement of the offer. For every four of these shares the Midland offers eleven shares of £2½ each, fully paid, which shares at present command a price of about £9, so that the price offered is equivalent to about £24 15s. per North of Scotland share."

Undoubtedly the bonus of nearly £10 per share was the price paid for desire to round off the representation of the leading bank in the United Kingdom.

This further aggressive seizing of the business of Scottish bankers undoubtedly provoked retaliation by one of the senior banks over the border, for early in the next month it was announced that the Royal Bank of Scotland had acquired the business of Messrs. Drummond and Co.— possessing excellent offices in London.

More interesting from the historical standpoint were the moves which produced the linking of Messrs. Childs' very old business to the distinguished house of Messrs. Glyn and Co. This happened in 1924, but in 1923 Glyns had taken over the business of Messrs. Holt and Co.—London army agents. The consequence is that Messrs. Glyn and Co., working on definitely individualistic banking lines, have very effectively consolidated their position. Along with Messrs. Hoare and Co. they alone represent the long line of once renowned and supreme London private bankers.

Other army and navy agents have been absorbed into the larger joint-stock firms, for Messrs. Cox and Co. and H. S. King, after joining together in 1922 (to some extent because of the illness of the principal partner in the latter named house), were taken over by Lloyds in the year following. It is interesting to note that Lloyds thereby secured some of the Indian representation which they were desirous of obtaining by the projected amalgamation with the National Bank of India in 1919. One reason for the absorption which will at once be apparent was that the business of army and navy agents, which flourished exceedingly during war years, was adversely affected by the conditions of the later post-war years, and alliance with a stronger institution was rendered desirable.   Messrs. Stilwell and Co. were absorbed in the same year by the Westminster Bank, and Messrs. Grindlay by the National Provincial.

The last-named bank was the only individual bank to show decided energy in this period.   This was probably accounted for by the fact that it was one of the smallest members, in point of size and resources, of the " Big Five," and it desired to secure more extended representation.   Amalgamations were made in 1920 with the Sheffield Banking Co., and in 1922 with two of the very few remaining private businesses in the land—Messrs. Dingley Pearse and Co., of London and Launceston.   None of these banks were of large size. Another amalgamation was made with the Guernsey Banking Co. in 1924.   Before it had long been accomplished, the Westminster Bank had seized on the remaining Guernsey Bank (the Guernsey Commercial)—an excellent evidence of the persistence of vigorous competition.

Three other agreements may be mentioned.   Lloyds in 1921 took the business of Messrs. Fox Fowler and Co., and the note issue which was forfeited in consequence was the last to be surrendered in accordance with the provisions of the 1844 Act.

In the same year the business of Messrs. Beckett and Co. of Leeds was disposed of to the Westminster Bank, and this was one of the largest and most renowned of all the provincial businesses operated by private firms.   It had survived fifteen years longer than its neighbours Leatham Tew and Co., mainly because it possessed a high-class West and East Riding business, but eventually it yielded to the tempting offers of its London agent.

Lastly, in 1923 Lloyds secured by purchase the bulk of the shares in the London and Brazilian Bank, and thereby acted extensively to its interests abroad.   As a result of a fusion later accomplished by the London and Brazilian, another bank operating in South America was absorbed, so that an even wider representation has been secured. Since then a controlling interest has been acquired in the Bank of British West Africa.   The effect of these definite moves made in 1920-4 has therefore been to add to the ramifications of Lloyds' foreign interests and to give it a supreme position in this field of banking enterprise.

To sum up the reasons governing policy in this period, it is evident that almost all the agreements were made under the influence of strong rivalry. This grew more intense with the years. Particularly does this explanation apply to the moves made by the large concerns, and to war years. The motive of geographical expansion was also prominent, and indeed more so than in any other period, for amalgamation was the readiest, and possibly the least expensive, of all methods of securing block growth. The acquisition of accounts of firms engaged in very various types of enterprise not only gave the gains cited earlier, but inevitably gave strength, first because the policy of a large bank may be more stable than that of a small, and second, because the specialised experience of bankers operating in areas concentrating on similar types of industry was focused under one, instead of many roofs. In the case of provincial banks regional expansion only was sought and secured. A common argument often advanced by bankers in earlier years was that amalgamation to increase resources was rendered necessary by the prior integration of industrial and commercial firms. The speed, too, of the fusion process is sometimes attributed to the speed of the opposed development.

Occasionally some joint-stock firms of lesser repute found difficulties of administration too stubborn to solve, and in a few instances it was deemed to be a wise step to seek protection, and absorption followed. With smaller banks, too, agency expenses became so greatly increased, owing to the necessity of increasing facilities to customers, that amalgamation with a larger concern able to give these directly was preferred. One or two small banks such as Stuckeys were led to amalgamate to use surplus funds more profitably than was possible in small—usually agricultural— areas. Other reasons figuring in individual amalgamations were the absence of London representation and the hindrance to progress caused by large capitals.

In the war period the use of the new " reconstruction " argument is found *ad infinitum*.   It was largely the product of psychological war-time conditions, and served as a very useful banking tool.   Other war and post-war amalgamations were due simply to the extraordinarily good terms offered by competing banks, directed by ambitious leaders.   From creating " national " banks the fusion idea has progressed to extension to foreign fields, and the chief argument cited in support has been the necessity of meeting foreign financial competition and of supporting English trading ventures, and this argument still prevails.

A description of the positions reached as a result of a hundred years of amalgamation policy, and the full effects of the multifarious moves and counter-moves upon the banking structure, must be left to the chapters following.

Part II.

CHAPTER VI.

EFFECTS OF AMALGAMATION.
(MAINLY STATISTICAL.)

OVER a period of one hundred years there have necessarily been many changes, striking and extensive in character, in banking. Easily the most notable of these has been the change over from the system of private banks, with a Bank of England monopoly, to that of a highly developed joint-stock system, with the Bank of England as the " Bankers' Bank." This change is well reflected by figures. In 1825 there were as many as 554 private houses, possessing altogether only 681 branches ; [1] in 1924 there remain only 2 private firms (both of which are to be found tucked away in one corner of London), possessing but two branches, compared with 13 joint-stock firms possessing 8,081 branches. [2] The contrast between the two periods is more strikingly revealed if it is remembered that in 1825 the census figures of the population may be estimated at 12,759,460, giving an average of about 18,739 persons to each banking office ; in 1924 the population may be estimated at 38,611,142, or an average of about 4,777 persons to each office. The gain in banking facilities is apparent, and this gain is very greatly magnified by the presence of an effective transport and communication system, which was not available a hundred years ago. [3]

[1] The enumeration of branches is taken from the *London Directory* of 1826, published by Kent.
[2] *Bankers' Magazine,* 1924 ; *Banking Almanack,* 1925.
[3] For instance, in the late eighteenth century there were no banks in a town of the size of Leeds. " Manufacturers in some of the remote parts of Yorkshire and Lancashire were compelled to conduct their business

To pursue the comparison—in 1825-6 and succeeding years the inefficiency of the prevailing system is shown by the number of failures which occurred repeatedly. In a few weeks in 1825-6 at least 63 private banks outside London failed,[1] while in the years 1839-43 the yearly failures were respectively 9, 24, 26, 12, and 11. On the other hand, there have been no failures of importance since 1890, notwithstanding that in 1914 the banking system was called upon to withstand a trial of great severity. On the score of safety, therefore, the superiority of the present system is evident.

It may also be mentioned that in 1825 banking was conducted principally, if not wholly, for the benefit of merchants and traders, and well-to-do people generally, whereas now the fullest banking accommodation is open to all members of the community ; and influence, which formerly played an important part in business, is now absent.

Lastly, a hundred years ago banking was conducted by individuals and groups of individuals in the neighbourhood where they lived in an arbitrary, unscientific manner, with no regard whatever for the national banking position ; now it is in the hands of companies working with logical accuracy, and well-tried practice, noted for its soundness and conservativeness, established in adequate—if not excessive—numbers, in all parts of the land. The private bankers worked in the dim light of privacy, took heavy risks, and sought large profits ; the companies are now administered under the incessant glare of strong criticism, seeking to minimise and spread risks, and driven by fierce competition to work on narrow margins of profit.

It is desirable to discover what share the amalgamation movement has had in this striking progress, and consequently an analysis of its various effects is necessary.

transactions at Nottingham, 70 to 100 miles distant from their dwellings and factories, because there were no banks at Leeds or Sheffield, or any of the intermediate towns."—Pamphlet, title-page missing, by H. Burgess (1828), p. 3 (Institute of Bankers).

[1] "In 1825-6 there were 770 country bankers, and of these 63 had stopped payment; out of the 63, 23 had subsequently resumed their payments and paid 20s. in the £, and of the remainder 31 were making arrangements for the payment of their debts, and there was a hope that every farthing would be paid."—Sir M. W. Ridley, House of Commons, June 3, 1828. This sanguine hope by no means materialised.

If all the totals of separate amalgamations recorded in the historical survey are added, the result is 552—made up as follows :

Period.	Private with Private.	Joint Stock with Joint Stock.	Joint Stock by Private.	Private by Joint Stock.	Totals.
Unknown dates .	—	—	—	17⎫	122
1825–43 . . .	23	6	—	76⎭	
1844–61 . . .	11	10	—	23	44
1862–89 . . .	31	40	1	66	138
1890–1902 . .	37	51	1	64	153
1903–24 . . .	1	58	—	36	95
	103	165	2	282	552

The Bank Amalgamations Committee of 1918 referred to " over 300 instances in the past." [1] This total was therefore too small. Even now it is possible that a few amalgamations have been omitted, since none of the banks of the present day possess complete records of events which involved the many institutions now merged in them (as shown in Chapter I).

From these figures it is evident that the movement has been responsible for carrying off more than five banks each year. The period averages are :

1825–43	.	.	.	.	.	over 6
1844–61	.	.	.	.	.	over 2
1862–89	.	.	.	.	.	over 7
1890–1902 .	.	.	.	.	over 11
1903–24	.	.	.	.	.	over 4

If account is taken of the reduced number of banks, these figures show that the latter half of last century is notable for the activity then prevailing, and that the modern movement may be dated from the passing of the Act of 1862. The

[1] Cmd. 9052. Vide Appendix III.

constancy and steadiness of the movement are shown by the fact that there have been one or more agreements recorded in 93 out of the 100 years. From 1851 to 1915 the only years without amalgamations were 1869 and 1885.

So many as 387 private concerns have thus disappeared as a result of the process. Bearing in mind that the total of 554 [1] was the highest recorded during the entire period, and that the toal number of new private banks set up since does not appear to be more than 11, while there are now only 2 private banks in existence, it would seem that of the full number of private banks which have disappeared from all causes, amalgamation has carried off 69 per cent. Further, it would be interesting to discover, were it possible, how many banks which were amalgamated would have been driven into failure if the fusion process had not been available. Some cases of this type have already received mention in the historical survey.

The total number of joint-stock banks which lost identity as a consequence of amalgamation was 167. The highest number in existence was 121, in the years 1873-4-5 and 1880. Since 1825 it may be estimated that altogether 233 joint-stock concerns have been launched. There are now 13, and allowing for these it is evident that amalgamation has caused the disappearance of 73 per cent. of the whole. Here again, then, the importance of the process is seen : of the 13 institutions remaining 5 are of very large size.

These generalisations made, attention will now be given to details, and first to those concerning capitals and reserves.

For the earlier periods figures are difficult either to secure or estimate. The difficulty arises from the fact that the banking capital of the country was formerly held by private bankers alone, who neither published accounts nor balance sheets. And any attempt to seek to evaluate capitals or reserves must be doomed to failure if only because private firms were usually engaged in some other business besides banking, e.g. especially brewing. [2] There is reason to believe

---

[1] This was the number in 1825.
[2] E.g. Barclays, Lacons, and Hanbury and Lloyds.

that they relied excessively upon their local reputations,[1] and were not greatly concerned as to the adequacy or otherwise of their capital funds.

It is astonishing how long this state of affairs prevailed, for even in 1883 no full accounts of private bankers were published, and by 1891 only 36 out of 149 made up a balance sheet for the inspection of the public. Even then it was rare to find capitals and reserves shown separately. Moreover, in the case of the joint-stock companies, although most of the earlier ones showed some accounts, their examples were not followed by the banks created when the joint-stock methods had won recognition and a measure of success, and in 1874 not many more than half their numbers published accounts. Lastly, for many years after 1880 the large West End banks in London maintained secrecy. But since particulars of the purchase price of private banks are not usually obtainable, and there had only been 33 amalgamations of one joint-stock bank with another in the fifty years preceding (at least half of which were caused by failures of those absorbed), the gap is relatively of no great importance. With the scare resulting from the serious failure of the City of Glasgow Bank in 1878, more companies and houses began to issue accounts, and in time the custom became more

---

[1] " The Country Banks of England have been a source of great derangement, and it is a matter of astonishment that they have been suffered to continue so long possessed of such vast privilege and vast power, without measure or control. . . . A general dealer getting into good trade and credit in a country town would separate a window off from his store and write ' Bank ' upon it, and then commence the issue of notes."—*Observations on Banks of Issue and the Currency* (1841), p. 15. Anon. In the collection of the Rylands library.

The extent and diversity of their trading risks are shown by the fact that the principal partner of the firm of Clark Richardson and Hodgson, of Whitby, was engaged as a draper, mercer, and wine merchant, as well as banker. Another Whitby bank was conducted by a lady—Margaret Campion—who professed also to be a general merchant, sail-cloth maker, and a wine merchant. Yet another man—Joseph Dresser—was the proprietor of banks at Thirsk and Ripon, and used his depositors' funds to work a water corn-mill, with the produce of which he controlled the corn markets at these towns.—Backhouse Collection of Documents relating to Yorkshire Banking.

Again, asked by Thomas Hankey—another well-known banker—how much capital there was in his business, Lord Overstone replied that all his capital was his desks, pens, ink, and books. " That is all my capital," he said, " the rest belongs to me. It has nothing to do with my banking business."—Quoted, *Bankers' Magazine*, 1879, p. 477.

and more widely adopted, so that from 1876 to 1891, inclusive, a sum of about £15,000,000 had been declared in addition.[1] After this latter year, too, there were other disclosures, e.g. the private firm of Messrs. Coutts and Co. adopted joint-stock form and declared capital at £1,000,000, while other private firms added a sum of £5,614,811 of capitals and reserves. In measuring the growth of the capital fund allowance must therefore be made for these additions.

In 1875 the total of capital was £31,460,000. In 1913 the total was £56,107,480—an increase of £24,647,480. The total of capital newly declared as a result of additions such as those mentioned above is at least £9,754,809. Allowing for this then, the net gain in the period is £14,892,671, or 47·33 per cent. The total capital at the end of 1923 was £85,528,131. This shows a net gain over 1875 of 140·8 per cent. Over the 1913 total it is a gain of 52·5 per cent.[2] In view of the fact that banking progressed notoriously since 1875 these gains do not appear to be large. Compared, too, with the increase in deposit totals, the gain does not appear proportionate, for as will be seen from the table of deposits on page 108 the 1913 figures show an increase on those of 1875 of 358·34 per cent., while the figures for 1923 (end) show an increase over those for 1875 of 713·4 per cent. In the case of the totals for 1913 and 1923 respectively, the gain in deposits is 127·2 per cent.[3]

Even if allowance is made for capital lost as a result of failures and withdrawals from business—£2,975,412—the statement that capital did not increase so quickly as deposits is nevertheless true. It is obvious, therefore, that to bring about this result some special cause has been at work. To discover this it is necessary to analyse the detailed figures affecting the yearly totals of capital, as specifically affected by amalgamations. This analysis shows that during the

---

[1] These and following figures are based on details contained in the *Bankers' Magazine.*

[2] In this case the gain is not subject to deduction for additions to capital.

[3] The figures for deposits need very little correction for additions other than those resulting from natural growth.

period 1875–1913 there was a total of 272 agreements of all types. Of these some were apparently so small, or the capital of the absorbing bank was so large, as to cause no change to be recorded in the volume of capital.

Since some private banks had previously shown capital and reserve as one sum, it is not possible to trace the exact changes in capital which resulted from amalgamation ; but it is certain that the general totals now to be cited were not greatly affected by such amalgamations, owing to the small size of such private concerns. Again, mainly because it is impossible to determine whether or not they were occasioned by the preceding amalgamations, later alterations in capital made by the banks engaged therein must be ignored. These qualifications stated, during the period 1875–1913, capital was decreased through amalgamations by £15,170,985, and increased by £2,311,466. On balance it was therefore reduced by £12,859,519.

In the years 1914–24 (inclusive), altogether 78 amalgamations were registered. The effect on capital was to decrease it by £3,653,351, and to increase it by £3,200,457. The net effect was therefore to reduce it by £452,894.[1]

The full statement as to the movements of the total fund of capital may now also be cited.

JOINT-STOCK AND PRIVATE BANKS OF ENGLAND AND WALES.

PAID-UP CAPITAL.

1836 [2] 90 Joint-Stock Banks (estimate)	£10,000,000
1876 (end)	32,875,000
1881	35,521,000
1886	39,838,000
1891	50,751,000
1896	54,450,000
1901	54,371,620
1906	55,236,000
1911	54,205,000
1913	56,107,480
1914	55,623,364

[1] These figures are based on details extracted from the *Bankers' Magazine*, the *Economist*, and financial newspapers.

[2] Estimate by J. W. Gilbart. Q. 1368. Report of Committee (1841)

PAID-UP CAPITAL (*continued*).

1915	56,654,762
1916	57,536,431
1917	60,113,105
1918	67,231,033
1919	68,961,242
1920	85,973,246
1921	86,872,399
1922 [1]	94,098,392
1923 [2]	85,528,131

It is easy to understand the reasons for seeking to lessen capital. Obviously large dividends could be paid far more easily on reduced capitals. Large dividends over a period of years served to give prestige to the institution concerned ; this in turn resulted in a high quotation being obtained for the shares. The benefit did not accrue simply to the contented shareholders. It enabled the fortunate bank to purchase other banks with larger proportionate capitals on terms which were not only favourable to the shareholders absorbed, but had also monetary advantages for those of the absorbing institution. Further, in many cases, it enabled amalgamations to be arranged, which allowed of even a further reduction of capitals, and this, again, made for improved prospects of expansion in the future ! Concrete examples will serve to illustrate the importance of low capitals. As already shown (page 72) the London and Westminster Bank had been precluded from amalgamating earlier because its capital was too large, the dividend was in consequence low, and this in turn caused a low market quotation. And when finally it did amalgamate it was compelled to suffer absorption at the hands of a neighbouring rival whose proportion of capital was lower. On the other hand the absorption in 1914 by the London City and Midland Bank of the Metropolitan Bank (of England and Wales) enabled the Midland Bank to make a capital reduction of £267,858, because, owing to its previous small capital, it was able to pay without difficulty a dividend of 18 per cent. free of income tax, and its shares of £2½ and £5 were respectively quoted at

---

[1] C.W.S. Bank £12 millions increase.
[2] C.W.S. Bank decrease £7 millions.

£9¾ and £21⅞. These prices were proportionately much higher than those for the corresponding £5 shares in the Metropolitan Bank, so that eleven Midland shares of £2½ each were given for seven Metropolitan shares of £5 each. The respective nominal values were therefore £27½ and £35. This represented an offer of £107¼ for £35 nominal—giving a value of £15½ for each Metropolitan £5 share. As might be expected, these terms provided a substantial bonus for the absorbed shareholders, while they would also receive an increased dividend in future. On the other hand, the Midland was able to save considerably in capital and reserve. This entirely satisfactory union was therefore made possible only by the relatively small but yet valuable capital possessed by the absorbing bank.

It should be pointed out that this is in no way an exceptional amalgamation. Indeed it was chosen haphazardly, and is only typical of the majority of examples which are to be found before 1914. In view, then, of the prestige and potential power which a small capital conferred, there is little wonder that the directors of progressive competing banks took no notice of occasional driblets of protest.

Not till the 1918 Bank Amalgamations Committee [1] did the matter receive very serious attention, but then it was pointed out that the relation of capital and reserve to deposits was not a sound one, as the former were together only 6 per cent. of the latter. It would seem that the bankers recognised the necessity of correcting the relation, since subsequently there has been a decided increase in the dual fund.

Obviously, the policy of holding proportionately low capitals, and of taking every suitable opportunity to reduce them, meant that the difficulty of building up high reserves was lessened. Incidentally, therefore, this provided another temptation for keeping small capitals, and the way was thus

---

[1] The Committee on Financial Facilities (1918) also took note of it. Its report said : "Moreover in recent years, in view of the decline of the ratio of paid-up capital and reserves to deposit liabilities, an increase is eminently desirable. From the evidence which has been placed before us, and from the trend of recent events in the banking world, we believe that bankers are, generally speaking, agreed upon the desirability of this increase. We recommend therefore that facilities should be given by the Government."

H

paved for the production of those " hidden reserves " about which so much has been written and so little is really known. Since the accounts of private bankers were not generally published until the last few years of the nineteenth century, and even joint-stock banks had no uniformity of practice in making up and publishing balance sheets until after the adoption of limited liability in the 'eighties and 'nineties, and generally for the reasons previously mentioned, it is not possible to make a correct statement of value on reserve funds before 1875. The joint-stock banks were slow to establish reserves of any size, for in early years they had to contend with many handicaps, not the least of which were the objections of their shareholders.[1]

The first figures in this case for the total number of joint-stock banks reproduced are those made up by Mr. J. Dun in August, 1875. They read :

JOINT-STOCK AND PRIVATE BANKS OF ENGLAND AND WALES.

RESERVE FUNDS.

				Percentage of Capital.
1875	113 Banks	.	£12,993,000 ..	42·0

The remainder are calculated from figures given in the *Bankers' Magazine*, and they include private as well as joint-stock banks :

1876	(end)	.	. £14,019,000	..	42·5
1881	.	.	. 17,182,321	..	48·7
1886	.	.	. 20,534,534	..	52·5
1891	.	.	. 24,076,102	..	47·0
1896	.	.	. 28,941,454	..	53·9
1901	.	.	. 31,010,964	..	57·5
1906	.	.	. 34,728,000	..	63·7
1911	.	.	. 34,494,000	..	62·9
1913	.	.	. 35,808,226	..	64·3
1914	.	.	. 35,828,208	..	64·3
1915	.	.	. 36,166,703	..	63·1
1916	.	.	. 35,804,132	..	62·1

[1] See, for instance, reports of Westminster and National Provincial Banks, 1840–50. The paid-up capital of three large London joint-stock banks in 1848 was £1,798,568, while their reserve funds were only £247,492 14s. 1d., equal to nearly 15 per cent.

RESERVE FUNDS (*continued*).

1917	.	.	.	35,995,287	..	60·0
1918	.	.	.	40,583,582	..	61·2
1919	.	.	.	53,751,068	..	79·6
1920	.	.	.	61,052,461	..	71·0
1921	.	.	.	62,335,474	..	71·7
1922	.	.	.	60,264,750	..	64·1
1923	.	.	.	60,468,814	..	70·7

Generally speaking, then, reserves increased slowly to 64·3 per cent. in 1913. The war years saw a decline in this percentage which, though slight, yet reflected clearly the neglect to increase capitals, and the reduction which occurred as a result of the amalgamation " boom " of 1918–19. The great increase in capital shown during 1922 by the C.W.S. Bank, which was offset by a notable reduction in the following year, is here shown by an exceptional disturbing of the figures. Otherwise reserves are now established at about 70 per cent. of capital.

As indicated before, so long as capitals increased so slowly, or even not at all, the yearly profits enabled the keeping of reserve funds to be accomplished with relative ease ; yet for a period of about fifteen years, even this task was rendered difficult because of the frequent necessity of applying substantial funds to depreciation of investments. This has been well shown in *Memoranda and Charts*—produced in 1911 to show certain statistical effects of amalgamation by Mr. A. H. Gibson. He shows that from 1897–1910 the following falls in price in the stocks mentioned had occurred :

Local Loans 3 per cent. . . .	$101\frac{3}{4}$ to $94\frac{5}{8}$
India 3 per cent.	$89\frac{1}{4}$ to $82\frac{3}{16}$
Metropolitan 3 per cent. Consolidated .	$101\frac{1}{4}$ to $91\frac{1}{2}$
Great Western Railway 4 per cent. Debs. .	$131\frac{1}{2}$ to 112
Great Northern Railway 3 per cent. Debs.	100 to $83\frac{1}{4}$

Such were the stocks principally held by bankers during this period, and the seriousness of the prolonged falls may be realised. Indeed, if amalgamation policy had not achieved the end of reducing capital, either the percentage of reserve would have suffered, or hidden reserves such as property would perhaps have been brought up to actual current values in each balance sheet. Certainly percentage profits would have suffered.

Detailed consideration indicates that, generally, reserves showed definite successive increases, with the exception of 1891 and 1911, from 1876 up to the last pre-war year. Not only do the percentages show increase, but the totals also. It would therefore appear that the influence of amalgamation policy has been favourable to the cumulative development of the element of strength in bank balance sheets generally.

This conclusion, however, needs some qualification. For during the 37 years covered by the period 1876–1913, the net increase in reserve totals is £21,789,226, or a yearly average of £588,330 8s. 8d. Bearing in mind the rapid growth of banking operations during this period, the increase does not seem to be a substantial one. Moreover, it is not actually net, since at least £4,000,000 must be deducted for additions to reserve made by the declaration of accounts (by companies and private firms) since 1876 (the exact amount may not be ascertained because the private firms which chose to publish accounts did not separate the totals of reserve and capital). Consequently the net increase cannot be more than £17,789,226, or a yearly average of £480,789 17s. 10d. This comparatively small increase corresponds with an increase in the percentage of capital of 21·8, so that in order to show a gain of 1 per cent. on the reserve fund it was only necessary to make an addition to it of approximately £816,020. Obviously, therefore, the diminished capital growth produced by amalgamation facilitated the percentage growth of reserves. This conclusion may be stressed if, for a moment, it is assumed that the capital fund had grown at the same rate as reserves actually did. Had this occurred, the 1913 total of capital would have been £74,460,550. If now reserves in 1913 were brought to the percentage of this new (hypothetical) total, the average annual increase necessary would be £915,111. That which actually occurred was £480,789, so that the extra amount annually required would have been £434,321, or 90 per cent. more than that which actually materialised.

During war years the percentage sank, but since then a pronounced recovery, leading to a definite percentage and total gain, has occurred. Partly this has been due to the response of the banks to the recommendations of the Bank Amalgamations Committee, and to the additions to reserves of substantial premiums realised by the necessary issues of fresh capital. Again, an analysis of the arrangements made as a result of the amalgamations announced, demonstrates that capital funds have not been depleted to the same extent as in pre-war years—as shown earlier. This statement appears to be a direct contradiction of the impression given in the fifth chapter of the Historical Survey. But it may be explained by the fact that the total number of amalgamations which had been carried through prior to 1914 had already lowered substantially the individual capitals of the banks concerned therein ; consequently, not only was a further reduction in capital improbable, but an increase was easily made.

BANKS IN ENGLAND AND WALES (JOINT-STOCK AND PRIVATE).

PERCENTAGE OF CAPITAL AND RESERVE TO DEPOSITS.

Year.				Capital.	Reserve.	Combined Percentage.
1875 (end	.	.	.	13·4	5·2	18·6
1881	.	.	.	12·8	6·1	18·9[1]
1886	.	.	.	11·5	5·9	17·4
1891	.	.	:	11·3	5·3	16·6
1896	.	.	.	9·9	5·2	15·1
1901	.	.	.	8·5	4·9	13·4
1906	.	.	.	7·9	4·9	12·8
1911	.	.	.	6·9	4·3	11·2
1913	.	.	.	6·5	4·1	10·6
1914	.	.	.	5·9	3·8	9·7
1915	.	.	.	5·3	3·4	8·7
1916	.	.	.	4·7	2·9	7·6
1917	.	.	.	4·1	2·5	6·6
1918	.	.	.	4·0	2·4	6·4
1919	.	.	.	3·3	2·6	5·9
1920	.	.	.	3·9	2·9	6·8
1921	.	.	.	4·0	2·9	6·9
1922	.	.	.	4·7 [1]	3·0	7·7
1923	.	.	.	4·4	3·0	7·4

[1] Partly estimated.

In judging the precise effect of the movement on reserves, then, it is necessary to remember that the progress of the fund was influenced by considerations other than amalgamation : e.g. especially, depreciation of investments. On balance, however, it is plain that movements of reserve have constantly been influenced and conditioned by movements in capital, and in this way the deleterious results of amalgamation policy have affected reserves similarly to capitals. The validity of this conclusion is evidenced by the table overleaf, which shows that, while the 1923 (end) combined totals of capitals and reserves was £145,996,945, this represents but 7·4 per cent. of deposit liabilities.

The next figures to be considered are those of deposits. Over the first few decades of the period the joint-stock banks were collecting deposits from new sources. Progress was irregular because sometimes joint-stock and sometimes private concerns secured the ascendancy. The repeated failures of the weaker firms also retarded the progress of the stronger. It is not possible to quote early totals of deposits since they were not published by any except London banks. Indeed the only information available for the very early

JOINT-STOCK AND PRIVATE BANKS IN ENGLAND.
Deposits (including Note Issues).[1]

Dick	1874	.	.	.	.	£242,102,000
	1883	.	.	.	.	284,841,000
	1891	.	.	.	.	451,089,000
	1896 (end)	.	.	.	559,565,000
	1901	.	.	.	.	636,484,000
	1906	.	.	.	.	700,631,700
	1911	.	.	.	.	799,012,900
	1913	.	.	.	.	866,818,700
	1914	.	.	.	.	948,431,300
	1915	.	.	.	.	1,057,854,500
	1916	.	.	.	.	1,226,143,200
	1917	.	.	.	.	1,449,735,900
	1918	.	.	.	.	1,672,388,400
	1919	.	.	.	.	2,062,419,200
	1920	.	.	.	.	2,154,762,200
	1921	.	.	.	.	2,165,606,400
	1922	.	.	.	.	2,003,452,000
	1923	.	.	.	.	1,969,318,300

[1] Calculated to the nearest £100.

years is an estimate contained in a pamphlet published in 1834 by Effingham Wilson, which gave the deposits of all the London banks as about £26,500,000. But as there were only a relatively small number of amalgamations among joint-stock banks during the period 1825–75 the omission is not serious. The first totals are taken from the calculations made by Mr. J. Dick in the *Journal of the Institute of Bankers*. It is notable that all three totals shown were, to a certain extent, dependent on estimate.

The figures produced by Mr. Dick were obviously incomplete, since the growth from 1883 to 1891 was no less than £166,248,000—an average of over £20,000,000 per year and at least 58 per cent. more than in 1881, which, in view of what is known as to the progress of joint-stock banks in this period, does not accurately represent the actual changes. Indeed the declaration of accounts by companies and firms hitherto silent accounts for some part of the increase, and this is true for the whole of the period up to 1913. When the various amalgamations were made by joint-stock firms with private firms which had previously not shown accounts, their figures were naturally swollen by the inclusion of the deposits which had not before been declared to the public. Between 1894 and 1913, for example, it may be estimated that the 46 banks which were thus amalgamated were responsible for an addition of about £47,000,000 [1] to deposit totals. On the other hand, deposit totals of country bankers were also included as part of those shown by their London agents, so that when amalgamation occurred, one total was eliminated, and consequently the whole was lessened by so much. This applies only of course when amalgamation occurred with a London bank, for otherwise the balances with London agents would not be affected.

The exact figures are not known, as in many cases the local bank did not publish accounts. For the present purpose, however, this does not interfere with calculations to any serious extent because the amounts are small in comparison with the gross amount of deposits. No large error will be

---

[1] There is little doubt that this estimate represents the minimum total, since the calculation has been based on minimum figures.

committed therefore if it is assumed that the total was approximately offset by the increases recorded as a result of previously undeclared deposits.

Another point connected with deposits occurs when it is assumed, as was often indeed the case, that a large firm of, say, contractors, which had various branches in England and Wales, used to keep accounts with different banks. Let it be imagined for simplicity that there were two branches each of which kept its account at a different bank. Assume further that A branch had a credit balance of £60,000, while B branch had only £10,000. The full total of deposits would then be £70,000. Now if B branch has power to overdraw up to £50,000 and exercised this power, the result will be that total deposits will increase to £120,000, while loans will figure as £50,000. If instead of B branch taking a loan the £50,000 had been withdrawn from A's account, the new position would have been a deposit total of £70,000, and there would have been no loans. The former position was the one which used to obtain in earlier years when there were many separate joint-stock banks in existence. The latter is often the result of the reduction of numbers by amalgamations. In so far as this process does actually happen, then, the effect of amalgamation is to reduce both loans and deposits. That it does take place there is no doubt, but there is no available method of measuring it. It can only be pointed out that it became of more frequent occurrence when the numbers of banks were seriously reduced by the later phases of the movement. In connection with this same point it is of interest to remark that where some branches of a firm (all the branches of which use the same bank) have overdrafts, it usually happens that each branch of the bank where they are obtained reports separate overdrafts to head office. The result is that deposits and loans are again increased as a result of appearing in separate totals, precisely similar to the last example. In other cases the bank's head office subtracts the total of loans from that of deposits and thus obtains a net total of deposits. This latter practice is, however, comparatively rare, so that deposit and loan totals are made to appear larger than actually they should be.

Passing to a consideration of the figures in the table it is evident that, unless withdrawn in cash, every loan or overdraft creates an additional deposit corresponding to the exact amount of each cheque drawn on the overdraft or loan account. The total of deposits, which may be called the " gross " total, therefore includes all sums which have been advanced by bankers. Since these are created by a process different from that which brings about the normal growth of deposits, it is necessary to subtract the amount of loans or advances if a correct " net " total measuring real deposit growth is to be secured. The result of doing this is to produce the table following. With this should be compared the table showing the percentage of advances to gross deposits :

GROSS TOTAL OF DEPOSITS CORRECTED FOR ADVANCES.

Year.	Gross Deposits.	Advances.[1]	Net Deposits.
1883 (end) .	£284,102,000	£232,044,000 [2]	£52,799,000
1891 . .	451,089,000	323,039,000 [2]	128,050,000
1896 . .	559,565,000	377,415,000	182,150,000
1901 . .	636,484,000	391,372,200	245,111,800
1906 . .	700,631,700	443,621,900	257,009,600
1911 . .	799,012,900	501,422,700	297,590,200
1913 . .	866,818,700	557,798,600	309,020,100
1914 . .	948,431,300	571,395,900	377,035,400
1915 . .	1,057,854,500	587,895,000 [2]	469,959,500
1916 . .	1,226,143,200	602,000,000	624,143,200
1917 . .	1,449,735,900	723,890,500	725,845,400
1918 . .	1,672,388,400	875,845,200	796,543,200
1919 . .	2,062,419,200	1,155,888,100	906,531,100
1920 . .	2,154,762,200	1,284,054,000 [2]	870,708,200
1921 . .	2,165,606,400	1,412,221,300	753,485,100
1922 . .	2,003,452,000	1,226,066,400	777,385,600
1923 . .	1,969,318,300	1,242,014,200	727,304,100

[1] Advances also includes Bills Discounted, as when a bank discounts a bill it is equivalent to making an advance to the person for whom it is discounted. Figures calculated to the nearest £100.
[2] These figures are estimated in part or in whole.

PERCENTAGE OF ADVANCES TO GROSS DEPOSITS.

Year.								Percentage.
1883 (end)	.	.	.	.	.	.	.	81·6
1891	.	.	.	.	.	.	.	71·6
1896	.	.	.	.	.	.	.	67·1
1901	.	.	.	.	.	.	.	69·9
1906	.	.	.	.	.	.	.	55·8
1911	.	.	.	.	.	.	.	62·9
1913	.	.	.	.	.	.	.	64·3
1914	.	.	.	.	.	.	.	60·3
1915	.	.	.	.	.	.	.	55·6
1916	.	.	.	.	.	.	.	48·7
1917	.	.	.	.	.	.	.	49·9
1918	.	.	.	.	.	.	.	52·4
1919	.	.	.	.	.	.	.	56·2
1920	.	.	.	.	.	.	.	59·9
1921	.	.	.	.	.	.	.	65·4
1922	.	.	.	.	.	.	.	61·3
1923	.	.	.	.	.	.	.	67·1

The table of " net " deposits reveals a strikingly regular growth over the period 1883–1919, which was not arrested until the later post-war years. The figures were then affected by the changed banking policy necessitated by post-war conditions, and the violent fluctuations in the nation's trading. Such regular progress merits attention, and it will be profitable to discuss the causes principally operating to produce it, and to discover the influence exerted on amalgamation policy. And first it will be advisable to consider the effect on the growth of deposits of the creation of bank branches. The most satisfactory method of doing this is to discuss the historical growth of the policy.

In early years it was not customary for a firm of private bankers to keep more than one or two offices. Ordinarily, too, these were situate in the same district as the residences of the partners, for banking was then of a local character only. Even the joint-stock banks in their early days seem to have been opposed to the practice of extension by branches.[1]

[1] A director of the Manchester Joint Stock Bank, in giving evidence to the 1832 Committee, thought branches " objectionable on the ground that one bank should be one bank, and that literally if it becomes many branches, it becomes many banks." (Q. 4233). Another contemporary view is contained in the pamphlet *A View of the Banking Question* (Anon., 1832), which says : " The establishment of Branch Banks is one of the

The consequence of this attitude was that the 554 private bankers of 1825 had only 681 branches, while in 1837 the 102 joint-stock banks had only 541. By 1844 the joint-stock banks had extended to 106 concerns possessing 604 branches ; but the 335 private bankers had only 428. The figures for this and subsequent years are based on the lists given in the *Bankers' Almanack*.

TOTAL BANK OFFICES OF JOINT-STOCK AND PRIVATE BANKS IN ENGLAND AND WALES.

				Offices.	Persons.
1851[1]	,,	,,	,,	96[2]	1 to 19,921
1858 (Palgrave) part estimate				1,195	1 to 16,644
1872 .	.	.	.	1,779	1 to 12,766
1874 (Dun)	.	.	.	1,863	1 to 12,211
1876 (end)	.	.	.	2,118	1 to 10,713
1881 .	.	.	.	2,413	1 to 11,283
1886 .	.	.	.	2,716	1 to 9,549
1891 .	.	.	.	3,383	1 to 7,788
1896 .	.	.	.	3,959	1 to 7,436
1901 .	.	.	.	4,762	1 to 6,787
1906 .	.	.	.	5,433	1 to 6,023
1911 .	.	.	.	6,267	1 to 5,630
1913 .	.	.	.	6,839	1 to 5,305
1914 .	.	.	.	7,037	1 to 5,153
1915 .	.	.	.	7,148	1 to 5,049
1916 .	.	.	.	7,089	1 to 5,058
1917 .	.	.	.	7,033	1 to 5,114
1918 .	.	.	.	7,040 [2]	1 to 5,106
1919 .	.	.	.	7,050	1 to 5,102
1920 .	.	.	.	7,307	1 to 4,923
1921 .	.	.	.	7,644	1 to 4,972
1922 .	.	.	.	7,882	1 to 4,832
1923 .	.	.	.	8,081	1 to 4,689

causes of the resources of industry in the country being lessened and dried up, and, from their most obscure and remote channels of usefulness, altogether withdrawn," p. 114 (Rylands Library). Again, from the 1834 report of the Sheffield Banking Co. : " At the time of the forming of this bank, it was the opinion of the directors, which additional experience and information has tended to confirm, that branch banks in general are not profitable, and that they are a source of weakness, rather than strength, to the parent establishment."

[1] Calculation by Easton in *Banks and Banking*, p. 60.
[2] Approximately.

The increase in the period of one hundred years is great—there were in 1924 (end 1923 figures) over fifteen times as many offices. Even since 1844, which is a sort of official date from which to measure progress, the increase has been nearly 800 per cent. From 1886 onwards the growth has been particularly striking, and reflects growing competition.

One of the main reasons for the adoption of the system by the joint-stock banks is precisely because the private banker was slow and unwilling to make use of the opportunities offered by it. It is evident from what Gilbart says as to the restrictive and exclusive practices of private banks, that it was greatly desirable that the joint-stock banks should widen the approach to the possession of a banking account. The best method of doing this, in the first place, was to open establishments in ground hitherto neglected or not adequately served by private banks. This, combined with the taking of steps to increase the scope of banking practice—e.g. by commencing in acceptance business, forming foreign departments, and opening a savings department for the deposit of very small sums—and assisted by the general development of manufacturing resources which is a feature of nineteenth-century history, caused deposit growth. Various set-backs were experienced, especially at times of crisis such as 1836, 1847, 1857, and 1866, but the sounder methods of administration supported the policy of branch extension so well, that progress was resumed without much loss.

At first attention was chiefly given to localities rather than to wide areas, with the consequence that some banks served purely agricultural districts (e.g. Stuckeys), while others grew up with the growth of industrial operations (e.g. Parrs, Lloyds, Manchester and Liverpool District). It was only by later amalgamation and extension of branches that the chief advantages of the branch system were realised, and representation was obtained in various types of area each of which served to offset the conditions prevailing in others. The result of this was that there was a more uniform and generally stronger demand for loans, and since these create deposits, totals expanded. Again, while the number of branches were few, banking operations were always attended with greater danger in consequence of the smaller margin of safety.   When the number was increased beyond a certain point, on account of the larger and steadier deposit funds, the bank was able to throw off some of the need for every caution, to move more freely and widely, to extend functions, and thus to earn more.   The increased earning power paved the way for further expansion, and gave prestige which was afterwards of no small value.   An example might be quoted of a bank which pursued this policy—the Capital and Counties.   In the course of twenty years its net profits increased from 1·49 per cent. to 1·50 per cent.   This is not a large increase, but it compares favourably with one which pursued an opposite policy.   This was the City Bank, and as a settled feature of administration, it refrained from opening branches and seeking the accretion of business to be obtained therefrom.   In the same period, and in the same length of time, its net profits declined from ·69 per cent. to ·54 per cent.

From this discussion it is clear that the branch system played an important part in the increase of deposit totals. If this thesis is established, it is but a step to the further one, that amalgamation policy, since it was intimately bound up with the expansion of branches, played no small part in assisting the growth of deposits.   One of our eminent bankers has said, indeed, " The system of branch banking is the direct outcome of the principle of consolidation." [1] The point at once arises as to how this has come about, and since the discussion is somewhat lengthy, it will be undertaken in the next chapter.

[1] Sir D. Drummond Fraser, *Journal of the Institute of Bankers*, 1908, p. 35.

CHAPTER VII.

EFFECTS OF AMALGAMATION (*continued*).

ONE of the reasons now advanced for the fact that amalgamation was, through its connection with the growth of bank offices, also concerned with the growth of bank deposits, is at first glance not very strong. Amalgamation represents only one branch of banking competition, but it undoubtedly reacted on that competition by increasing and intensifying it. For when one bank made a bold stroke and captured a business possessing a number of branches, its rivals were stimulated also to seek expansion, in order to protect the gains they had made previously. Perhaps the best example of this retaliatory kind of competition is also a recent one, for when in April, 1914, the news of the alliance of Lloyds with the Wilts and Dorset Bank was received, one of its rivals—the London City and Midland—had within 24 hours made arrangements to open, with the minimum of delay, no fewer than 17 new branches in the same area.[1] This was not the only example, although this extreme type of competition prevailed more extensively in later years.

Secondly, in view of what has been said before on the methods pursued by the private bankers, it is obvious that they did not aim at securing maximum deposits in any certain area. Actually they were more concerned with the merchants and traders and large farmers than with all classes equally, for their largest operations were the issuing of notes (since this gave them most profits), and the making of acceptances. It should be noted that, owing to the necessity of maintaining a London agent, and owing to their inability to spread their funds so as to offset the low profits of one type of area by the higher profits of another type, and to their

[1] *The Evolution of the Money Market*, 1385–1915, p. 453, E. T. Powell.

incapacity to utilise the principle of division of labour like their joint-stock rivals, they required higher profits, and this tended to prevent them expanding the range of their business. And this, in reflex fashion, also operated to bring about the necessity for higher profits. Again, in many cases, private bankers worked with limited capitals,[1] so that here too they were unable to accept increases of business above a certain limit.

When, therefore, their businesses were in due course acquired by joint-stock concerns, the latter were able to secure a much larger amount of deposit funds from the same area. An illustration of this is shown by the absorption by the National Provincial Bank in 1842 of the business of the Dover Private Bank ; for the report of that year says : " . . . The Directors have much pleasure in stating that the valuable connexion, to which the bank has thus succeeded, has considerably increased since the junction took place."

Precisely a similar result occurred when a large, well-established, and well-connected joint-stock bank took over a local, small, and inefficient member of the same class. Most of these instances are to be found in the years of last century, when transport was clumsy, and communication with the metropolis was not easily made. Then, as shown in the history of the period, not a few small joint-stock banks were driven to the wall as well by inefficiency and inability to take full advantage of local conditions, as by utter mismanagement. Referring to one instance of this, the report of the National Provincial Bank for 1847 says :

" Shortly after the last annual meeting the business of the Stockton and Durham County Bank carried on at Stockton and Guisborough was incorporated with that of this company at those places. This arrangement has been attended with a valuable increase of connection from amongst the Agricultural Interests of that District."

The process had a further effect which was not visible until the amalgamation had been long completed. In many

---

[1] " Accustomed for a century and a half to the small capitals of the private banks, few could rise above the tradition, and initiate a fund of capital proportionate to the trade they expected to finance."—W. Graham, £1 *Note in Scotland*, p. 226.

instances, for example, amalgamation was effected by a bank in an area hitherto unknown to it. It subsequently happened that opportunities presented themselves for further extension, using the original branch as a centre of operations. In time more branches were opened, and the resultant accretion to deposit totals was considerable. A case in point happened when one of the London banks, keen to extend, opened in Middlesbrough, as a result of amalgamation, about the time when the first iron deposits were discovered. After a few months working it was found that there was need for banking accommodation at Darlington, and later at Durham.

In any case, it is important to observe, the opening of branches, either in insufficient or excessive numbers, never reduced the amount of deposits, but it always heightened the possibility of increasing them, if merely because of the advertisement resulting.

Lastly, amalgamation was a means of increasing branches more rapidly than otherwise would have been practicable ; for it is far easier, as well as much cheaper, to take over branches already existing, however unsuccessful they chance to be at the time of amalgamation. This reason is often cited as a predisposing cause of amalgamation activity, in speeches made by the chairmen of absorbing banks. Additionally it must be remembered that the opening of single branches, particularly in new areas, was a slow, difficult, and expensive business. It was expensive because a substantial sum was usually paid for a suitable central site, the building of a suitable branch designed to impress the public on the score of strength and solidity was a heavy charge, and rates, taxes, salaries, etc., were all disproportionate items during the first few years. The fact that amalgamation made possible the acquisition, if need be, of scores of branches at one stroke, at a cheaper rate than independent establishment, meant that the money which was saved in consequence could be devoted to working up the business. That this usually happened there is no doubt, for it is frequently mentioned in bank reports.

Another cause of growth is to be found in the general

adoption and extended use of cheques.   The reasons for this were various, but the chief one is that cheques have proved a more suitable medium of exchange, and have conduced to a safer, and therefore more economical, working of the English credit system than the local notes used in the early part of last century.   The explanations of this are that the cheque, in addition to being suited to local use, is a national and international instrument.   When the credit system is wisely controlled, and the time of clearing is reduced to a minimum, it is also a more acceptable method of payment.   Almost equally important is the fact that bank-notes are limited to one fixed amount ; no such restriction impedes the use of cheques.   Again, the improvement of the law relating to cheques has given them greater security than bank-notes possess, while the use of cheque currency during the last eighty years has probably been the main factor in achieving a credit system which is only maintained by the support of a developed commercial morality.   Lastly, the cheque lends itself to an easy and simple book-keeping method involving very low administration expenses.

The fact that London banks were by law forbidden to issue their own notes doubtless assisted materially to secure the adoption of payment by cheque.

Amalgamation was responsible for assisting the growth of cheque currency mainly because it assisted the reduction of the note issues controlled by banks other than the Bank of England.   To recapitulate, under the principal provisions of the 1844 Act :

(a) If any private bank increased its partners to more than six the right to issue notes was forfeited.

(b) If two banks joined, each of which had a right to issue, one issue was forfeited.

(c) If either of two amalgamating joint-stock banks had an office in London, or within 65 miles, the right to issue was lost.

(d) If a joint-stock bank having a right of issue allied itself with a private bank in London or the radius, the issue lapsed.

In 1844 the original state of the note issue was fixed by Peel's Act as:

207 Private Banks	. . . .	£5,153,417
72 Joint-Stock Banks .	. . .	3,478,230
		£8,631,647

The rate of diminution is shown by the following table:

1868.	125 Private Banks	. . .	£4,042,626
	50 Joint-Stock Banks	. .	2,738,640
			£6,781,266
1880.	107 Private Banks	. . .	3,588,528
	50 Joint-Stock Banks	. .	2,493,595
			£6,092,123
1891.	81 Private Banks	. . .	2,927,691
	38 Joint-Stock Banks	. .	2,042,161
			£4,194,250
1896.	56 Private Banks	. . .	2,220,048
	35 Joint-Stock Banks	. .	1,974,202
			£4,194,250
1901.	30 Private Banks	. . .	1,147,938
	25 Joint-Stock Banks	. .	1,470,527
			£2,618,465
1906.	12 Private Banks	. . .	482,744
	17 Joint-Stock Banks	. .	1,084,836
			£1,567,580
1911.	10 Private Banks	. . .	423,749
	7 Joint-Stock Banks	. .	245,731
			£669,480
1915.	7 Private Banks	. . .	307,294
	4 Joint-Stock Banks	. .	94,425
			£401,719

1917.	6 Private Banks	.	.	.	273,076
	3 Joint-Stock Banks		.	.	61,744
					£334,820
1919.	6 Private Banks	.	.	.	273,076
	2 Joint-Stock Banks		.	.	32,267
					£305,343

1921. Nil.

Although many lapsed issues were due to causes other than amalgamation, e.g. failures and withdrawals from business, speaking generally, amalgamation was the major cause of their disappearance. It is interesting, on this account, to note that the progress of the movement is well reflected in the declining figures, e.g. the decline in the number of banks from 1880–91 was 26, compared with 51 from 1891–1901.

Digressing for a moment from the main point, another incidental effect of the lapse of over £8 millions of country note issues was to increase the Bank of England's fiduciary issue from £14 millions to £19,750,000, and the effect of this has therefore been to reduce the reserve of gold, since the £5,750,000 is only issued against securities. Whether or not this is significant may be seen by comparing the percentage of reserve on the assumption that the increase had, and had not been made against a corresponding increase of gold. The return dated August 14, 1924, showed that the reserve was 16·87 per cent. of liabilities. If the Bank had been required to issue the extra £5,750,000 notes against gold, the percentage would have been 21·5. The effect of amalgamations has therefore been to lower perceptibly the Bank's reserve of gold. Before the war such a reduction meant much more that it does to-day ; for the extraordinary measures rendered necessary by war expenditure have given a great prestige to the Bank, and this possibly carries much more weight than figures, which, after all, are only presumptive evidence of that stability and soundness which the events of the war undoubtedly displayed.

There is a third reason for the growth of deposits. This is to be found in the greater safety of banking and the more scientific character of the methods attached to modern practice. The former is evidenced by the comparative absence of failures over the modern period.[1] The year of the Baring Crisis saw the last event of its kind which is worthy of note, and even this was different from earlier crises, inasmuch as it was met by the joint-stock banks with a united front under the guidance of the Governor of the Bank of England. The joint-stock banks, having given undertakings to be guarantors for certain definite sums, rigidly held to their obligations, and this enabled the ensuing difficulties to be met with ease.

The reasons for the increased safety of banking are many. For instance, the practice of banking has been put on to a scientific basis, and has regularly become more and more logicalised. A comparison of the methods of the private bankers who functioned in local spheres and issued excess local notes with no regard to the position from the national perspective, and with certainly no regard to an adequate reserve, with those of the highly centralised joint-stock companies not working in the dim light of privacy, but in the glaring light of publicity, knowing well that a deviation from policy commands instant criticism, reveals a great contrast. The maintenance of a never-ceasing competition which was hardly felt by the private banker, has necessitated not only a cautious policy on the part of the joint-stock concerns, but also a progressive, exact, and non-faltering adherence to sound banking, and the provision of all possible facilities for the public. In this, amalgamation has had a share.

To no small extent, this is obviously shown by the absence of failures—especially during the last war period. Then, undoubtedly, the truth that a small number of large banks can combine more readily than a large number of small

---

[1] An example of the unsound nature of the banking carried on so late as the 'fifties of last century is given by Morier Evans in a *History of Commercial Crises*, 1857–8. On page 37 he says : " When it appeared that a house which offered 2s. in the £1 was a debtor to the Liverpool Borough Bank for £30,000 unsecured, who could say which was the more culpable party ? " Another is provided by the fact that the chief cause of the failure of 240 private banks from 1814–16, inclusive, was the lending of money on farm mortgages for agricultural improvement and development. (*Vide* p. 4 of the text.)

banks in times of crisis, was demonstrated [1]—and large banks have been produced by means of amalgamation.

To compare with 1814, for instance, in that year there were 940 private banks, but by 1825, 398 had disappeared—most of these having failed. Mr. J. F. Smith (of Edinburgh) published a tract in 1839 showing that between 1814 and 1816, 240 banks were swept away. Subsequently to 1844 there were other similar cases. And an instance in the modern period occurred in 1911, when Barclays Bank took over the Stamford and Spalding Bank—the latter having become too much involved in the troubles of a local industry.

Perhaps the most convincing part of this narrative is that the number of weak banks has grown less with the succession of years, until now balance sheets present a uniformity of practice which is indicative of strength. Additionally, with the progress of years, the absorbed weak banks have shown positions which have been relatively less weak.

Taking leave of deposits and deposit movements, the figures next claiming attention are concerned with the separate amounts of investments and cash. Both sets of figures represent totals, inasmuch as investments include both British Government and other types of investment, while cash includes cash in hand, and at the Bank of England. Before 1883 it is impossible to obtain totals which are sufficiently authoritative for consideration.

The private bankers do not seem to have been at all uniform in respect of the types of investments they kept, or the amounts of cash holdings in proportion to liabilities which they maintained. From what information it has been possible to gather it seems as if they were not careful to maintain a strong holding in gilt-edged securities, and certainly they appear to have trusted overmuch to their London agents to supply them with actual cash.

[1] *Vide The Times*, December 17, 1917: "In financing the Great War, the large banks have been able to do much more than they would have done had they been split up into a number of small unrelated units."

[2] *Vide* the amusing stories contained in Maberley Phillips' *History of Banks, Bankers, and Banking in Northumberland, Durham, and North Yorkshire.* He gives many descriptions of the excitement caused by reliance on too small a proportion of cash, none of which are more graphically told than that on page 148, where he describes the

PRIVATE AND JOINT-STOCK BANKS IN ENGLAND AND WALES.

INVESTMENTS AND CASH.

(000's omitted.)

	Invest-ments.	Cash.	Percent-age of Invest-ments to Deposits.	Percent-age of Capital to Deposits.	Total.
1883 (end) .	41,754	54,846	14·7	19·3	34·0
1891. . . .	109,374	107,357	24·2	23·8	48·0
1896. . . .	163,051	163,748	29·1	29·1	58·2
1901. . . .	146,984	163,631	23·1	25·8	48·9
1906. . . .	141,058	186,801	20·1	26·6	46·7
1911. . . .	145,189	218,820	18·1	27·4	42·5
1913. . . .	134,491	242,924	15·4	27·9	43·3
1914. . . .	159,760	284,969	16·9	29·9	46·8
1915. . . .	323,367	275,196	31·5	26·1	57·6
1917. . . .	336,510	459,946	23·2	31·7	54·9
1918. . . .	336,950	500,968	21·9	29·9	51·8
1919. . . .	426,871	466,409	20·7	22·6	43·3
1920. . . .	384,016	470,631	17·9	21·8	39·7
1921. . . .	395,559	459,076	18·0	21·3	39·3
1922. . . .	448,577	441,151	22·4	22·1	44·5
1923. . . .	425,636	422,273	21·5	21·5	43·0

This table shows numerous fluctuations. · Generally speaking, however, it indicates that the first decade saw the gradual definite improvement resulting from the continually strengthening position of the joint-stock banks, in the ratios to deposit totals, followed by a loss of this improvement in the second decade due to the widespread depreciation of investments. The effects of war finance are fully seen in the early war years, for then cash was strongly increased, and the total of investments jumped up with alacrity. The succeeding years portray the gradual return to more normal conditions. The decline in investments in the second decade

triumphant balancing of the cash accomplished by Messrs. Backhouse when they rushed in with the necessary coin just in time to save a panic, with the cash balanced so as to allow the vehicle to run on one wheel—the other had broken!

extended over the period 1897-1912, and during that time
the banks were compelled to write them down by no less
than £10 millions.   The gains of the war period are due
principally to the purchasing of Treasury Bills and similar
investments, as well as to a great extent to the purchases of
War Loans both by the banks and their customers.

The growth in the ratio of cash is not so favourable as that
of investments, since even in 1883 the percentage was 19·3
per cent., whereas in 1923 (end) it was but 21·5 per cent.,
although during and since the war Treasury notes have been
ranked as cash.   Obviously they hardly possess a gold backing.   Such a result is caused by the war-time developments
and is in no way connected with amalgamation.

It is apparent that movements both in investments and
cash are not so much influenced by amalgamation policy as
by the prevailing state of public opinion, and the prevalent
and future banking requirements.   Hence amalgamation is
no cause of short-period irregularities.   Is it possible that,
in some subtle manner, the process had some connection
with long-period changes ?

It may be conceived, and it actually was the case, that the
small local banks were not accustomed to hold so sound a
selection of investments as the large London concerns.   In
this they often lacked the knowledge, and consequently the
power, given by the possession of an office in the metropolis.
This was detrimental in many ways, but especially did it
result in the country bank not possessing a scientific investment scheme designed to use exact portions of the funds
which were available for investment.   It often happened,
then, that on a country bank being absorbed by a London
concern, the investments had to be drastically overhauled to
bring them into line with those of the absorbing bank.[1]
Even when the investments of the small provincial house
were tolerably well arranged it was usually found that
they were not written down to actual market price at the
date of the balance sheet, but were taken at the original cost !

In the matter of cash it may be interesting to trace the

[1] Modern bankers with experience of amalgamation readily testify
to this.

result of the taking over of a country banker by a London concern. Usually the former held about 15 per cent. of his deposits in cash. Thus, if his deposits were £100,000, he would keep £5,000 in his till, and about £10,000 with his London agents. Against this £10,000 the London agent would keep in turn a reserve of 15 per cent. or £1,500. Thus the total amount of cash held against the £100,000 deposit was not 15 per cent., or £15,000, but £6,500. When the banks decided to join, the London banker still kept his regular proportion of cash—viz. 15 per cent., and so really £15,000 would then be held against the £100,000 deposits. This explains, to some extent, the reason for the increased cash held against deposits, as shown in the table.

When a country banker absorbed a London institution—since the former then became a member of the London group of banks and therefore became exposed to competition both enlarged and of a more severe type—it was found necessary to hold increased cash reserves. In such cases it was rare that the new bank lost on the transaction, for it was enabled to save the fees hitherto payable to its London agents, since it could now employ the money direct in the money market.

Examination has now been made into some of the results of amalgamation policy and the reasons for these in respect of movements in capital, reserve, deposits, branches, cheques, and notes, and liquid assets. It is now desirable to discover the effect of the policy on working expenses, and profits, and to discover what, if any, were the economies resulting from the process.[1]

In attempting to do this, a difficulty at once appears, for, as the result of inquiries made at the large joint-stock banks, it was discovered that no statistics had ever been prepared by bankers who had engaged in amalgamation to show whether or not definite economies were secured. The difficulty is enhanced by the fact that now the figures shown in bank balance sheets are neither so exhaustive nor so detailed as those published when the joint-stock bankers

---

[1] The substance of the matter relating to this topic has previously appeared in the *Economic Journal*, vol. xxxv. pp. 583-9, from which it is now abstracted by permission.

were facing the keen competition of the private houses.
In those days, Gross Profit, Net Profit, and Working Expenses
were all revealed by the majority of joint-stock banks.   Now
only Net Profits are shown.   Speaking of this the *Bankers'
Magazine* for February, 1923, says (p. 179) :

"Most of the banks nowadays content themselves with a
bald statement of the net amount of profits, the gross profit and
expenses no longer being disclosed, a movement which is to be
regretted, and hardly seems to be in the interests of the banks
themselves, now that the question of reducing established charges
is very much in the foreground."

For the early years of the period a typical record of the
relations of gross profits, net profits and expenses may be
obtained by taking the balance sheets of the London Joint
Stock Banks then existing, and a representative group of
provincial banks.   It is impossible to give figures for private
banks as these were not published.   The following are figures
for the London Banks :

TABLE I.

ALL LONDON BANKS.[1]

Year.	No. of Banks.	Net Profit. Percentage.	Expenses. Percentage.	Gross Profit. Percentage.
1861 (end) .	6	1·12	·74	2·02
1866 . .	11	1·74	·86	3·25
1871 . .	13	1·33	·72	2·49
1876 . .	15	1·04	·70	1·94
1881 . .	14	1·62	·79	2·76
1886 . .	14	1·37	·88	2·65
1891 . .	15	·92	·68	1·90
1896 . .	12	1·12	·94	2·46
1901 . .	10	1·30	1·04	2·63
1905 . .	10	1·16	1·08	2·57
1911 . .	9	1·02	1·18	2·74
1913 . .	4	1·06	1·31	2·53
1914 . .	4	·90	·96	2·26

This table reveals substantial fluctuations.   Some of the
years, e.g. 1866 and 1913, were exceptional ones, for in the

[1] Based on reports supplied by some of the banks, the *Economist*, and
Position and Progress of the London Joint Stock Banks (Crump).   In this
and following tables the percentage on total working resources is used.
These include paid-up capitals, reserves, deposits, and acceptances.   Acceptances include all bills accepted by the banks.

former the high profits shown were occasioned by the speculative mania prevailing before the Gurney failure ; while in the latter banking profits were assisted by the strength of the trading activity then prevalent. Similarly again, the year 1891 well reflects the stagnation consequent on the Baring crisis.

With these qualificatory remarks in mind it is nevertheless clear that expenses regularly increased over the period. And net profits showed a distinct decline, while gross profits (necessarily the most fluctuating item) also loomed up large in the latter years of the period. The two most interesting and significant items—Net Profits and Expenses—may profitably be compared, and to do this the next table shows them in juxtaposition.

TABLE 2.

ALL LONDON BANKS.—EXPENSES AS A PERCENTAGE OF NET PROFITS.

Year.						No. of Banks.	Percentage.
1861 (end)	.	.	.	.	.	6	66
1866	.	.	.	.	.	11	49
1871	.	.	.	.	.	13	54
1876	.	.	.	.	.	15	67
1881	.	.	.	.	.	14	49
1886	.	.	.	.	.	14	64
1891	.	.	.	.	.	15	74
1896	.	.	.	.	.	12	84
1901	.	.	.	.	.	10	80
1905	.	.	.	.	.	10	93
1911	.	.	.	.	.	9	116
1913	.	.	.	.	.	4	124
1914	.	.	.	.	.	4	107

The result of this comparison is striking, for it shows plainly that while expenses increased, net profits were correspondingly reduced during the period of nearly sixty years. Had it been possible to obtain figures for a sufficient number of banks after 1914 (1915 figures) the comparison would possibly have been more striking. It is again necessary to ignore minor deviations from the general movements, noticeable in 1881, 1901, and 1914.

In view of the fact that the London banks might conceivably present special cases of the changes in the relations of gross and net profits and working expenses, it is desirable to give attention to those which occurred among banks in the country as a whole. Unfortunately the number of banks which published figures in comparison to the total number is small, especially in later years. This was occasioned by the fact that they were not directly under the focus of a strong London financial opinion, and therefore responsive to its criticisms. It is believed, however, that those now cited in Table 3 will serve as representative figures, especially since the majority of concerns which failed to show results were small provincial concerns, e.g. Yorkshire banks were notoriously deficient in this respect.

TABLE 3.

JOINT-STOCK BANKS IN ENGLAND AND WALES.

Net Profit as a Percentage of Total Working Resources.

Year.	No. of Banks.	Percentage. (Weighted Average).
1874 ⎫ . (end)	63	1·88
1883 ⎬	90	1·67
1891 [1] ⎭	95	1·13
1896	124	1·13
1901	63	1·21
1906 [2]	—	1·07
1911	37	·96
1913 [3]	37	1·13
1914	32	·94
1915	32	·86
1916	30	·82
1917	29	·73
1918	20	·71
1919	16	·69
1920	15	·79
1921	15	·63
1922	15	·58
1923	14	·57

[1] Based on figures compiled by Mr. J. Dick, quoted *Journal, Institute of Bankers*, April, 1897.

[2] Based on figures prepared by Sir D. Drummond Fraser, quoted *Journal, Institute of Bankers*, 1907.

[3] This and following figures abstracted from the *Economist.*

Comparing these with the figures for London concerns the same story is told, only in more certain fashion. The apparent deviation in 1913 was due to the extraordinary character of banking operations in that period, resulting in large profits. The slight deviation of 1920 is due to a similar cause : for even after bankers had employed surplus profits in adding to established reserves, and in creating new ones, they still showed record figures. On the whole, then, the decline in net profits is a well-marked feature.

The next table shows the relations of working expenses to net profits, and to total working resources. The number of banks is small for the reasons mentioned above.

TABLE 4.

JOINT-STOCK BANKS IN ENGLAND AND WALES.

Expenses as a Percentage of Total Working Resources and Net Profits.

Year.	No. of Banks.	Percentage of T.W.R.	Percentage of N.P.
1881 (end) . . .	54	·86	52
1886	54	·88	60
1891	51	·89	60
1896	41	·89	77
1901	30	·95	82
1906	23	1·08	89
1910	20	1·09	101
1911	20	1·08	103
1912	9	1·03	94
1913	7	1·06	89
1914	8	1·02	97
1915	5	1·04	111

From this table it is clear that all the banks detailed show movements largely synchronous with those for London concerns. The movements are not so pronounced, but this may be accounted for by the fact that provincial firms did not find the increase to be so heavy as the more important metropolitan concerns. To no small extent this was possibly due to the relatively small number of branches controlled by country houses, and partly to the fact that they were not often engaged in amalgamation.

Although the absence of a full statement for every bank is

an argument against, yet it is believed that the table as it stands is an accurate representation of the general variations which occurred over the period.

The figures for 1891 and 1896 require some explanation. They were influenced by the large number of branches opened at this time,[1] and the extremely low interest rates which prevailed for about five years. Really the first is to some extent the result of the second, for when profits were small, banks were impelled to extend to the country. The low rates caused, additionally, a reduction in the progressive increase in " real " deposits, since this was only £54 millions as compared with £63 millions in the succeeding five years, and £75 millions in the preceding eight years. This produced a serious reduction in the amount of total working resources (which includes deposit and current accounts, capitals, reserves, and acceptances), and therefore a higher ratio of expenses. The greatest increase in expenses was shown by the London banks, and as it is notorious that they were the greatest sufferers from low rates, it points to the accuracy of the explanation offered above. Lastly, as pointed out later, Mr. J. Dick, the banking statistician of the period, ascribed the increase largely to the many amalgamations carried out in this period.

A comparison of the present table with that for all London banks leads to the inference that, since they were always the most active amalgamators, and since the dimensions of their businesses were larger by far than their provincial brethren,[2] expenses increased with the years, and in particular during the last forty years. And as this period coincided with the modern movement in amalgamation—which is much more significant than the early movement [3]—it is permissible to deduce that as amalgamation progressed, the burden of expenses increased.

After 1911 it is difficult to draw any conclusions which are justified by the figures, owing to the small number of banks

---

[1] Between 1891–6, 576 new branches were opened.
[2] Even in 1873, for example, the 16 London banks (joint-stock) had 398 branches.—*Utley's London Directory.*
[3] In this period the number of groupings was 279, or more than half of the total for 1825–1924.

which declared expenses. The only resource is to attempt to judge by results. Too much significance must not be attached to the fact that banks began to withhold figures, but evidently there was a reason for it, and it is possible that expenses were looming up large. One of the results of the 1918 movement was that bank staffs combined to form the Bank Officers' Guild to protect their interests. The explanation of this is that large amalgamations meant that impersonal methods were substituted for the more personal ones which obtained before the day of great banks, and banks were somewhat tardy in assisting their staffs to bear the increased cost of living engendered by war. It is notable that the efforts of the Guild have resulted in a very substantial increase in salary scales, and since this is the most considerable item in the expenses account, it is only logical to assume that expenses have increased almost in proportion. Rates, taxes and rents have also heavily increased. In view of the fact, too, that nearly 1,000 extra offices and branches have been opened since 1914, and that the expense of opening these must have been considerable, it is clear that expenses have increased in more than the normal ratio. It is not surprising, therefore, to find that in 1921 the great banks announced that the rates for deposit money were to be altered from $1\frac{1}{2}$ per cent. below bank rate to 2 per cent. below bank rate. As this is a favourite method of arranging rates, it may be presumed that the taking of such a measure was only done on account of rising expenses, particularly since banking competition was then very keen.

It is interesting to point out that the conclusion reached was also that reached in earlier years by two banking statisticians—Mr. J. Dick and Mr. A. H. Gibson. Mr. Dick prepared figures of expenses for 1883, 1891, and 1896. Speaking of these he said (*Journal, Institute of Bankers*, April, 1897) :

" Every one of the London banks has arisen (i.e. in expenses), and there is no sign that amalgamation has done them any good so far as this part of the business is concerned. . . . The same remark applies to those London and Provincial Banks which have increased their business in the same way."

Later he says: " The decrease of net profits in 1896 compared with 1891 has arisen entirely from increased expenditure." [1] A glance at the chronological table in appendix I reveals that the period of 1883–96, inclusive, saw a total of 128 amalgamations, or about 9 per year. Making allowance for the fact that the results of some of these could not be revealed in so short a period, it nevertheless appears to be a reasonable assumption that the increased expenses had a direct relation to the number of amalgamations. If this is so, Mr. Dick's explanations seem to be justified.

Mr. Gibson's Memoranda Sheets were drawn up in order to show the effect of banking developments from 1885–1911. His tables include the following headings : Capital, Reserve, Year, Dividend, Mean Share Price, Number of Branches, Deposit Totals, Net Profits, Amalgamations. By a process of comparison he finds that the banks making most progress were the London and South Western and the London and Provincial. These were general London concerns of moderate size. The Lancashire and Yorkshire Bank ranked third, and this was a provincial bank. He points out that if no account is taken of the small amalgamations carried out by the last-named bank, these banks were not built up by amalgamations. Closer investigation reveals that in the case of both the first two banks net profits increased continuously over the whole period of 26 years. Of no other bank was this true. He therefore concludes that expansion was possible without resort to amalgamation.

Later he states that those banks which had absorbed others should be expected to show gradually increased earning powers as a result of economies, but such was not the case. He suggests as explanations that

1. The small banks were accustomed to keep a small percentage of liquid assets, and after amalgamation they have to be ranked with the standard of the large bank. This may result in reduced earning power.

2. Bad and doubtful debts may have leaked out after amalgamations.

[1] Page 203.

K

3. Rates allowed on deposits have been growing, and deposits bearing no interest had been diminishing.

4. Continued depreciation of investments (since 1897) had eaten into profits.

5. Larger banks work on much finer rates ; therefore the benefit of large amalgamations, or amalgamations which create large banks, reverts to the public.

The first two and the last of these refer directly to amalgamation policy ; the remaining two refer to general banking conditions. Mr. Gibson thus takes the view that amalgamation does not necessarily make for more economic working. Consequently he agrees to all intents and purposes with the conclusions set out above.

In view of the importance of this aspect of the subject it is now proposed to examine more closely this item of expenses.

From inquiries made at all the existing joint-stock banks and from leading bankers, it appears that no changes of importance have occurred in the items constituting expenses in the period 1874–1924.

This evidence points to the conclusion that if expenses have altered in amount, the alteration is, to all intents and purposes, confined to the same items as appeared in the charges of fifty years ago. [1] These items may be cited as :

Group 1.	Group 2.	Group 3.
Salaries.	Insurances.	Law Charges.
Directors' Fees.	Provident Funds.	Licences.
Rents.	Light and Fuel.	Tea Money for Staff.
Rates.	Other Stamps.	Auditors' Fees.
Taxes.	Travelling Expenses.	Advertising.
Stationery.	Agency Charges.	
Postages.	Telephone Charges.	

It is not customary to class interest payments as an expense.

The charges are arranged in three groups according to their respective importance.

Of the whole number of items probably the only new ones for all banks in the last year recorded were expenditure on

---

[1] "Banks' expenses are to-day the same as fifty years ago, so far as the items are concerned, with the addition of pensions."—Sir D. Drummond Fraser in letters to me.

advertising and extra insurances. Provident Funds were in existence so early as the 'eighties of last century. The expenditure on these two items is not so important as to be the means of causing the large general increase in the total, now being discussed. Indeed a certain amount of advertising was done in these early years, as the columns of the financial newspapers bear witness. Also, against the increase shown on account of these items, must be set the reduction in agency charges. In 1874 there were many more separate banks than in 1924 : consequently the amount paid in agency fees must have been much larger in the former year. Again, the large reduction in the number of banks has not been brought about without the numbers of directors [1] and auditors suffering reduction. The items of Tea Money, Licences, and Law Charges are comparatively so small and have probably varied so little in the period that they may be omitted without further attention. This reasoning shows the increased expenses to be due to one or more of the remaining items : Salaries, Rates, Rents, Taxes, Stationery, Postages, Light and Fuel, Travelling Expenses, Telephone Charges. Of these the most important are Salaries, Rents, Rates, Taxes and Telephone Charges, since it is only to be expected that Stationery charges have been lessened as a result of amalgamation. Additionally, the customers are usually debited with postages made on their account, and the remaining charges are relatively small.

Obviously, then, the extra expense on account of these items is due mainly to the opening of branches, since these items are the main features of branch expenses. It has been shown in earlier pages that amalgamation was a great cause of the swift and expansive creation of branches, and therefore the process is shown to result in increased, and not reduced, expenses.

In concluding the discussion, it is proposed to cite for the purpose of illustration one or two cases in which the history of expenses can be traced. Generally speaking, it is very

---

[1] The additions of the totals of directors shown in the *Bankers' Almanach* for all the English joint-stock banks shows that in 1900, 1913, and 1923 the numbers were respectively 580, 423, and 390.

PERCENTAGE OF EXPENSES TO TOTAL WORKING RESOURCES.

Union Bank of London.

	Percentage.	
1879	·53	
1880	·51	
1881	·54	
1882	·62	
1883	·59	
1884	·61	
1885	·62	
1886	·64	
1887	·63	
1888	·66	
1889	·66	
1890	·66	
1891	·66	(Chasemore, Robinson & Sons)
1892	·69	
1893	·70	
1894	·61	
1895	·57	
1896	·63	
1897	·66	
1898	·65	
1899	·73	
1900	·76	
1901	·76	
1902	·80	(Smith Group)
1903	·93	(London & Yorkshire) (Prescotts) (Wigan Mercer & Tasker) (London Commercial and Cripplegate)
1904	·93	
1905	·96	
1906	·95	
1907	·96	
1908	·95	
1909	·90	
1910	·91	
1911	·95	
1912	·97	
1913	·93	

difficult indeed to get adequate information, with the result
that the selection of instances is unduly restricted. The
Union Bank of London is a suitable example because it has
published detailed expenses since 1879. The table on page
136 indicates the percentage of these to total resources, and
also the dates of the amalgamations in which it was concerned.

This bank serves as a good instance for illustration, as for
over twenty years it was engaged in but one amalgamation,
and that only a small one. Again, it did not open many
branches during the period. During all this time the
expenses rose but slightly, and this was almost entirely due to
increases made in staff salaries and directors' remunerations.

Its remaining amalgamations prior to 1918 were made in
two consecutive years. In 1902 six separate private businesses, all controlled by the Smith family, were added ;
while in 1903 four other distinct amalgamations were made,
three of which were with banks of substantial size. The
increased expenses are reflected in 1903 and succeeding
years quite definitely, and—which is of importance—they
persist up till 1913.

Similar figures can be presented for the London and
Westminster Bank. They are :

PERCENTAGE OF EXPENSES TO TOTAL WORKING RESOURCES.

London and Westminster Bank.

	Percentage.	Branches.
1880	·34	8
1881	·27	8
1882	·28	9
1883	·36	9
1884	·29	10
1885	·32	10
1886	·33	14
1887	·32	14
1888	·32	14
1889	·32	15
1890	·33	16
1891	·33	17

LONDON AND WESTMINSTER BANK (*continued*).

	Percentage.	Branches.
1892	·38	17
1893	·37	17
1894	·36	17
1895	·34	18
1896	·37	22
1897	·39	27
1898	·39	33
1899	·41	33
1900	·43	34
1901	·44	35
1902	·46	35
1903 . . . . , . .	·49	35
1904	·45	36
1905	·47	36
1906	·38	37
1907	·46	37
1908	·46	37
1909	1·08	(Amalgamation with London and County Bank)
1910	1·07	
1911	1·03	
1912	1·18	
1913	1·26	

For earlier periods it has been deemed advisable to indicate the number of branches. The only amalgamation recorded during this period was the large one with the London and County Bank. The figures therefore are very interesting. It is evident that as the number of branches grew, so did the expenses and the percentage expenses. This concrete illustration of the conclusion of a few pages earlier is also of no little significance.

Without doubt, however, the main interest lies in the jump shown in the figures when the amalgamation occurred. This not only persisted but grew in the succeeding years. In order to show that the jump was not caused by the figures of the London and County Bank, the figures of that bank for five-year periods may be subjoined. These are :

LONDON AND COUNTY BANK.

Percentage.

1879	.	.	.	.	·62
1884	.	.	.	.	·56
1889	.	.	.	.	·56	1891, Amalgamation with Hove Banking Co.

1889 . . . . ·56   1891, Amalgamation
                            with Hove Banking
                            Co.
1894 . . . . ·59
1899 . . . . ·55
1904 . . . . ·59   1907, Amalgamation
                            with F. Burt and Co.,
                            a small London
                            private bank.
1909 . . . . 1·08
1909   Amalgamation with London and Westminster.

Both the amalgamations were very small ones, and hence it is not likely that the figures of the London and County were greatly affected.

Connected with expenses are the statistics of net profits. Beginning with so high a percentage as 1·88 in 1874 these show a persistent fall both for London banks and the other English banks up to 1913. In that year a definite gain is recorded. After 1913 the fall is resumed, to be arrested again in 1920. Both these deviations have already been explained. The lowest point touched was ·57 per cent. in 1923. As compared with 1874 this shows a reduction of 69 per cent. for all banks.

The reasons for so regular a decline include the fact that for the latter part of the period there occurred the heavy and regular depreciation in gilt-edged securities to which reference has been made already.[1] The increase in the rate of income tax was another, for banks usually pay income tax on the salaries of their staff, as well as on profits. The competition of Municipalities, Building Societies, Discount Houses, Thrift and Friendly Societies, the Post Office Savings Bank, mill loans (especially in Lancashire), and other investments, has curtailed the increase of deposits, and

---

[1] This applies mainly to earlier years, since the predominant practice of modern bankers is to make allowance for investment depreciation after net profits have been struck.

taken with the strong competition among the banks themselves, has necessitated higher rates of interest. Interest
is now allowed on current accounts even by some London
banks, and on a more extensive scale than before by provincial concerns, and this militates, like other items, against
the obtaining of good profits. There is no doubt, too, that
inter-banking competition has reduced commission and overdraft rates, both of which are essential for profits. Account
must be taken of the new avenues of profit opened by the
innovations of engaging in acceptance and discount business,
foreign business, and trustee business, but there is no doubt
that this extension of functions has proved relatively less
profitable than the old and principal function of loaning.
Lastly, a certain amount of weight must be given to the fact
that banks now make larger appropriations to contingency
funds such as Provident Funds, Reduction of Premiums, and
Staff Widows Funds.

But it is not to these reasons that we should look so
much as to the fact that expenses have shown a continual
increase over the period. The great difference between
gross profits and net profits shown during the last few years,[1]
especially, indicates the heaviness of this burden, and the
evidence of banking authorities confirms this deduction,
e.g. Sir D. Drummond Fraser says : " I think the reason that
net profits have suffered is that expenses have increased." [2]
And as it has been shown that amalgamations have undoubtedly increased expenses, they have reduced net profits in consequence. This means that dividends, paid on
reduced capitals, have been less than otherwise might have
been the case, allocations to reserves have necessarily been
smaller, and the disbursement of profits generally has been
affected.

[1] An illuminating example is the report of Barclays Bank for 1924.
Expenses were reduced from 1923, but even so, Gross Profit was
£7,508,514 14s. 2d. ; Net Profit, £2,067,281 9s. 4d. ; and Expenses totalled
£5,441,223 4s. 10d. Gross Profit was thus 363 per cent. of Net Profit,
while Expenses were 263 per cent. of Net Profit.
[2] In a letter to the writer.

Part III

CHAPTER VIII.

ADVANTAGES AND DISADVANTAGES OF AMALGAMATION.

THE preceding chapters have dealt with the history of the movement towards amalgamation from the date of its association with the new development of joint-stock banking enterprise ; with the causes predisposing to the making of the various types of agreements ; and with the economic effects of the movement.

It is now proposed to come to the heart of the problem and to consider the case for and against amalgamation.

The arguments arising from the analysis in Chapters VI and VII will first be considered, and later various points not implicated in this analysis will be discussed.

The arguments relating to capitals and reserves demand first consideration. Those usually employed by bankers to defend the low ratios of capital to liabilities have laid stress on the amount of " reserved liability," i.e. the amount of capital callable in case of emergency as first provided by the Companies Act of 1879. It has been shown that this was in excess of paid up capital, and if called, would give a sub-stantial backing to liabilities. This argument had force in the days when banking was conducted by thirty or forty joint-stock companies of many sizes and interests, none of which were so large as to tower high above competitors. It had strength also when the proportion of capital to deposits was both steady and comparatively reasonable ; for banking is largely based on " habit " and " convention." But when banks became restricted to a dozen concerns of large size and a greatly extended list of shareholders (the increased numbers being drawn largely from people of less substantial means), the position became changed, since the possible dangers resulting from the failure of any one bank were also increased. And after the percentage of capital to deposits fell, as a result of amalgamation schemes hastily conceived and executed, the problem took on a serious aspect. (For when in 1918 the percentage sank to 6 per cent., it must be remembered that 3·2 per cent. only was actual capital. The remainder consisted of reserves, which, though sometimes regarded by bankers as the equivalent of capital, are only undivided profits liable to be trenched upon). Again, the failure of one or two of the speedily growing banks such as existed in the early years of the war, would have involved the others, and these, though substantial in size, were actually not big enough to withstand serious losses. This aspect of the problem may be considered somewhat theoretical, but on grounds of equity alone objections can be raised against an over-low percentage of capital. For under the present system of deposit repayments the claims of depositors, which in 1919 totalled £2,062,419,216 for safety, should rank equally high with that of the proprietors for dividend payments. And 6 per cent. is not a safe limit on which to work.

For the sake of comparison, the practice of foreign systems may be considered, although, since there is no complete analogy between industrial and financial conditions here and abroad, results should not be expressed dogmatically. In Germany, for instance, in 1916, eight German credit banks, including the Dresdner and Deutsche groupings, had capitals and reserves averaging 30·7 per cent. of deposits.

The contrast with English banking at the time was a striking one, for the percentage of capitals and reserves to deposits was only 7·6 per cent. Besides the Bank Amalgamations Committee, the Committee on Financial Facilities after the War also was opposed to the low percentage. Notable support is therefore given to the necessary conclusion that the movement which allowed reductions to be successively made, and to so great an extent, must on these accounts be criticised.

Interviews with bankers reveal that they do not regard the question with seriousness.   They believe that so long as balance sheets are kept in a liquid condition there is little to fear on the point of security.   To this argument the reply must be that it is manifestly desirable to preserve liquid balance sheets ; yet the bankers' duty does not end here. The success of any banking machine depends entirely on whether or not it enjoys the full confidence of the community which it serves.   Consequently everything should be done to produce and maintain this confidence.   Neglect to maintain a reasonable ratio between proprietors' and depositors' funds detracts from safety and therefore endangers the relations between bankers and public.   Provided that a reasonable ratio can be determined, there is thus a strong reason for doing so ; and this can be done with little attendant disability.

Reduction of capitals, then, is a disadvantage attendant upon amalgamations.   The problem was more serious in the later years of last and the earlier years of this century, since in 1918 and succeeding years there has been some attempt to increase the ratio.   Yet it is again becoming serious as a result of the steps since taken by Barclays Bank of extinguishing all uncalled liability on its various types of shares.   To do this is to remove one of the safeguards on which bankers in the past laid stress, and as there is no compensatory gain, the seriousness of the problem of capital is increased.

The question of reserves is inseparably bound up with that of capital.

Another development for which amalgamation was responsible to no small extent, has been the rapid growth of bank offices.   Only for a short period during the war was this policy not pursued, but since then, the fierce competition generated by the reduction of banks to a very small number of large concerns (which was a direct result of speedy amalgamations) has caused an over-rapid development on these lines.   This aspect of growth received comment so early as 1903, for Mr. A. S. Harvey, a notable banking authority, declared :

" Indeed, so completely have the existing institutions responded to the call for branches that England as a whole, may be said to be well-nigh overbanked, while in the suburbs of London the branches of two or three well-known banks compete for the accounts of the solvent trader."

At the time of this declaration the numbers of branches in England and Wales and London (including suburbs) were approximately 5,000 and 480 respectively.[1] In view of the fact that population has increased but little since then, the number of offices existing at the end of 1924, namely 8,081 and 859 respectively, demonstrates how in the space of twenty-one years, banking competition has further increased and excessive branch banking has occurred. With respect to the present position the *Manchester Guardian Commercial* says : " One may suspect that this competitive opening of branches has been overdone, and that the banks themselves are beginning to see that the lust for record figures may be gratified at too great a cost. . . . Many of the branches erected at the time of maximum prices are certainly not yet paying their way." [2] The competition prevailing to cause this receives condemnation in the *Natproban* (November, 1923)—the organ of the National Provincial Bank. Mr. J. Darge, speaking of present day practice, says : " Banking strategy, where new branches are concerned, seems to be as simple as that of sheep at a gap in a hedge—where one goes the other follows."

Lastly, the detailed table on page 113, Chapter VI, and the one here given, demonstrate the unique growth which has occurred.

---

[1] The figures for 1901 were 4,762 and 452.
[2] August 2, 1923.—Further, Dr. Walter Leaf, speaking at the annual meeting of the Westminster Bank, January 29, 1925, said : " The only persons who have any right to complain are the shareholders, whose profits are devoted in some measure at least to the opening of fresh branches which take a long time before they can pay their way and in some cases, one may fear, are not likely ever to pay at all. Before the war a new branch, if established in a growing region, should pay its way, we used to find, after some three to five years of existence. Now, owing to the rise in overhead expenses on the one hand, and the severe cutting of profits on the other, that period is about doubled."

NUMBER OF ENGLISH JOINT-STOCK AND PRIVATE
BANKS AND BRANCHES IN LONDON AND SUBURBS.

Year.	Number.
1861	72
1871	120
1881	180
1891	303
1901	452
1911	596
1913	615
1921	763
1924	859

All these opinions and figures are responsible and weighty.
But more convincing, perhaps, are the actual facts testifying
to the excessive competition.   If, for instance, the amounts
of deposits in 1921 of 11 of the largest banks are taken, the
total is £1,905,316,000.   The number of branches possessed
by these concerns was 7,565.   The average deposits per
branch were therefore £248,700.   The same banks consisted
of 30 banks in 1911, when they possessed 5,259 branches.
Their total deposits were then £634,282,000, or an average
for each branch of £120,600.

Obviously, however, the 1921 figures suffered from the
inflation of the war period.   Allowing for variations in money
values, the corrected average per branch in 1921 was £113,045.
When this is compared with the 1911 average of £120,600,
and it is remembered that the branches in London had been
increased by 167, and that the average deposits of these
branches are much above the average for the whole country,
it is evident that country branches opened in this period
have collected a diminished amount of deposits.   Since, as
shown in Chapter VII, expenses have risen considerably, it
is evident that the newer branches are not so remunerative
as the older.   This is testimony to the over-development
of branches.   And the conclusion is strengthened by the
fact that if net profits are calculated as a percentage of
deposit totals for the same banks in 1911 and 1921 the
result is respectively 1·175 per cent. and ·907 per cent.

In so far as amalgamation has been a strong cause
of branch opening, it must be regarded as assisting

an economic development which has lost its beneficial character by being carried to extreme points. Not only does this result in loss to the banks, but the safety and quality of banking are affected. Over-competition tends to reduce margins beyond the limits of desirability, and sometimes practicability ; it also encourages such practices as " touting " for accounts, the only eventual effect of which is to reduce the prestige on which banks set great store. If persisted in, the eventual result will be that the meagre profits obtainable on straightforward, ordinary business will necessitate extension of the banking field, with possible engagement on a large scale in foreign business, with its additional risks ; or the adoption of the German method of becoming partners in, and not merely lenders to, business enterprise. If this latter were to result, it would immediately lay bankers open to the charge of unduly supporting certain specific branches of production, and their lack of scientific and technical knowledge might cause the directors to contract bad debts. Lastly, all the evils of interlocking directorates and financial trusts would become rampant.

Or, on the other hand, over-competition might lead to a series of agreements among the great banks to work in close concurrence, and this, with banking still under private control, must be deprecated.[1]

Enough has perhaps been said to show how serious a problem is bound up with this topic, and the reasons why the over-development of branch policy, largely resulting from amalgamations, is disadvantageous. It should not be overlooked that in so far as branch offices were developed to meet the desires and needs of the community, and in so far as they have brought banking facilities to areas where they were required, they have been of distinct value. For capital

---

[1] Hartley Withers points out that the Scottish banks now work in close co-operation. He says : " In Scotland . . . coherence and co-operation among the banks are carried to an extreme of which the mercantile community frequently complains. The banks are few and stand together like a close corporation ; they agree absolutely and arbitrarily among themselves as to the rates they will allow to depositors, the rates at which they will advance or discount, and the terms and commissions for which they will do business for customers."—*English Banking System*, p. 49.

thereby acquired a mobility which otherwise it would not have possessed. Surplus cash could then be transferred with maximum speed to districts where there was the slightest call for it. The invaluable habit of thrift received encouragement. The local trader, on whom even now much depends, might then lay claim to all the banking facilities enjoyed by the companies and larger traders established in areas of greater importance. And when, through amalgamation, the local branch of a small bank became connected with an institution sufficiently large, the facilities were somewhat increased in scope, and speeded up. As examples of this last point may be mentioned the issue of " Circular World Letters of Credit " first inaugurated by the Midland Bank ; and foreign exchange dealings of all descriptions. Post-war conditions necessitated a great deal of this type of business and since it is better transacted on a large scale, the policy of amalgamation which assisted, say, the Midland Bank to establish a foreign department in which 2,000 clerks are now employed, is a beneficial one in this particular respect.

Where amalgamation was responsible for joining areas in which already both amalgamating banks existed, it was an unsound development.[1] This occurred in some of the amalgamations recorded in 1918 and 1919, and in earlier years also ; and the actual number of places at which banks overlapped as a result of the whole number of amalgamations registered since 1914 exceeds 450. While some of this was unavoidable, if the excessive speed of 1918 and 1919 had been moderated, the amalgamations might have been arranged on a wiser basis, and the great saving consequent on pure geographical expansion, viz., the increased mobility of money, would then have been secured.

Another consequence of the spread of offices has been shown to be the growth in the use of cheque currency. Of this little but good can be said. In addition to giving increased prestige to Bank of England notes through the

---

[1] The 1918 Bank Amalgamations Committee also deprecated this, as may be seen by a glance at the report in Appendix III. Their objections were mainly founded on the destruction of effective competition.

reduction of country notes (in spite of the fact that the Bank's cash reserve was reduced), it has made possible the evolution of a delicately shaped banking system, based on credit, which is strikingly economical. In witness of this the 1922 report of the London Clearing House shows that the proportion of the whole cash transactions which required coin, was only 0·7 per cent. of the whole ; whereas in 1865 Sir John Lubbock told the Royal Statistical Society that out of £1,000,000 paid into his bank 2·7 per cent. was in coin. Cheque currency, too, has assisted the growth of a high code of commercial morality, the value of which may hardly be estimated.

One of the main effects of the movement is in the equalisation of interest rates, loaning rates, and charges, over the whole banking field. In the case of individual banks this statement is only true when one bank possesses a number of branches, and it particularly applies when the proportion of branches to head offices is large. Since this position has been reached in England mainly by amalgamation it will be of interest to glance at the process.

In the days of the private bankers, who were generally located in their own single districts, there was little uniformity of rates.[1] In evidence to the 1875 committee Sir Inglis Palgrave ascribed this to the differences in the relative wealth of different districts. But further, when the number of private bankers ran into hundreds, with no organisation to link them, it is patent that variations were bound to occur, since no one banker had knowledge of what all his fellows were charging and allowing. Again, certain of their number were able to secure a monopoly

---

[1] " There existed no regulation absolutely fixed and uniform, except that of 5 per cent. per annum for the interest on loans ; all other charges varied according to the risks encountered and the customary profits of bankers ; those who derived profit from the circulation of their own promissory notes rarely made any charge beyond 5 per cent. for the interest on the sum advanced to the borrower. When the Bank of England established its branches the Directors fixed a uniform charge which was 4 per cent. per annum for discounting bills at not exceeding 90 days' rate." —*A View of the Banking Question.* Anon. (1832), p. 105 (Rylands).

" Among the country bankers various modes are adopted for remunerating the banker for his trouble and expense. In some cases a banker allows interest on deposits, charging a commission on all transactions with his customer."—Wilson, *Capital, Currency and Banking*, 1847, p. 32.

charge for their services, since there was no competition. In the early joint-stock banks more uniformity is to be seen, although even here there were differences between the practice of London, provincial and local banks. For many years it was not customary to allow interest on current accounts in London ; in the provinces interest was allowed.[1] Again, practices varied from branch to branch of the same bank. With the increase of the number of branches belonging to one bank (particularly since the '90's of last century), and the growth of associations of bankers,[2] rates and charges have tended to become more uniform and to be reduced.[3] This tendency has now been crystallised into effective practice by the development of competition. Such competition, as pointed out before, has been progressively in evidence since the opening of the present century. While, therefore, it is improbable that loaning and interest rates ever varied so widely in the more compact banking area of England as in the heterogeneous divisions of America (where rates in the pre-federal reserve bank system varied as much as from 2-6 per cent.), undoubtedly the differences were sufficient to be economically undesirable. For the share that the amalgamation movement has had in creating larger banks and thereby bringing about equalised rates, it must therefore be credited.

To discuss more fully the increased facilities now at the disposal of customers. The phrase " increased facilities " was often used by bank chairmen in discussing prospective amalgamations. Ostensibly it means that all branches of the two banks were fused into one system, and this gave the effect of there being, as it were, one bank only. The incidental benefits resulting from this process were the more concrete gains however. For instance, if a London bank

---

[1] 1875 Committee—Qq. 1856-60.

[2] The Institute of Bankers, established 1879. The Association of English Country Bankers, reconstituted 1874.
Central Association of Bankers, set up 1895. These also are now amalgamated.

[3] " The reduction of profit is due to some extent to the reduction of charges, commissions, etc., which the public now enjoy from the great body of bankers."—J. Dun, *Journal Institute of Bankers*, 1897, p. 230.

joined with a country bank, the excess deposits of the former were used to give additional accommodation to the latter [1]—and occasionally *vice versa*. Another incidental gain—of a minor character it is true—was that of the saving of time in making the clearings of cheques. When the two banks were separate entities, all country cheques had to pass through the regulation country clearing, which occupied three days. As one bank instead of two, the cheques could be sent through head office or direct to the branches on which they were drawn, with the result that one or two days were saved respectively. The gain to customers is that the " fate " of the cheque was therefore known earlier, and the time occupied by the negotiation of transactions was speeded up. Another change is that, in some cases, cheques received by a bank from any of its own branches were debited with a smaller number (sometimes even none at all) of decimals than in the case of cheques received through the country clearing. Therefore, unless the account was worked by the method of " Contract Commission," there resulted slightly reduced charges to the customer. This gain is offset however by the fact that customers' accounts are debited one day or more earlier than under the previous method. The credit balance is thus reduced and the debit balance increased, and the interest accordingly reduced or increased.

The special clearings of Scotch and Irish cheques have also been affected by the amalgamations which English banks have made with banks in those countries. Formerly, since these cheques used to take four or five days to clear, and the banks of those countries combined effectively to charge at high rates,[2] extra decimals were debited for clearing cheques on Scotch and Irish banks. In some cases, too, extra charges were made at the end of the banking half-year if the customer had a large turnover. With amalgamation, these charges have been reduced, with advantage to the English trader. To some extent, too, it has had the effect of breaking up the

---

[1] Liverpool Union with Lloyds in 1900. Stuckeys with Parrs in 1908 is the opposite case.

[2] This is mentioned even in the evidence given to the 1875 Committee (Q.1098). The eleven Scotch banks were then shown to be working in effective combination.

combinations of bankers who formerly insisted on heavy charges. Yet the evidence on this point is hardly sufficient for definite assertion. The operation of clearing does not now occupy so long, notwithstanding, and this is a distinct gain.

Another change affects particularly the position of firms or companies which have branches in many different towns. When banks were smaller and had fewer branches the regular receipts and withdrawals made by these widespread firms, necessitated the charging of commissions to those banks which acted as agents of the bank with which the account was kept. This charge was passed on to the customer. After amalgamation most of these commissions were no longer payable, with the result that sums of money could be paid or withdrawn from a larger number of places, at reduced charges. Again, it was customary to advise the bank with which the account was kept of the various payments and withdrawals. Now this is no longer imperative, since such items may be included on the " Daily Statement " transmitted to Head Office by branches. In this case heavy postage charges are also saved. It should, however, be remembered that usually the agency charges of two banks were to some extent offset, the one against the other, so that the gain here is not unqualified.

Another point parallel to those already discussed, is that if customers formerly banked with local banks not possessing direct agents abroad, it was necessary to arrange such business through London agents, who made a heavier charge— because they all worked separately—than is now made when the large banks have their own offices abroad, or when all the foreign business is brought together and transacted more cheaply as a result of its greater dimensions. All of the large London banks now have special departments dealing with the foreign business.

In discussing the effect of amalgamation on movements in deposits, it was shown in Chapter VII that, by its great influence on the growth of branches, amalgamation was to no small extent responsible for the decisive increase which has occurred.

More indirectly, perhaps, the movement was responsible for increasing deposits because it made for the ascendancy of joint-stock over private concerns ; and because, with the destruction of the note issues and the strength acquired by the combination of the strong companies, the introduction and development of the cheque currency was made possible. With respect to this it should be remembered that it was the speedy progress of joint-stock methods, largely made possible through amalgamation, which made the use of cheques a reality instead of a theoretical possibility.

The third reason for deposit growth—the strength and safety of banking—has also been shown to be mainly a consequence of amalgamation.

In promoting the increase of deposits in these ways, there is much to be said in favour of the movement. It is obvious that deposits are a fundamental necessity of banking operations, and, further, the usefulness of banks to the community is dependent on the expansion or diminution of real (or net) banking deposits. For the English joint-stock banks control nearly the whole amount of the credit which is created to serve the needs of industry and commerce, and the adequacy or shortage of this is necessarily of vital concern to all trading operations. It is of the highest importance that banks should be able to support industry and commerce up to the limits of prudence at all the varying stages of the trade cycle, and since bankers are now prone to work by the somewhat arbitrary limit of 50 per cent. advances to deposits, it is essential that the total of deposits should be a maximum total. For then the elasticity of the advances which bankers can give is increased, and this may be offset against the wide fluctuations in monetary requirements caused by the oscillations resulting from the variations comprised in the extremes of a trade cycle.

Discussing this item of advances more closely, it is apparent that up to 1913 there had been little change compared with 1891—the best measuring year. Also, that during war years the percentage sank, to rise again until at the end of 1923 practically the same percentage was being lent as in 1891. Judging solely from the figures, it may be presumed that amalgamation rather tended to reduce the total volume of advances over the period. But it must be remembered that trade conditions exert a dominant influence over the demand for accommodation, so that a special factor must be considered. Consequently some part of the decline is ascribable to this—e.g. 1913 was a year of active trading operations and the demand for loans increased ; similarly in 1920–1 ; but 1906 was a year of depressed trade, while 1918–19 saw the slow recovery after the war. Actually amalgamation tends to increase the capacity of the banks to advance in three ways. First, because of the increase in real deposits over the period—which it has been pointed out was governed to a considerable extent by the direct and indirect results of amalgamations. Second, because a large bank is able generally to lend more proportionately than a group of small banks, having equal resources, since it may work with smaller reserves, and in practice does so. Third, because amalgamation has resulted in greatly reduced capitals, and has tended to increase deposits, lower rates may be charged for accommodation ; and under the stress of the extra competition caused by the reduction to a small number of banks, this has actually resulted. The increased safety of modern banking has, however, undoubtedly tended to restrict heavy loaning done without security and this, together with the variability of demand for accommodation generated by the different phases of the trade cycle, and the tendency of bankers to work on customary methods, probably accounts for the fact that, throughout the period, loans have decreased in percentage volume rather than otherwise. The conclusion is therefore that amalgamation was not responsible for the diminished percentage of advances shown in the table in Chapter VI.

It is this aspect of banking activities which nevertheless has received most criticism. The objection most frequently made has been that the absorption of the private country banker has brought a change in the method of granting loans. It is shown that the private banker used to be a member of the local community, not only known by all, but knowing all. He was therefore in intimate touch with all the affairs of the district and knew its exact requirements. And he knew how much exactly he might safely advance to each individual. With this first-hand knowledge he developed sympathy with customers' requirements, and gave them loans, usually on personal reputation or without taking a legal charge.[1] When the business was sold to a joint-stock concern the banking partner or proprietor was replaced by the manager, who in the majority of cases had passed his earlier life elsewhere. The substitute had therefore little knowledge of local conditions and peculiarities. He came, too, not with plenary powers, but simply as the salaried agent, whose position, and therefore whose salary, were dependent on the methods with which he carried out the codified system of his superiors. Instead of giving advances on personal security, he required that, wherever possible, tangible security of a high character should be produced. Land and buildings were discovered to have a strangely less value in his critical eyes than those of the private banker friend. Generally, too, the security must provide a margin over and above the loan. Lastly, before the advance could be definitely fixed, sometimes a balance sheet and detailed particulars were required by Head Office.

Had it not been that joint-stock concerns were not so well organised in earlier years as they are now, and that a certain amount of compromise was shown by them the change would have been drastic. Even so, there were many complaints that it was for the worse ; that the introduction of security discipline was killing enterprise.[2] Most of them

---

[1] For instance, Mr. G. C. Glyn told the 1832 Committee, " The London (private) bankers frequently allow a customer, if he be a respectable trader, to overdraw his account, merely upon the opinion they have of his good character."—*Banks and Banking*, Hardcastle, p. 291.

[2] A typical one is taken from the columns of *The Times*, viz. : " Perhaps few people realise from what agriculture is suffering to-day. Is it not from the amalgamation of the big banks, and the position that they have taken up with the farming industry, namely, that of practically affording no financial assistance to farmers ? What is the position of the tenant farmer to-day when he wants an overdraft ? In the old days his landlord was, directly or indirectly, his banker, insomuch as he, the landlord, was out to help his tenant. Who to-day takes his place ? The local corn merchant, the manure merchant, and the coal merchant—all good people to whom the farmer has to mortgage his crops before they are harvested. What is again wanted is local banks with managers who know something of agriculture, and perhaps the farmer will come into his own again."

stressed that the large joint-stock banks did not apportion a
sufficient part of their loans to particular industries and
trades, and also, in general, that they did not lend enough.
Becoming very numerous, in September, 1914, Mr. Ernest
Sykes, Secretary of the Institute of Bankers, was constrained
to deal with them.   Writing in the *Associated Accountants'
Journal* he summarised some of the remaining complaints as
(1) " the banks lend too large a proportion of their funds in
financing the London Money Market, and that the industrial
and commercial classes are starved of the accommodatio
necessary for the successful carrying out of their projects."
(2) " There is a general complaint that the volume of money
available for borrowing by the public is restricted by the
bankers, and that they do not lend enough."

The arguments pointing to the distinction between a local
resident partner and an imported manager shows that sentiment took no little part in former dealings between banker
and customer.   The change is regretted, and rightly so.
Yet, from the standpoint of scientific and safe banking, it is
for the better.   The element of personal bias disappears, to
be replaced by impartial consideration.   By this banking
has become safer ; for many times the private banker with
his small capital supported some person or firm beyond
danger point, and disaster followed.[1]   To require security
is a step to safe banking also.   It has the disadvantage of
restricting enterprise, but it tends to discourage speculative
business.   That the requirement has not been enforced
harshly as yet is evident from the evidence given to the
Bank Amalgamations Committee, and from the report of
the Westminster Bank for 1923.   The latter pointed out that
28 per cent. of the borrowers had secured loans, while a
further 13 per cent. only gave partial security.   It is not
unreasonable to assume that a similar state of affairs exists
in other banks, and especially in the smaller provincial
concerns.

As to the complaints made by agriculturists, it seems to be
a penchant of farmers to grumble.   Without doubt, modern
managers are not so thoroughly acquainted with the needs of

[1] *Vide* the earlier chapters of the History.

farmers as individual private bankers. It is necessary to remember, however, that in the case of branch private banks the conditions did not vary very much from those existing now. It is mentioned in the speech of the chairman of Lloyds Bank in 1923 when he said that where twenty years ago a certain private bank was giving overdrafts of £15,642, Lloyds in 1923 gave sanctioned limits to £63,550, of which full advantage had not been taken. In this particular instance, therefore, the farmers had benefited rather than lost. Thoroughly to prove the case, full statistics would be required from all banks, but as these are not obtainable it must be sufficient to mention that in 1923 Lloyds were giving 12,800 farmers £14,000,000 in loans, or an average of over £1,000 each. Again, none of the banks are specially opposed to advancing to farmers, for the risk is certainly less than in other businesses, and inquiry at leading banks has elicited the reply that there was no ground for complaint by the agricultural interest.

Mr. Sykes answered the complaints cited above by pointing out that the amount of money which a bank might lend depended on the state of trade and the financial outlook. This proportion was in turn regulated by the amount of deposits it received, i.e. it depended on the thrift of the people. Bearing in mind that bank loans also create deposits, he showed that if only £100 out of each £1,000 advanced found its way back to the lending bank, its balance at the Bank of England was reduced by £900 and its loaning activity thereby restricted. Applying this logic to the present position, it is evident that when banks are fewer and larger, a higher proportion of the loans made returns to the lending bank, since it has many more customers who are likely to receive the cheques drawn on the loan account. Not finding its balance at the Bank of England reduced, it is able to lend more than before. The conclusion is that over-lending rather than underlending is likely to occur as a result of amalgamation.

He also points out that banks must keep a certain amount of money in the Money Market to maintain their liquid assets. Since the rates are low, they do not keep there more

than they can help.   Lastly, he mentions that people suffer
from the common illusion that banks withhold money in
times of prosperity simply because they do not remember
that there is then an increased demand for it.

To pass to some of the disadvantages resulting from amalgamation, affecting the loaning of money, it is but necessary to
mention that the number of banks having been seriously
reduced, there is a tendency for banks to grant large loans
to comprehensive firms and to neglect the small man.   This
is an almost inevitable effect of the working of the machinery
of coded rules.   Preference is naturally given to those who
can guarantee the bank against loss by offering security, even
though it be purely collateral in type.   The individual who
may have the ability to rise to a higher level than the normal
trader, but who has no financial backing, is apt to receive
less assistance than he received under the old private system.[1]
The formation by most of the banks of boards of local
directors is a valuable antidote, but the conditions prevailing before have hardly been reproduced, since the
districts are generally as large as the whole areas formerly
controlled by provincial joint-stock banks, and consequently
the same personal touch cannot be obtained.

Again, trade depression—and especially a severe depression extending to many types of industry—shows one of the
worst features of loans made by a few great concerns.   The
machine-like London control is not only slow to respond to
prospective openings made by individual entrepreneurs,
but its scientifically devised time-limits tend to detach some,
if not all, of the support given to industry just at the time
when perhaps it is most needed to pass through the middle of
the depression before there is a definite turn for the better.
And when the support is withdrawn, it is not now possible
to turn to a number of other competing banks with the total
number of concerns at 13, as when the number of banks was,
say, 50, and especially if it is recollected that of these 13
only 5 are represented throughout the country.   During these

---

[1] E.g. The late Lord Leverhulme, who has declared that banks are
merely " rabbits " in respect of capacity to venture funds.   And yet it
cannot be overlooked that bankers have loyally supported, for example,
the cotton industry, during the present unexampled time of difficulty.

periods, too, values both of finished commodities and fixed capital fall, and since the great London banks make it a matter of policy to insist on the maintenance of adequate security in order to protect their own position, traders are thrown into unforeseen difficulties.

On page 124 of Chapter VII it has been shown that the liquidity of banks underwent during the period of about forty years, numerous flunctuations, but no great change was finally recorded. If anything, the decline in the total percentage shows a slightly worsened position at the ending of the period, but nevertheless one which is still very liquid. It has been mentioned, too, that amalgamation had little concern with this aspect of banking, except that the change from private and small local banks has undoubtedly tended to strengthen the general position, for all the existing banks now exhibit much greater uniformity in presenting high standards of liquid assets, whereas before there were some individual banks which were always weaker than the rest. The absence of severe failures since 1866 testifies this. For its share in the comparatively minor changes which have happened, amalgamation is therefore rather to be looked on with favour than disfavour.

The last point dealt with in Chapters VI and VII now requires discussion. This concerns the item of expenses and net profits. The discussion on these topics resulted in the conclusion that while net profits have strongly decreased over the period, expenses have correspondingly increased.[1] Very definitely amalgamation is largely responsible for this. In the case of expenses it is apparent that the expected economies so often stressed in chairmen's speeches have not materialised, and consequently what was a strong argument in favour is actually a strong argument against the policy. Most bankers still seem to consider that more economies than diseconomies have resulted, and consequently do not seem to be alive to the results of their actions. From the point of view of the community this results in direct loss, for the charges are finally borne by individual

---

[1] The results of the large railway re-groupings has been similarly productive of increased expenditure.

customers in the shape of reduced deposit rates and increased loan rates. With the lowering of the deposit rate to 2 per cent. instead of $1\frac{1}{2}$ per cent. below bank rate in 1921, already a proportion of the extra expenses has been passed on to the public, and it is likely that if further large amalgamations occur, expenses and therefore charges will again be increased. Additionally, since the banks have here a common meeting ground (for from details available it is evident that the rise is not confined to one or two concerns), it is possible that arrangements to increase charges will lead to combined working in other aspects of banking, and the value of virile competition will be lost. On the other hand, it should be pointed out that a portion of the enhanced expenses is due to the payment of larger salaries to the 52,000 employees of the various English banks. In so far as the raising of salaries has served to effect a desirable reform of economic working conditions it is to be welcomed ; and if this brings forth a higher standard of work and attracts a more efficient type of labour in time, the loss to the community arising from that item will probably be offset. Of the other items, e.g. expenditure on buildings, it is impossible to speak with equal certainty. In any case it is evident that banks should investigate carefully their individual positions with respect to the item of expenses, and endeavour to reduce the cost of providing the national banking service. Since the reduced net profits are almost entirely occasioned by the increased expenses it is evident that attention to this latter item is essential if the fall is to be stopped. In this connection it should be observed that partly greater expenses are the result of enhanced competition, to which they are a testimony. So long as this is not overdone, by such steps as the opening of an excessive number of branches, it is economically good, as the benefit accrues to the customers. Since the majority of the shareholders are also customers,[1] the gain likewise also accrues to them. Consequently there is no reason to deprecate healthy and regular competition, so long as the banks are controlled

[1] Amalgamation has increased greatly the number of shareholders, by reason of the splitting of capital which it has caused, e.g. in ten large banks over 300,000 separate share accounts were open in 1924.

by private enterprise. Most of the competition hitherto prevailing has been of this type so that in so far as amalgamation has been responsible for it, the movement must be credited. If further re-grouping occurs as a result of amalgamation between one or more of the great banks there may be a tendency to increase net profits by monopolistic methods—a thoroughly undesirable development.

This exhausts the discussion of the points arising from the analysis of Chapters VI and VII, and attention will now be devoted to various points not yet treated. First as to details of the 1918 Bank Amalgamations Committee's sitting. It is possible to offer criticism that the witnesses were not a representative group, for half of them exactly were concerned with banks. The remaining half included only five witnesses who were concerned in active trading operations of any sort, and such staple industries as agriculture, cotton, iron and steel, mining, woollen, electricity, and shipbuilding, had no representatives. Indeed, while the trading interests of the country were represented by two members of London merchants, the manufacturing interests gave no evidence whatever. This was due perhaps to the necessity for dealing quickly with the problem, and this view would seem to be borne out by the fact that no witness submitted evidence of any length or was examined at more than one sitting. Actually, all the twenty-two witnesses were examined in eight meetings, and the report states that " Unfortunately time did not permit of our taking oral evidence from more than a limited number of witnesses." Again, only one witness was called to state the case for the accepting houses, and his firm was more active in making new issues than in accepting : but written evidence was taken from various sources such as the Association of Chambers of Commerce, the Stock Exchange, and some manufacturing companies. Certainly, however, it was not wise to appoint Sir R. R. Vassar-Smith, the late chairman of Lloyds Bank, to the committee, and to leave out gentlemen who occupied similar positions in other banks. Indeed, no bank chairman should have been appointed to sit.

Owing to the fact that the evidence was taken under secrecy it may not be discussed. A reading of it, however, gives the impression that the question was surveyed hurriedly, and that the full implications of banking combination were not therefore touched upon : e.g. the full effect of amalgamation on the distribution and possible redistribution of loaning was not considered, possibly because the trading interests were not adequately heard. In particular, also, little attention was given to the historical development of the process, with the result that such questions as the scale of compensation to absorbed shareholders were not investigated. Again, the problem of the effect of the movement on expenses and methods of administration received but spasmodic mention, so that one of the not unimportant aspects of the policy did not receive the weight to which it was clearly entitled. As pointed out earlier, the fact that the committee sat in an atmosphere such as was engendered by war-time conditions, necessarily partly determined the method of attacking the problem : but it must not be overlooked that the excessive speed of the 1918 moves and the necessity of quickly reaching a decision on the problem also weighed with the committee.

To these criticisms should be added the fact that the appointment of two independent gentlemen to arbitrate on future proposals has not proved adequate. In the first place a committee of two is not sufficient to deal with a question so important as this. Second, since both gentlemen had strong banking interests (as well as commercial), *a priori* their appointment was not designed to allay the apprehensions of the public with regard to possible future developments. Third, the fact that in effect only one amalgamation has since been actually disallowed, and that in 1919 a high average number of fusions and agreements was recorded, has led the public to believe that the arbitrators' powers were not fully employed—especially since the committee's findings were unfavourable to the uncontrolled growth of the movement. Fourth, the proposed Parliamentary Bill dealing with the future regulation of amalgamations was so badly drafted that it has never passed into law. In view of all these considerations, and the fact that the movement is likely to persist, there is clearly a need for a new, and full, survey of the problem and its implications.

Even though it is not possible to discuss the evidence submitted to the committee, before passing to discuss other aspects of the process, the arguments of the late Sir Edward Holden, who was long recognised as the leader of amalgamation policy, call for discussion. Since the chief of these were included in his speeches at the meeting of the Chambers of Commerce on April 8 and 9, 1918, and at the meeting called to sanction the amalgamation between the London City and Midland and the London Joint Stock Banks in September of that year, they may be extracted therefrom :

(1) " The first benefit accruing to the large banks from these big amalgamations is a large increase in their capital ; and a large increase in their resources ; but if you are going to stop amalgamations, they will not be able to increase their capital any more on that line."

(2) " Big Banks will help to increase our commercial exports abroad, and to offset an unfavourable trade balance after the war."

(3) " Every development of amalgamation has rendered the banks more stable, and our recent immunity from the distresses consequent on bank failures has been due to the strength of the banks by amalgamation."

(4) " But for the amalgamations the banks could not possibly have given adequate assistance to our enormously increased trade."

(5) " We have not had a single instance in which the accommodation given by a bank taken over by us has not been much greater after amalgamation than it was before the bank was taken over."

(6) " The deposits of this country can be more effectively lent if they are concentrated than if they are scattered."

The first two quotations are taken from the speeches to the Chambers of Commerce, the last four from his speech at the confirmatory meeting.

Taking the arguments seriatim it is obvious that (1) applied to amalgamations generally is inaccurate. Banking resources could not possibly be increased by the merging of two banks, and it has already been shown that in a long period banking capital actually decreased considerably as a direct result of amalgamations.   Again, the Midland Bank at December 31, 1917, had the smallest ratio of capital and reserves to liabilities of any existing bank, viz.—4½ per cent. ! The second argument is couched in general terms.   Apparently it implies that because banks are made big, the results indicated will follow.   Such an argument is not conclusive, for if two large banks combine to make a " great " bank, their lending powers are increased but slightly, as shown earlier.   Consequently one bank is little more efficacious than two banks in increasing commercial exports or offsetting an unfavourable trade balance.   Argument (3) is similarly couched in general terms.   As mentioned previously, by weeding out weaker banks, and creating a few large banks situated in London for the greater part (thereby rendering practicable the co-operation necessary at times of crisis), amalgamations have made for stability.   Even so, had there been a bank failure say in war years, when they were not actually large enough to bear heavy losses, the crash might have had severe effects.   The fourth argument is a qualified truth only.   Mere bigness, as the report of the Bank Amalgamations Committee pointed out, is not necessary for giving assistance to trade.   But in so far as amalgamations resulted in the displacement of many small banks by fewer strong provincial and London banks of moderate size,[1] it enabled banks to meet the position resulting from the change in the type of its customers from individuals to companies, and from small to large combinations of customers.   It therefore allowed the banks to keep pace with the industrial integration which it seems correct to assume occurred prior to banking integration in pre-war years.   Argument (5) contains a statement of exceptional importance.   It only applies to the Midland Bank, however, for no other bank has declared thus.   It implies that after every amalgamation the Midland Bank increased the total of its loans.   So long as the proportion of liquid assets was

---

[1] The 1914 position represents this ; there were then 38 Banks, mainly of moderate size.

preserved there can be no possible objection to this. But it must be observed that totals only are given. It is to be suspected that they were swollen by extra loans granted to the many large customers possessed by this bank, which a smaller bank could not before undertake, e.g. corporation accounts. It would be interesting to learn of figures referring to the numbers of loans, and especially of increased small loans. The last statement (6) is obviously a strong one. It stresses the benefit resulting from the control of numerous branches well distributed over the various types of area in the country. The only problems which arise are those concerning the utilisation of the deposits in a proper and effective manner. On this point one writer affirms that large banks prefer to employ depositors' funds in London in purchasing discountable bills; in giving loans to large commercial and well-known firms who can deposit market collateral; and in advances to stockbrokers.[1] Apart from a few isolated complaints, there is no convincing evidence of this, while many bankers have testified that there was no alteration in the distribution of loaning in 1918.

Again, in a review by Mr. Sykes, Secretary of the Institution of Bankers, of Mr. Minty's *American Banking Methods*, he quotes from page 181 as follows:

" Taking their size into consideration, the New York Banks have at their disposal larger short term credit resources to lend to the markets than the banks in London, which are much larger. This is mainly due to the fact that the New York banks are the main depository of the surplus funds of the out-of-town banks who lodge money in them, payable at call."

His comment is that " This is a counter-argument against those who affirm that concentration of banking among a few large banks with Head Offices in London has resulted in a drainage of provincial money for use in the London Money Market." Again quoting, page 205 : " Banks are individually smaller and individual *concerns* are, compared with English industrial enterprises, much larger." These statements show the favourable position, compared with American con-

[1] Article—" Banking Amalgamations and the State " (*Sperling's Journal*, 1918), by Arcturus.

cerns, of the English banks, and serve to support the conclusions stated earlier.

Turning to other points, it is clear that when amalgamations such as that of Lloyd's Bank with the Capital and Counties Bank resulted in overlapping as shown on page 82, this was bound to result in loss to the community. Again, there have been many instances where excessive prices were paid for the businesses acquired, mainly because it was usual to offer compensation to absorbed shareholders in all amalgamations. The reason for this is hardly apparent, for the absorbed shareholders were always offered a participation in the fortunes of the new bank, except in cases where the absorbed bank was liquidated or in a difficult position at the time of fusion. Consequntly, to act on the principle of equality was the only fair method, and since market prices were always available before amalgamation was announced, to do so would have involved no difficulty. There is no record that because of paying an excess price for an absorbed business the absorbing bank was driven into failure,[1] but it is known that some of the bargains made had not resulted successfully ; and in any case, an excess price is only a handicap to the new concern. For this waste, competition amongst the banks themselves is mostly to blame. When this became so strong as to cause amalgamations to be arranged very speedily, as was the case particularly in 1918 and 1919, the leaders of the banks who were responsible laid themselves open to criticism. Yet obviously the difficulty of avoiding this waste was a great one for banks which were determined to maintain their position relative to rivals.

The plea for the necessity of a retention of the personal element in banking, a plea which has been put forward by Lancashire bankers, is an interesting one. This had reference to the special nature of Lancashire industries, such as cotton. It is difficult to see wherein these industries differ from others in the country similarly worked in a compact area, e.g. the

---

[1] With the possible exception of the amalgamation of the Consolidated Bank with the Bank of London in 1863.

M

West Riding woollen trade, in respect of banking requirements. For the company form of industry prevails, and there are many excellent examples of the working of combines in cotton and associated industries.[1] Probably the sturdy independence of the Lancashire character has no small relation to this attitude. Wherever possible, it will be agreed, the retention of personal methods is desirable, so long as the full benefits accruing from amalgamation and association are not withheld. It would be interesting to discover if these smaller banks were at any time compelled to refuse very large advances ; if not, it is evident that some of the London banks are already overdeveloped in the matter of size. Even if future developments in the industrial and commercial world are such as to produce larger units than now exist, after a point it is clear that nothing tangible will be gained by similar moves in the banking field. For the argument, referred to by the Bank Amalgamations Committee, that even in the improbable circumstances that the present-day banks do not possess sufficient resources to undertake loans of the sizes which may be demanded, still has validity—i.e. recourse may be had to more than one bank. Indeed this method would probably be the safer of the two, since the risks would be spread between two or more concerns, each of which pursued its own individual policy (and this almost certainly would vary from that pursued by its competitors), instead of being concentrated on one firm with one policy alone. Again, it must be remembered that the size of the banking unit which conduces to the most economical and efficient working, by reason of the specialised nature of banking operations, is not so large as correspondingly efficient and economical trading units, owing to the different nature of their functions.

Another point which arises is the possibility of the growth of a system of interlocking directorates. The trend of events since 1918 has been for many of the directors of English joint stock banks to meet regularly on the boards

---

[1] Fine Cotton Spinners ; Bleachers' Association ; Calico Printers' Association. The " loom and power " system is to be found in the West Riding as well as in Lancashire.

of other banks and corporations, particularly colonial banks, as shown by the table below.[1] The result is that rival directors are thrown into each other's company, and this in time may tend to breed a spirit of association finding means of expression in some types of working agreements in respect of policy at home.   This likelihood is enhanced by the fact that one or more of the home banks have interests in banks trading abroad and in similar areas of the same countries. The extra risks and dangers, to say nothing of the increased difficulties attendant upon foreign banking, might have the tendency of causing the home directors to work together. But the most significant development as yet has been the joining of Lloyds and the National Provincial Bank in working branches of these banks in France.   This actually brings together on to one board, what are nominally strong rival boards in respect of home banks.   There seems to be a probability that the joint working will sooner or later bring the two banks together on matters of policy affecting English banking.   If this occurs, the example will speedily be imitated in other institutions.   It is this feature of the effects of the policy of extensive fusion which is the least desirable (if it results), for then a condition of effective

---

[1] TABLE OF DIRECTORS OF COLONIAL AND FOREIGN BANKS.

Bank.	Banks which have representives on the Board.
Colonial Bank . . .	Barclays ; Westminster.
National Bank of New Zealand.	Barclays ; Midland ; Lloyds ; National Provincial.
Banque d'Athênes . .	Barclays ; Midland.
British Trade Corporation .	Barclays ; Midland ; National Provincial.
National Bank of South Africa	Barclays ; Lloyds.
Standard Bank of South Africa	Midland ; Lloyds ; Westminster.
London and Brazilian . .	Midland ; National Provincial.
P. and O. Corporation . .	Lloyds ; National Provincial ; Westminster.
British Italian Corporation .	Lloyds ; National Provincial ; Westminster.
Bank of Australia . . .	Lloyds ; National Provincial.
Union Bank of Australia .	National Provincial ; Westminster.
Chartered Bank India, Australia and China . . .	National Provincial ; Westminster.

Representative directors of six English banks also meet regularly to conduct the affairs of the Yorkshire Penny Bank, of which they form the board.

monopoly will prevail. There has been ample testimony that the system of combined working operative for many years in Scotland has been a disliked feature of that system ; [1] if it appears in English banks, the effects will be much worse and more serious because they are much larger and more widespread. Combination among the great London banks will necessitate similar action on the part of the Lancashire group ; or, what is perhaps more likely, those smaller banks will be driven to amalgamate to save their positions.

[1] German banking conditions before the war also testified to the undesirability of combined working of large groups of banks. In 1912 a Bankers' Congress was held in Berlin, which adopted a resolution that private banks were indispensable for offsetting the effects of such group working, and that they were an indispensable link in the organisation of banking, stock exchanges, and credit. Thus a strong protest was uttered against the bad effects of combined group working.

CHAPTER IX.

ADVANTAGES AND DISADVANTAGES OF AMALGAMATION (*continued*).

It is now desirable to discuss the effect of the movement on the Bank of England, the Money Market, and the Discount Market.

Fairly to do this, it is necessary to cast a glance backward, to 1863. A quotation from the *Bankers' Magazine* of that year runs : " Bankers merely look to the Bank of England returns, and tacitly follow in the wake of that mammoth establishment " [1] (p. 323). The Bank of England was then so strong that it could have absorbed all the other London banks, their capitals and reserves, and yet its own capital would not have been exhausted. Rather curiously, by far the greater part of the foreign exchange business was then transacted by the London private banks, their joint-stock rivals not yet possessing the London representation or even the resources to carry out such business. [2] Again, foreign banks are not to be found before the Franco-German war. After that time, however, they invaded London and managed to secure a large share of business on account of working on extraordinarily keen margins. Meanwhile, as shown in the historical survey, the joint-stock banks obtained a strong

[1] With this might be linked Bagehot's well-known quotation to the effect that ordinarily there was not enough money in Lombard Street to enable all bills to be discounted without recourse to the Bank of England.

[2] Illustrated by the following quotation : " The London private banks have long ceased to be banks of circulation. Their capital is principally employed in discounting mercantile paper, a branch of business, into which, as has been shown, the Bank of England does not enter very extensively, and with regard to which, even so far as it does go, it acts to a considerable extent through the agency of the London Private Bankers."
—*Banks and Banking*, R. Hildreth, Boston, 1840.

Again, in 1900 the acceptances of the London private banks amounted to about £240,000,000—about 90 per cent. of the whole. Those of the London Joint-Stock banks did not much exceed 1 per cent. of the whole.

grip of London business, partly by amalgamation, and partly as a result of ordinary expansion and the development of banking. It was not till 1905, when Sir Edward Holden opened a foreign department of the Midland Bank that an attack was made on the business which had been almost monopolised by the branches of foreign banks. Two years later, the London and County Bank followed this lead, and in 1913 Lloyds went so far as to open a foreign branch in Paris. The war not only brought about the disappearance of enemy foreign banks, but brought with it a great extension of foreign business in many countries. The English joint-stock banks therefore gained experience which assisted in the post-war extensions.

Reverting to the position of the Bank of England in 1874 the *Economist* pointed to the decline of the once largest bank.[1] Indeed, so changed had its relations (in the matter of size) become, to its competitors, that their combined deposits were now larger than those of the Bank. The significance of this is realised from Sir R. Inglis Palgrave's statement showing that between 1844 and 1877 there were 61 occasions when the Bank's reserve " was not sufficient to meet the London Bankers' balances." The process continued on a larger scale in the years following because of the increased scale of joint-stock business. At last, in 1918, Sir Charles Addis declared in the *Edinburgh Review* (July, 1918) that :

" It may be questioned whether the gigantic size they have already attained does not constitute a menace to the pre-dominant position which the Bank of England has hitherto enjoyed as the Bankers' Bank. How will the Bank of England be able to maintain its supremacy surrounded by banks in-dividually greater and more powerful than itself, especially when the object in view is by raising the rate of interest to prevent an internal or external drain upon our gold reserves ? "

In his lately published book on the " London Money Market " Mr. Spalding also refers to the large compar-ative size of the joint-stock concerns. Obviously, then, there is a latent danger in this, although as yet there are no signs of any attempt to make such an undesirable

[1] " The Bank of England is now only *primus inter pares*, though once it had distanced every competitor " (December 5).

use of their huge resources. So far undoubtedly it has been prevented by the undisguised opinions of the City and by public opinion in general, and so long as these views are accepted and preserved its occurrence is highly improbable. Yet there is no doubt that, from the point of view of the preservation of the status and authority of the Bank, further large combinations are undesirable.

The effects of the amalgamation process on the Money and Discount Markets must now be treated. It has been mentioned that the acceptance business was formerly in the hands of the London private bankers and private discount and acceptance firms. This virtual monopoly was broken up by the absorptions of the private by joint-stock concerns, not only in banking but also in the discount world ; for even the private firms often amalgamated so that they might better resist the force of competition. And when the monopoly no longer existed it was a recognised feature of Money Market practice that joint-stock banks did not enter into it, but preferred to buy and sell their bills through the agency of the three joint-stock discount houses and ordinary bill brokers. This practice prevailed into the first decade of the century. The lead taken by the Midland Bank in 1905 resulted gradually in the making of acceptances by the joint-stock banks themselves, and thus one of the branches of money market business was interfered with. So highly valued did a bank's acceptance eventually become, that this business has developed extensively. The heavy boycott of foreign banks during the last war further assisted its expansion, and although, by reason of the growth of telegraphic business and other reasons, the volume of acceptance business dwindled during the war, the banks were well equipped to take a substantial share of that passing after 1918. A statistic will show the alteration since 1900.

1900.   Total Acceptances, £250 mills.   Joint-Stock Banks £2¼ mills.
Aug. 1914.   ,,   ,,   350   ,,   ,,   ,,   ,,   50 ,,
    1919.   ,,   ,, again 350   ,,   ,,   ,,   ,,   170 ,,

The respective percentages of the total made are 2·7 per cent., 14·3 per cent., and 48·6 per cent.

Owing to the difficulty of distinguishing between the businesses of merchants and merchant bankers it is hard to show whether the number of private acceptors has increased or decreased. By some it is thought that the number of *bill brokers* has increased during the period. If, however, the opinion expressed in the report of the 1918 Bank Amalgamations Committee that the number of private firms has decreased is accepted, and it is borne in mind that Sir Ernest Maes Harvey [1] holds a similar belief, and that in each case the reduction is ascribed to amalgamation, the working of the movement calls for adverse criticism. For in the entrepôt city of the world, the process of reduction must have serious effects. The evil was so apparent in 1918 that, since discount firms would not take more than a certain amount of the paper of any one bank, on grounds of safety, it was necessary to create new banks or new accepting houses to restore the lost names to the City, in order to safeguard London's position as the financial settlement house of the world. It might be expected that the private accepting firms would use the opportunity to increase their numbers, but the process has rather been for the existing houses to extend substantially their resources ; e.g. Messrs. Lazard and Co., Messrs. M. Samuel and Co., Ltd., and Messrs. H. and S. Lefèvre are all larger than before the war. Again, there are one or two additional companies such as the London and Foreign Banking Corporation Ltd. This firm was established in May, 1924, and in its circular, issued privately, declared that— " during the last ten years credit facilities have been greatly reduced, as many important Bank and Banking Houses have been absorbed, and the London branches of various foreign banks have ceased to exist." It later absorbed the old private firm of Messrs. Arthur H. Brandt and Co., after the latter had been joint-stocked.

Turning to another aspect of the effect of amalgamations on the private and public discounting and accepting houses, it is clear that the curtailment of credit mentioned by Sir

---

[1] He declares : " The loss of names is a real loss to the City. It was the number and use of first-class names that gave London her outstanding financial importance."—*Times Trading Supplement*, Banking Number, 1923.

Charles Addis was in evidence so early as 1909.[1] Further
protests of the same kind were made in later years, but
probably the process was accepted as more or less inevitable,
so long as the absorptions were neither very large nor accomplished quickly. But when the race began in 1918 *The
Times* (of July 3), a supporter of previous policy, was moved
to declare that " One thing may be said quite plainly, and
that is, that the announcement of more bank fusions has
produced a distinctly uneasy feeling in the discount market."
In the same month as this was written, the article by Sir
Charles Addis, referred to earlier, appeared in the *Edinburgh
Review*. This showed that since modern banking depends
for its success on the way in which risks are divided—and not
concentrated—the bill-broker was forced to borrow in pre-
war days from several banks in order fully to satisfy his
wants. The reduction of the number of banks was always
felt, but when the reductions were numerous and occurred
after previous fusions had left the total very low, then the
hardship became pronounced. Again, the process affected
the stock jobber in similar manner, for he was not able to
advance as much to the broker.

To the disturbing effect of the amalgamations must be
added the unfavourable effect on the total of acceptance and
discount business of the greatly extended use of telegraphic
transfers for supplying the currency of foreign trade, and the
heavy depression in foreign trading after 1920. This total
has already been quoted, but to some extent it is accounted
for—though how much may not be known—by the fact that
when home banks absorbed foreign banks, a certain amount
of acceptance business was forfeited. For, if the absorbed
concern were to draw on its principal, a " house " bill would
be created, e.g. Lloyds, and the London and River Plate
Bank Ltd. It might confidently be expected that the great
increase in the dealings in foreign exchange *vià* the tele-

---

[1] Mr. Doxet, speaking at the meeting of the National Discount Co.,
said : " The amalgamations of the City and Midland with the North Wales
bank, thus further contracting the supply of free money, are somewhat
unfavourable events for the discount market, which has already suffered
considerably of late years from similar amalgamations " (1909).—
Economist, p. 209.

graph, on the part of the joint-stock banks, would to some considerable extent have reduced the proportion of acceptance business passing through banks. Early in 1924, for instance, the Midland Bank had over 2,000 officials then employed in the foreign branch alone. Obviously the inference must be that the banks have obtained a stronger grip than before on exchange business, and this is borne out by the figures quoted.

It is necessary to decide if the changed position is desirable or not. In the first place there is no doubt that acceptance by a bank is beneficial to traders, inasmuch as it is the best guarantee to a foreign trader that he will receive payment at maturity, if only because bankers always work on the principle of safety. Apart from this, their practice does not vary much from that of the private and joint-stock discount firms. In discount business they do not insist, for example, as does the Bank of England, on the requirement that a bill should contain two English names of which one must be the acceptor. They therefore do not place restrictions on the making of bills. Probably they are keener to reject " accommodation " bills, and this certainly is for the good. Again it cannot be doubted that many embryo crises have been detected and arrested by banks, for they are careful to detect excess " paper " of any particular house.

But arguments have been levied against these advantages. For instance, much of the bankers' knowledge of the quantity and quality of the bills in the market is supplied by the brokers and officials of the discount houses. And with the present organisation of banking there is no doubt that the benefits arising from the present specialisation are solid and substantial. No bank official can pretend to possess the varied knowledge of bills which the bill brokers or discount companies possess. The training must be long and thorough, and it is safe to say that it is not now possessed by any bank officials. Additionally, banks are concerned with the safer sides of bill-broking, and refrain from taking risks which sometimes are indispensable to business. On the other hand, if they were so disposed, there is nothing to prevent the banks organising themselves to undertake all classes of business, and there is little doubt that it would be possible to dispense with the service of intermediaries.   The real problem is to be found in the question as to the desirability of this occurring. The answer seems to be that the present organisation of the money market is one which has resulted almost entirely as a result of the process of evolution so that it is a complete example of the " survival of the fittest." [1]   And on this ground, the private brokers and public discount companies with their specialised functions have justified their share of the processes of the market.

In discussing this aspect of the problem, it must not be forgotten that in consequence of the amalgamations with foreign banks, English banks have tightened their grip on the acceptance business, because their member banks abroad are in direct touch with the foreign traders, and therefore conversant with the details of their commerce.   Power to ascertain the nature and extent of transactions entered into by individual firms and business groups is therefore increased, and this cannot fail to strengthen the basis of security on which such business is based.   Obviously the only weakness is that there are yet many independent foreign banks, most with London representation, to which English banks have no closer relation than that of agents or correspondents.

The existence of the three public discount companies must not be overlooked.   Before the war these companies transacted a little less than half of the total discount business. In 1923 they transacted about one half, so that their position has not been greatly affected by war-time fusions.   It has been pointed out by Mr. D. Spring Rice that they operate at a disadvantage as compared with the banks, for they, along with other members of the discount market, have to take good bills from any reputable firm offering them ;   the banks, on the other hand, may, and do refuse bills if they wish.   In view of the fact that banks compete with the members of the market for the supply of bills coming from similar sources, this is a privilege which does not seem to be merited.

---

[1] Demonstrated by Ellis T. Powell in his book, *The Evolution of the Money Market*, 1385–1915."

In gathering together the points of the discussion it is evident that the amalgamation movement has inflicted harm on the working of the money market by the restriction of names, the discouragement of specialist enterprise which is essential to its successful working, and the very large control obtained by the great banks over the acceptance business. Against this must be set the extra security which results from bank acceptances, the discouragement of accommodation business, and the fact that the banks do not possess a monopoly or control over operations. On balance it would appear that the arguments against are somewhat stronger than those in favour, so that the amalgamation process is injurious in this respect. And the size to which the great banks have attained is a potential source of danger to the position of the Bank of England, although on this point there is little call for pessimistic anticipation.

Another vital point is the trading of English banks in foreign countries. In the historical survey it is mentioned that Lloyds was the first bank to open abroad by the absorption of Messrs. Armstrong and Co., of Paris, in 1913. This move provoked opposition,[1] not only in England, but also from French bankers and financiers. Yet it was not long before the London County and Westminster followed the example set. Now all the great banks with the exception of the largest—the Midland—are represented abroad. The advantages of this include the fact that foreign branches may be obtained by the easiest, though not necessarily the least expensive, method. This in turn enables the home banks to procure reliable information on the state of trade abroad. Again, it facilitates the dealing in foreign currencies, which is an integral part of foreign business. Inevit-

---

[1] The *Economist* of 1913 said : " Banking in the provinces has undoubtedly been strengthened by the absorption of the comparatively weak local institutions by the big London banks. But the strength of our banking system which centres upon the big London concerns and the Bank of England, lies entirely in the confidence of the public. That confidence has been built upon the open independence of the big banks, and it is by no means certain that the system as a whole is going to be strengthened by the new move " (p. 768), and " The balance of advantage is against the new enterprise " (p. 552).

ably it has given an extended range of business to the English banks operating out of this country, and particularly so since English currency and therefore prices have fluctuated less than those of other European countries. By reason of this, foreign business men have preferred to transfer their balances from a less to a more stable unit of value. Lastly, some saving of commissions and agency fees has probably occurred. Against these must be set several disadvantages which are apparent. For instance, in view of the meagre proportions of proprietors' funds to deposit totals, it is inevitable that the latter must be ventured in the new trading ventures abroad. This cannot be as safe as home business, and the loss of £460,000 referred to by Sir Charles Addis was the result of trading in Russia by the Westminster Bank.[1] Again, as before pointed out, a certain amount of acceptance business is forfeited on account of the " house " bills which would be created by a home bank drawing on its foreign subsidiary, and vice versa. Thirdly, if the enmity of foreign bankers is not aroused, their good will is not increased ; e.g. Dr. Leaf, speaking of his own bank's foreign extensions said in 1921, " This rapid growth is not without its signs of jealousy among some of the native bankers—notably in Spain." [2] Lastly, since foreign banks require to be worked as separate foreign companies on account of the high taxation of invading concerns, they are to all intents and purposes private companies, whose balance sheets are not published, and details of whose working are not forthcoming. And this is merely a reversion to the old type of private banking.

Consideration has already been made of the effect of the new developments on the business of the acceptance and discount markets. It only remains then to point out that the

---

[1] In the light of these developments it is interesting to compare the attitudes formerly taken by English banks to foreign business. In reply to Q. 7320 (Committee of 1875) a director of the London and Westminster Bank said : " Speaking for the London and Westminster Bank we hold that the public entrusts us with large deposits and large funds and that the security of our property should be here on the spot, and not broadcast over the world."

[2] Several Spanish branches have since been closed on account of the opposition demonstrated, including Barcelona, Bilbao, and Valencia.

Midland Bank, which has no branches abroad, yet transacts more foreign business than any of its rivals. The Chairman, speaking in 1921, said, " We have no branches or affiliations abroad. We have refrained from competing with our foreign friends in their own country, and I cannot help thinking that we have gained in favour in consequence. We have no present intention of deviating from this policy, which besides having the merit of enabling us to extend our relations with foreign banks gives greater security to our domestic depositors, by restricting our activities to the home field." This declaration points to the highly controversial character of this aspect of banking development. The success of the Midland Bank is a strong argument against ; the opinions of many bankers and traders are in favour. On balance it appears that there is a gain resulting from representation abroad which can hardly be secured by agents alone. It is notorious that before the war English merchants did not receive all possible help from their own banks in the matter of opening up new markets abroad, largely owing to conservatism. But it is possible to overdo foreign banking, and this danger should not be overlooked, if only because of the increased risk entailed.

Other excursions made by home banks away from the home areas need consideration. Both Scotland and Ireland have been invaded, as mentioned in the history. Respecting the moves to the latter country, Mr. R. J. Eaton says in the *Journal of the Irish Institution of Bankers* (1919) :

" The operations were affected in both cases by a purchase of shares on terms very advantageous to the Irish shareholders. Banking opinion in Ireland is on the whole inclined to resent the invasion, as it seems to imply an accusation that the Irish Banks do not give sufficient support to the industries in this country. A good deal of public criticism has been aroused to this effect, that Irish banks do not treat their customers as generously as the English banks, or employ so large a proportion of their resources in loans and advances. There is a certain amount of truth in these statements, but it is often forgotten that banking conditions in the two countries are different. The Irish banks are more highly capitalised in proportion to their working resources than the English banks, and find it harder to pay a high rate of dividend, as their profits must be distributed over a larger area. They are also on a much smaller scale as regards their working resources, and consequently have higher expenses of management per unit of business transacted. For both these reasons they cannot pay as high rates for deposits as the English banks. As regards lending rates it is doubtful if any great disparity exists, but if it does, it is chiefly accounted for by the better nature of the security offered in certain cases in England, such as the discount of first-class trade bills."

Summing up, he says:

" The Irish banks will, nevertheless, be justified in resenting any further penetration from across the channel, as there is no reason to suppose them incapable of giving to Irish industry all the assistance their future development is likely to require."

Side by side with this may be considered the following extract from the 1919 report of the Westminster Bank.

" The increase in the business of the Ulster Bank since the purchase is remarkable. At the time of the agreement the bank had 83 branches and 87 sub-branches—together 170. The number has now risen to 92 branches and 125 sub-branches—a total of 217. The deposits too have risen rapidly. In the balance sheet of August 31 last which we circulated to you,[1] they stood at £12,877,000. On January 1, they were £14,914,000, an increase of £2,037,000 in four months."

These quotations show that the existing Irish banks were not able to compete with their English brethren who possessed lesser proportionate capitals, and larger resources, and who were able to offer more competitive terms by reason of the greater volume of business which they conducted. Probably a good deal of the extra business secured was obtained by highly competitive rates, and possibly some undercutting ; for it must be remembered that there was more than one English bank at work. The mere fact that so many extra branches were opened is evidence of the heightened competition, but a map of new branches, which it has not been deemed necessary to reproduce, shows that new areas were opened up. In Scotland, considerable hostility was displayed by the bankers over the border. It was thought that banking integration had completed its course in Scotland, since the remaining 8 banks had developed

[1] Apparently during a period marked by unusual deposit growth.

a system of common working, which implied that Scottish banking had been reduced to a sort of routine. It would appear that there was little room for expansion there as the number of persons per bank was in 1924 just over 3,000,[1] this being fewer even than in England, where it has been shown that offices are in excess of those actually justified on economic grounds. Beyond the fact that charges in Scotland tended to be kept up as a result of co-operative working, there seems to have been no reason for the invasion of English banks. The best test of the desirability of both these types of amalgamations is similar to that which has been used to judge of the desirability of amalgamations in England. The main component of this is the gain resulting from a necessary geographical extension of area secured without much overlapping. In the case of Ireland this appears to have been accomplished, but not in Scotland. Another component is the provision of a more economical banking service with increased facilities. This, too, appears to have been realised in Ireland, but not in the sister country, inasmuch as rates have moved in favour of the customer in the one case but not perceptibly in the other. From the point of view of the English banks the amalgamations can only have resulted in success if the new management has resulted in the achievement of better results all round than the old. If increased profits testify this there is no doubt that it has occurred ; but without a full knowledge of the particular results it is impossible to judge from this one item alone. From what evidence is available, it is perhaps possible to say that the Irish amalgamations were economically desirable, but not so the Scottish groupings. The criterion to apply to projected future amalgamations is as to whether or not they would tend to reduce competition and cause the overlapping of areas, for similar principles exactly govern these as further amalgamations in England and Wales.

Another problem yet untouched upon, is the difficulty of organisation which results from the creation of very large banks by amalgamations. This was pointed out by Mr.

[1] In 1920 there were 1,283 bank offices in Scotland and 8 banks.

Hartley Withers in the *Spectator* (Banking Supplement), July 26, 1924. He said :

"While the banks have gained enormously through the amalgamation process in the magnitude of the resources that they wield, they have lost something of the elasticity and adaptability for which they were famous, and a tendency to red tape, that is almost inevitably associated with great size, is a danger against which they will have to strive by every possible improvement in organisation."

The problem has many aspects and complications. Not only does it involve, for example, the successful functioning of the many hundreds of branches controlled by one bank, but also the successful welding together of large staffs, working on harmonious lines. It may be said without hesitation that there is no deficiency of actual organisation in the new banks. The routine character of banking has facilitated this, and in many respects the acquisition of a new bank has simply resulted in the enlarging of operations transacted on well-defined lines, e.g. every branch sends a Daily Statement of its transactions arranged in summary form, to the Head Office. In some cases where London banks have been absorbed the former head office still receives these summaries and deals with them on but slightly different lines. But an enumeration of the various departments of a " great " bank will give some idea of the amount of organisation and specialisation necessary to provide smooth working. These may be stated as :

> The Board of Directors.
> General Managers.
> Assistant General Managers.
> Secretary.
> Registrar.
> Branch Inspectors.
> Chief Accountant.
> Chief Inspector.
> Coupon Department.
> New Issues.
> Bill Office and Brokers' Loans.
> Stock Office.

N

Clearings.
Head Office Correspondence and Circulars.
Supervision of Branch Accounting.
Income Tax.
Premises.
Safes and Securities.
Stationery.
Legal.
Intelligence.
Credit and Opinion.
Staff.

Slight variations occur from bank to bank, but in general this enumeration illustrates the prevailing type of separation. The Foreign Department, the Shipping Department, the Executor and Trustee Departments, are usually considered to be separate entities.

The most difficult problem of all, is to relate and co-relate the work of the various departments. To overcome this difficulty necessitates elaborate machinery for purposes of communication, and it is probably here that a great proportion of the enhanced working expenses arises.[1] It must be borne in mind that many of these various staffs work in different buildings, and consequently rarely, if ever, see other staffs. This severing of the personal link which existed formerly in smaller banks has important effects on smooth working which at first sight do not seem so important as actually they are. To appreciate this it is but necessary to pass from a London bank to one of the Lancashire provincial concerns. The departmental method of organisation tends too to impair efficiency because of the specialised training it involves, and in time it will inevitably create the problem of supplying a pronounced shortage in thoroughly well-trained bankers—instead of departmental heads.

The greatest disability attendant on the formation of great banks notwithstanding, is the severance of real connection between head office and the branch staffs. In smaller provincial concerns some sort of personal touch was possible

---

[1] Even a transitory visit to banking head offices shows how much personal time is lost in passing from one department to another.

simply because the number of branches to a head office was relatively small. Now, all the great institutions have branches ranging from 900 to over 2,000. With respect to the staffs employed at each branch, progress reports are sent in yearly by branch managers on individual members of staff. There are usually groups of inspectors working in local areas under deputy staff superintendents and one chief staff superintendent. The reports pass through their hands, and in some cases a classification scheme is adopted, e.g. A, B, C, D. It is on the basis of this that remuneration is based and promotion is made.

Even with the existence of numerous regulations, it is manifestly impossible that each separate staff inspector's mind should work alike, and when reports pass through many hands, it is possible that any first distortion may be magnified. Consequently organisation, however perfect, can never secure the same fair results which a more unified personal system previously gave. Amalgamation has therefore created some very large problems of organisation the present solutions of which do not approach in satisfaction the conditions prevailing under the pre-amalgamation system.

The greatest grievances have been in respect of salaries. In the amalgamations which date from the eighties of last century, no uniformity of practice is observable as to the method of treating absorbed staffs. Not till the groupings became larger and occurred more frequently apparently was there an approach to uniformity. In later years the practice was to bring the scales of all absorbed banks up to the absorbing bank's scale, if the former was lower, or to continue at the same rate if it was higher. This was found to be the best method of avoiding friction, although it will be realised that the members of the absorbing bank's staff never gained by such an arrangement. It will be seen that there has been much heart-burning over the question of salaries after amalgamations, and this was one of the reasons for the formation of the Bank Officers' Guild in 1919. Since this date the activities of the Guild—which is not yet recognised by the banks[1]—have been indirectly responsible for causing

1 1924.

the large banks to bring the many staffs together on the point of salaries, but even now it is not accomplished. In the endeavour to resist the organisation set up by the staff the banks formed separate internal guilds consisting of members of the staff sitting on a special committee, with representatives from the directors. Of this committee the Staff Superintendent is generally an ex-officio member. It makes recommendations on general lines but the actual increases or other alterations of salary are usually decided by a special Management Committee. Therefore the banks have resisted strongly any efforts on the part of their staffs to set up a defensive organisation which for one reason was caused by the de-personalising effect of amalgamations. Since already there are over 30,000 members of the external guild out of a total of about 52,000 bank officials, it would appear that eventually the latter must be recognised, when claims for salary increases and other amenities will probably be pressed home.

An incidental effect of amalgamations affecting administration has been the award by most of the large banks of bonuses for the satisfactory passing of the examinations conducted by the Institute of Bankers. The effect of this, combined with that of amalgamations, has been to cause a rise in the number of candidates. In 1924 over 10,000 clerks sat for the examination compared with just over 3,000 a few years ago. If nothing else, this demonstrates that staffs are feeling the difficulties of securing recognition by means of yearly reports, and are striving to increase their status by means of examination. The development is a welcome one, and benefit results from the training given in practical subjects. Yet this method can never be so satisfactory as that which permits of a wide training based on experience in many departments of bank work ; and the increased size of bank offices necessitated by amalgamation has closed down some of the possible sources of this. Again, it is but necessary to compare such a system with that of smaller provincial banks ; in some northern banks, for instance, promising juniors and others are noted by the chief inspector, who regularly arranges for a few months' varied experience at head offices and branches of different sizes, for those who he believes will benefit by it. The result is that the provincial banks will in time possess staffs more completely fitted for undertaking general banking work.

Related to this aspect of administration is the question of the effect of amalgamations on the actual work done by the staffs. The creation of large banks (especially in London and large provincial centres) has induced an over-specialisation of work—as just cited. This means that one clerk is required to perform what is more or less repetition work in the particular department to which he or she is attached ; e.g. it is the lot of many a junior just entering a bank to be set to copy for the whole of the day the particulars of bank-notes handled by the bank into a Register of Bank Notes, or for a ledger clerk to be occupied in working on one small section of the ledgers. Others again are employed in listing particulars of cheques received in to Bill Books. Such work is monotonous in character and does not necessitate the use of the higher faculties. The advantages of education and ability and initiative are therefore seldom called for, with the effect that lack of interest and a diminished sense of responsibility result. Since much bank work now partakes of this nature, and since it is generally asserted that the reduction of banks has reduced the opportunities of securing promotion, a spirit of unrest is generated which has been especially in evidence during the last few years.[1] Meanwhile, bank administrators have not solved the problem of the new working conditions, with the result that little has been done to alter the character of the work. For example, banks have always been extraordinarily conservative in the use of machinery. In America, mainly owing to the high cost of labour, machinery is used extensively ; in England up to the end of 1924 machinery for ledger posting was in use only in two firms, both in London. That for the performing of those mechanical operations which involve repetition work it is

---

[1] " Another serious objection is the inevitable effect on the morale of the staff. . . . Cashiers now do their business as disinterested machines, whereas they used to be the friends and advisers of the banks' customers." —Article on " Bank Amalgamations " by Sir Ernest Maes Harvey. *Times Trading Supplement*, Banking Number, 1924.

necessary, there is no doubt ; e.g. writing up ledgers, pass books, copying correspondence, sorting cheques, extracting periodical balances, making statements of account, and transporting books from office to safe, etc.

Other disadvantages attendant upon large amalgamations, and particularly those which were styled " fusions " and " affiliations," include the difficulty of reading with under-standing the balance sheets now submitted, for the balance sheets of affiliated institutions are maintained separately from those of the concern by which they are controlled. Again, the totals now involved are so large, that the details submitted are inadequate to convey a correct impression of the assets, liabilities, and general working of the banks issuing them ; e.g. there is no indication of the amount of loans and overdrafts, while the item of bank premises figures in the balance sheets as just so many millions without explanation of how the value is arrived at. Again, only one bank in the British Isles shows a statement of the details of the profit and loss account including gross profit as well as expenses. Great publicity on this score is necessary if just estimates of the working of such great concerns are to be made. Further details would necessarily reveal aspects of working which it is necessary to present to public scrutiny for the maintaining of confidence. Reticence is dangerous, and it is therefore desirable that informing accounts should be rendered.

CONCLUSIONS AND REMEDIES.

The discussion of the previous chapters may be summarised under the following heads :

1. Amalgamation has caused the regular reduction of capitals and reserves.

2. It has fostered the growth of deposits through the regular development of branch policy, the reduction of note issues, and the emergence of large, strong banks. It has tended to make deposit figures more truly representative of prevailing conditions, by the elimination of duplication. Both these results are thoroughly desirable.

3. Cash holdings and cash reserves have been slightly increased, while investments have become more scientifically arranged, so that greater liquidity, stability, and safety have been secured.

4. The progress of the system of branches, widespread over the United Kingdom, has in large measure accrued from the amalgamation policy pursued over the period of one hundred years. Up to a point, the results of this have been economically and socially beneficial, not the least important of these being the growth of effective, keen, and incessant competition. Of late years both the opening of branches and competition have been carried beyond desirable limits, and this has been produced by amalgamation moves the justification for which was questionable.

5. On the whole, amalgamation has increased the capacity to make loans : but the mechanical and impersonal control imposed by the organisation necessary in great concerns has tended to reduce the initiative of smaller entrepreneurs and business men, and is an obstacle to quick recovery from acute trading depression. Greater insistence on partial and full security caused by extra organisation following on large fusions, is not an unwelcome effect.

6. The emergence of large concerns has made for more stable working and rendered possible that degree of combined action which is occasionally of especial value.

7. The process incidental to amalgamation has financially benefited many thousands of shareholders possessing holdings both in absorbed and absorbing concerns. The prices paid for businesses acquired (especially at " boom " periods) have usually been high, and often undesirably so.

8. Amalgamation has perceptibly reduced the smooth and elastic working of the Money Market, and affected the effective work done by private firms. Further, the rearing up of great banks is not without dangers to the position of the Bank of England.

9. Probably some of the members of the " Big Five " are already over-developed in size and capacity to deal with the financial needs of the community. The undesirable features of over-organisation and unwieldiness with their accompanying dangers, are therefore apparent. An important consequence is the effect on bank staffs, their happiness in work, their promotion, and their salaries. Some of the later amalgamations did not produce increased facilities, beyond those generated by ultra-violent competition.

10. English banks have extended into foreign countries. The moves to Europe and to Ireland appear to be justified ; but there was probably no balance of gain in taking over the Scottish banks.

11. One of the most undesirable consequences of excited amalgamation policy has been to produce ,the growth of expenses of management. Mainly this has been the consequence of the unwise development of branch policy, typifying wasteful competition ; and part of the enhanced charges has been made the burden of the community.

12. The prospect of combined working has appeared.

13. The remedy propounded by the Bank Amalgamations Committee has not achieved its object, because the number of independent arbitrators was too few, they were not well chosen (in view of their banking and commercial connections), and the promised legislation has not matured.

In discussing remedies it is essential to accept the developments which have already occurred, whether or not they have been wholly desirable.

There is no doubt that banks should increase their capitals. The step would have few disadvantages, and the benefits secured would be such substantial ones as increased confidence, fairer sharing of the ratio between depositors' and shareholders' funds, and a rate of dividend corresponding more accurately to the actual rate of profits earned.

With respect to future developments of amalgamation policy it is clear that there is no necessity for further amalgamation on the part of at least three of the " Big Five." These are the Midland, Lloyds, and Barclays. Each of these possesses offices numbering respectively over 2,000, over 1,700, and over 1,600. The National Provincial and the Westminster Banks possess over 1,100 and over 900 respectively, so that, while they have no pronounced deficiency in resources, they have not the same extended area over which to spread their activities. Were amalgamation possible with banks in unoccupied areas, for reasons of securing greater competitive equality and perhaps slightly extended facilities, it may be desirable, although the probability of any other gains appears remote.

For similar reasons the great disparity which now exists in the competitive power possessed by members of the Lancashire group might be to some extent remedied by judicious amalgamation. It is difficult to see how this could be accomplished without much overlapping, but the greater gain would require to be set off against the lesser, in view of the facts as to the present situation. In any case these banks are not so violently competitive as the great London concerns. It must be borne in mind too that the existence of this group gives head offices which are situate at Manchester and Liverpool, and that this will in future be a means of preserving a state of competition in banking, there can be no doubt. It will be beneficial also because the provinces have the benefits derived from a management working in the midst of provincial and local conditions, maintaining responsive and intimate touch with industrial changes.

Assuming some such developments to occur it is plain that

the number of banks will be reduced then to the minimum necessary for the maintenance of competitive conditions.

If they become reduced below, say, seven concerns, the possibility of combined working may become a reality, and in view of the general economic axiom that competition is preferable to combination, and the particular fact that banking—the hub on which the wheel of commerce revolves —is a specially important link in commercial and trading operations, steps should be taken to circumvent such a policy. It is conceivable that at first no apparent dis-advantages to the community would result ; that indeed a reduction of the excessive competition now prevailing would tend to reduce expenses, but it is hardly likely that this phase would long endure, without the disadvantages attend-ant upon combination becoming evident. When it was observable that the community was suffering from a lack of the benefits obtainable under a competitive régime, it would obviously become necessary for the State to endeavour to remedy the evils. Then there would at once arise a very intricate, difficult problem. In this book only the principle governing the steps to be taken may be cited, as well for reasons of space as for the absence of a knowledge of the precise circumstances which will arise. It is clear that the history of anti-trust legislation (especially in America) is not one of success, chiefly because evasion of some sort is usually possible. It is hardly likely to meet with more success in England as applied to banking, and consequently not much reliance can be placed on its efficacy. But on the issue as to whether the State should take over all the banks (including the Bank of England), and run them as part of the national civil service scheme, there should be no hesita-tion in deciding against. To all acquainted with banking, it is patent that whatever the State might do with the tasks of routine work, it could not attempt successfully the opera-tions of loaning, accepting, and discounting. At all costs these must be divorced from the influence of political parties, and controlled by the best brains to be found among bankers. Hence State action, if it becomes necessary, should be limited to public control as opposed to public ownership.

This would involve the drafting of regulations which should aim at interfering as little as possible with existing machinery and its operations (except perhaps in the closing of supernumerary offices and further great extension in foreign fields). Mainly such regulations should aim at controlling the rate of profits so that bank customers should not be exploited. There would be no insuperable difficulty in determining a " fair " rate of profits, since these are comparatively stable, and banking is largely a routine occupation.

Notwithstanding the mention of methods of control, however, it is to be hoped and expected that English bankers, who possess a deserved reputation for sound methods and cautious practice, will not be so unwise as to attempt to exploit the community's interest by perpetrating a policy of combination designed to do so. It may therefore be presumed that effective competition will be maintained, and particularly if the remaining small banks take the step of banding themselves together to provide that healthy rivalry which is the germ of all desirable competition.

APPENDIX I

CHRONOLOGICAL TABLE OF AMALGAMATIONS
1825-1924

Year.	Private Bank with Private Bank.	Joint Stock absorbs Private Bank.	Joint Stock with Joint Stock.	Private Bank absorbs Joint Stock.	Totals
1826	6	3	—	—	9
1827	—	—	—	—	—
1828	—	1	—	—	1
1829	1	3	—	—	4
1830	—	—	—	—	—
1831	1	1	—	—	2
1832	—	2	—	—	2
1833	—	2	—	—	2
1834	—	6	1	—	7
1835	3	5	—	—	8
1836	4	26	2	—	32
1837	—	3	1	—	4
1838	2	1	—	—	3
1839	1	2	—	—	3
1840	—	5	1	—	6
1841	3	3	—	—	6
1842	2	6	—	—	8
1843	—	7	1	—	8
1844	—	1	1	—	2
Unknown dates.		17	—	—	17
1845	1	1	1	—	3
1846	—	2	2	—	4
1847	—	—	—	—	—
1848	1	1	—	—	2
1849	—	4	—	—	4
1850	—	—	—	—	—
1851	1	1	1	—	3
1852	1	—	1	—	2
1853	1	—	—	—	1
1854	—	2	—	—	2

Year.	Private Bank with Private Bank.	Joint Stock absorbs Private Bank.	Joint Stock with Joint Stock.	Private Bank absorbs Joint Stock.	Total
1855	1	2	—	—	3
1856	1	—	2	—	3
1857	—	2	—	—	2
1858	1	1	—	—	2
1859	1	1	1	—	3
1860	1	2	—	—	3
1861	1	2	1	—	4
1862	—	1	—	—	1
1863	1	4	3	—	8
1864	1	7	2	—	10
1865	1	5	2	—	8
1866	1	5	1	—	7
1867	1	1	1	—	3
1868	1	2	—	—	3
1869	—	—	—	—	—
1870	1	2	2	—	5
1871	1	2	3	—	6
1872	—	3	—	—	3
1873	1	4	1	—	6
1874	—	2	1	—	3
1875	—	3	1	—	4
1876	2	—	—	—	2
1877	3	1	2	—	6
1878	2	6	2	—	10
1879	3	—	—	1	4
1880	2	1	3	—	6
1881	—	1	1	—	2
1882	1	1	2	—	4
1883	1	4	5	—	10
1884	2	2	2	—	6
1885	—	—	—	—	—
1886	1	1	1	—	3
1887	—	4	—	—	4
1888	3	4	1	—	8
1889	2	1	4	—	6
1890	3	4	4	1	12
1891	12	12	3	—	27
1892	1	3	4	—	8
1893	—	5	4	—	9
1894	1	7	3	—	11
1895	—	3	1	—	4

Year.	Private Bank with Private Bank.	Joint Stock absorbs Private Bank.	Joint Stock with Joint Stock.	Private Bank absorbs Joint Stock.	Totals.
1896	15	3	2	—	20
1897	—	4	6	—	10
1898	1	2	5	—	8
1899	—	1	6	—	7
1900	1	7	4	—	12
1901	1	2	5	—	8
1902	2	11	4	—	17
1903	—	4	5	—	9
1904	—	2	3	—	5
1905	—	2	3	—	5
1906	—	2	5	—	7
1907	—	2	2	—	4
1908	—	2	2	—	4
1909	—	2	2	—	4
1910	—	1	2	—	3
1911	—	1	2	—	3
1912	—	1	—	—	1
1913	—	1	2	—	3
1914	1	2	3	—	6
1915	—	1	2	—	3
1916	—	—	—	—	—
1917	—	—	3	—	3
1918	—	1	8	—	9
1919	—	1	9	—	10
1920	—	4	3	—	7
1921	—	—	1	—	1
1922	—	2	—	—	2
1923	—	3	2	—	5
1924	—	—	1	—	1
					552

APPENDIX II

LIST OF AMALGAMATIONS EFFECTED IN THE PERIOD 1825–1924.[1]

This has been compiled from all available sources, and the term " amalgamation " has been interpreted to include all agreements for fusion, irrespective of the individual circumstances governing each agreement : e.g. banks which were in difficulties or had actually failed are included. Where deemed necessary or expedient, the location of various banks has been indicated. The concerns absorbed are shown in the first column.

For the purpose of the Chronological Table in Appendix I only those agreements which have been ascertained as certain and complete amalgamations have been counted.

BARCLAYS BANK, LIMITED.

Year.	Names of Banks Amalgamating.	
1832	B. Birks & Co.	with Wakefield and Barnsley Union Bank.
1836	Hutton & Co.	became basis of Swaledale & Wensleydale Bank.
1836	Hordern & Co.	with Wolverhampton & Staffordshire Bank.
1845	Gillett & Tawney	with T. R. & E. Cobb.
1847	Leatham Tew & Co. (Doncaster)	with Sir W. B. Cooke & Co.
1849	Simpson & White	with Stamford, Spalding & Boston Bank.
1853	Gile's (Rochford) Bank	with Sparrow Tufnell & Co.
1855	Copeman & Co.	with Gurney & Co.
1856	Ransome & Co.	with Bouverie & Co.
1861	Everard & Co.	with Gurney & Co.
1863	Norfolk & Norwich Bank	with East of England Bank.
1864	East of England Bank	with Provincial Bank.
1864	Peckover Harris & Co.	became Bradford Old Bank.
1864	Call, Marten & Co.	became Smith Marten & Co.
1864	Day, Nicholson & Stone	with Provincial Bank.
1864	Lock, Hulme & Co.	with Bank of Wales.
1864	McLean & Co.	with ,, ,,

[1] It has been found impracticable to reproduce diagrams indicating the historical development of the amalgamations.

Year.	Names of Banks Amalgamating.	
1865	Bank of Wales	with Provincial Bank.
1865	Spooner, Attwood & Twells	with Barclay, Bevan & Co.
1868	Fisher, Johnstone & Co.	with Mortlock & Co.
1870	Provincial Bank	became London & Provincial Bank.
1870	Crown Bank	purchased by Gurney & Co.
1871	Fincham & Simpson	with London & Provincial Bank.
1875	Harrison & Co.	with Bradford Old Bank.
1876	T. Ashby & Co.	with La Coste & Co.
1878	Alexander & Co.	with Gurney & Co., becoming Gurney, Alexander & Co.
1878	North Kent Bank	with London & Provincial Bank.
1878	Lock Hulme & Co.	with ,, ,, ,,
1879	Union Bank of Helston	purchased by Bolitho & Co.
1880	Huddleston & Co.	with Gurney, Alexander & Co.
1880	Barclay, Bevan, Tritton & Co.	became Barclay, Bevan, Tritton, Twells & Co.
1881	Midland Banking Co.	with Birmingham, Dudley & District (formerly Birmingham Town & District).
1886	Dendy & Co.	became Halstead, Woodbridge & Co.
1887	Hall, Smith & Co.	became Woodbridge, Lacy, Hartland, Hibbert & Co.
1888	Jarvis & Jarvis	with Gurney, Alexander & Co.
1888	Eland & Eland	with Stamford, Spalding & Boston Bank.
1888	Barclay, Bevan, Tritton & Co.	became Barclay, Bevan, Tritton, Ransome, Bouverie & Co. after amalgamation with Ransome, Bouverie & Co.
1888	Jas. Sewell & Co.	with Union Bank of Manchester.
1889	Wolverhampton & Staffordshire Bank	with Birmingham, Dudley & District Bank.
1889	Birmingham, Dudley & District Bank	became Birmingham District & Counties Bank.
1889	Robins, Foster & Co.	with Bolitho, Sons & Co., becoming Bolitho Foster Coode & Co.
1889	Hodge & Co.	with Bolitho, Williams, Coode, Grylls & Co.
1890	Willyams, Willyams & Co. (Truro)	with Bolitho, Williams, Foster, Coode, Grylls & Co.
1890	Williams, Treffry & Co. (St. Austell)	with ,, ,,
1890	Williams, Williams & Grylls (Falmouth)	with ,, ,,

O

Year.	Names of Banks Amalgamating.	
1890	Batten, Carne & Carne (Penzance)	became Batten, Carne & Carne's Banking Co.
1890	Hughes & Morgan	with Birmingham District & Counties Bank.
1890	Mills & Co. (Colchester) (failed) were taken over by Sparrow, Tufnell & Co.	
1891	Round, Green, Hoare & Co. (Colchester)	with Gurney, Alexander & Co., becoming Gurney, Round, Green & Co.
1891	Eaton, Cayley & Co. (Stamford)	with Spalding, Stamford & Boston Bank.
1891	Bain, Field, Hitchins & Co.	with Bolitho, Williams, Foster, Coode, Grylls & Co.
1891	Gilletts & Clinch (Witney)	with Gillett & Co. (Oxford).
1891	Sparrow, Tufnell & Co. (Withen)	purchased by Gurney, Round, Green & Co!
1892	Simpson, Chapman & Co. (Whitby)	with York Union Bank.
1893	Halstead, Woodbridge & Co.	became Millbanke, Woodbridge & Co.
1894	Pease's Old Bank (Hull)	with York Union Bank.
1894	Pease & Sons (Beverley)	with ,, ,, ,,
1894	Hall, Bevan, West & Bevans (Brighton)	with Barclay, Bevan, Tritton, Ransome, Bouverie & Co.
1896	Goslings & Sharpe (London)	with ,, ,, ,,
	Gurney & Co. (Norwich)	with ,, ,, ,,
	Gurney, Alexander & Co. (Ipswich)	with ,, ,, ,,
	Gurney, Round & Co. (Colchester)	with ,, ,, ,,
	J. Backhouse & Co. (Darlington)	with ,, ,, ,,
	Bassett Sons & Harris (Bedford)	with ,, ,, ,,
	Fordham, Gibson & Co. (Royston)	with ,, ,, ,,
	Gibson, Tuke & Gibson (Saffron Walden)	with ,, ,, ,,
	Molineux, Whitfield & Co. (Lewes)	with ,, ,, ,,
	J. Mortlock & Co. (Cambridge)	with ,, ,, ,,
	Sharples, Tuke, Lucas & Seebohm (Hitchin)	with ,, ,, ,,

Year.	Names of Banks Amalgamating.	
	Sparrow, Tufnell & Co. (Essex Bank)	with Barclay, Bevan, Tritton, Ransome, Bouverie & Co.
	Veasey, Desborough, Bevan & Tillyard (Huntingdon)	with ,, ,, ,,
	Goodall, Hebden & Co. (Scarborough)	with ,, ,, ,,
	All these firms became Barclay & Co., Ltd.	
1896	Batten, Carne & Carne's Banking Co.	with Bolitho, Williams, Foster, Coode, Grylls & Co.,
	becoming Consolidated Bank of Cornwall.	
1897	Woods & Co.	with Barclay & Co., Ltd.
1898	Smith, Marten & Co.	became Marten, Part & Co.
1899	Nottingham & District Joint Stock Bank	with Midland Counties & District Bank.
1899	Swaledale & Wensleydale Joint Stock Bank	with Barclay & Co., Ltd.
1900	Woodbridge, Lacy, Hartland Hibbert & Co.	with ,, ,,
1900	Parsons, Thomson & Co. (Oxford)	with ,, ,,
1900	Millbanke, Woodbridge & Co. (Chichester)	with ,, ,,
1902	J. & J. W. Pease (Darlington)	with ,, ,,
1902	Marten, Part & Co.	with ,, ,,
1902	York Union Joint Stock	with ,, ,,
1902	Roper & Priestman	with ,, ,,
1904	E. Yates & Co. (Liverpool)	with Union Joint Stock Bank of Manchester.
1904	Midland Counties District Bank	with Birmingham, District & Counties Bank.
1904	Thos. Ashby & Co.	with Barclay & Co., Ltd.
1905	Hammond & Co. (Newmarket)	with ,, ,,
1906	Leatham, Tew & Co. (Wakefield)	with ,, ,,
1906	Consolidated Bank of Cornwall	with ,, ,,
1906	Wakefield & Barnsley Union Bank	with Birmingham, District & Counties Bank.
1907	Downes & Co. (Nantwich)	with Union Bank of Manchester.

Year.   Names of Banks Amalgamating.
1907   Bradford Old Bank   with Birmingham, District &
                                   Counties Bank,
               becoming United Counties Bank.
1909   Wootten & Co. (Oxford) with Barclay & Co., Ltd.
1911   Stamford, Spalding, & with   ,,   ,,
       Boston Bank.
1913   J. & C. Simonds & Co. with Barclay & Co., Ltd.
       (Reading)
1914   Neville Reid & Co.   with   ,,   ,,
1915   United Counties Bank   with   ,,   ,,
1917   Halifax Permanent Bank with Union Bank of Manchester.
1918   London & Provincial with London & South Western
       Bank   Bank,
         becoming London Provincial & South Western Bank.
1918   London Provincial & with Barclay & Co., Ltd.
       South Western Bank
1918   East Morley & Bradford with Union Bank of Manchester.
       Deposit Bank
1919   Gillett & Co.   with Barclay & Co., Ltd.
1919   British Linen Bank   with   ,,   ,,
       Union Bank of Man-   with   ,,   ,,
       chester
              (Both these banks were affiliated.)
1920   Tubb & Co. (Bicester) with Barclay & Co., Ltd.
1920   Anglo-Egyptian Bank   with   ,,   ,,
       (affiliated)

          NATIONAL PROVINCIAL BANK, LIMITED.

1826   Elton, Baillie & Co. with Cave, Ames & Co. (Bristol).
       (Bristol)
1828   Percival & Co.   with Northamptonshire Union
                                   Bank.   ˎ
1828   Corser & Co. (Whit- with Northern & Central Bank
       church)   of England.
1834   Bristol City Private with   ,,   ,,   ,,
       Bank
1834   Mare & Eaton   with   ,,   ,,   ,,
1835   North Devon Bank   with National Provincial Bank.
       (Barnstaple)
1836   Rotton & Co.   with   ,,   ,,   ,,
1836   Pyke & Co.   with   ,,   ,,   ,,
1836? Blossome & Co.   with   ,,   ,,   ,,
1836? Vye & Co.   with   ,,   ,,   ,,
1836   Skinner & Co. (Stockton with   ,,   ,,   ,,
       & Darlington)

Year.	Names of Banks Amalgamating.		
1836	Northern&Central Bank of England (failed)	with National Provincial Bank.	
1837	Rugely Tamworth & Lichfield Joint Stock (failed)	with ,, ,, ,,	
1839	Husband & Co. (Devon-port)	with ,, ,, ,,	
1840	Hulke & Co.	with ,, ,, ,,	
1840	Haythorne & Wright (Bristol)	with ,, ,, ,,	
1840	Fryer, Andrews & Co. (Dorset)	with ,, ,, ,,	
1840	Harris & Co. (Dartmouth)	with ,, ,, ,,	
1841	Fector & Co. (Dover)	with ,, ,, ,,	
1841	Hammersley,Greenwood Drewe & Brooks	with Coutts & Co.	
1842	Cole, Holroyd & Co. (Exeter)	with National Provincial Bank.	
1843	Ley & Co. (Bideford)	with ,, ,, ,,	
1843	Loveband & Co. (Torrington)	with ,, ,, ,,	
1843	Pretor & Co.(Sherborne)	with ,, ,, ,,	
1843	Isle of Wight Joint Stock (Newport)	with ,, ,, ,,	
1846	Stockton & Durham County Bank	with ,, ,, ,,	
1852	Barnard & Co.	with Dimsdale & Co., becoming D. Drewett, Fowler & Barnard.	
1854	Kinnersley & Sons (Newcastle-under-Lyme)	with National Provincial Bank.	
1857	Laurie & Co.	with ,, ,, ,,	
1858	Wm. Moore (Stone)	with ,, ,, ,,	
1859	Dixon, Brooks & Dixon	with Union Bank of London.	
1860	Ledgard & Co.	with National Provincial Bank.	
1860	Robarts & Co.	with Lubbock, Foster & Co.	
1867	Crawshay, Bailey & Co. (Monmouth, etc.)	with National Provincial Bank.	
1868	Bailey & Co.	with ,, ,, ,,	
1870	J. & C. Robinson & Co.	with Sheffield Banking Co.	
1871	Morris, David & Son (Carmarthen)	with National Provincial Bank.	
1871	Robinson & Co.	with S. Smith & Co.	
1877	Miles, Miles & Co. (Bristol)	with Cave, Baillie & Co. (Bristol).	

Year.	Names of Banks Amalgamating.	
1878	Bank of Leeds	with National Provincial Bank.
1880	Godfrey & Co. (Newark)	with S. Smith & Co.
1887	Moxon & Percival	with Northamptonshire Union Bank.
	Hewitt & Moxon	with ,, ,, ,,
	Wallis & Hewitt	with ,, ,, ,,
	Whitworth, Wallis & Hewitt (All of Towcester)	with ,, ,, ,,
1891	Prescott, Cave, Buxton & Loder (London)	with Prescott, Dimsdale, Cave, Tugwell & Co.
	Dimsdale, Fowler, Barnard & Dimsdales (London)	with ,, ,, ,,
	Miles, Cave, Bailie & Co. (Bristol)	with ,, ,, ,,
	Tugwell, Brymer & Co. (Bath)	with ,, ,, ,,
	Geo. Moger & Sons (Bath)	with ,, ,, ,,
	Deane & Co. (Winchester)	with ,, ,, ,,
	Harwood & Co. (Thornbury)	with ,, ,, ,,
1891	Cane, Chasemore, Robinson & Sons (Croydon)	with Union Bank of London.
1892	Bulpett & Hall (Winchester)	with Prescott, Dimsdale & Co.
1898	C. Hopkinson & Sons (London)	with ,, ,, ,,
1899	County of Stafford Bank	with National Provincial Bank
1900	Cripplegate Bank	with Union Bank of London.
1900	T. Butcher & Sons (Tring)	with Prescott, Dimsdale & Co.
1901	Milford, Snow & Co. (Exeter)	with Sanders & Co. (Exeter),
	becoming Sanders, Snow & Co.	
1902	Sanders, Snow & Co.	with Prescott, Dimsdale & Co.
1902	Hilton, Rigden & Rigden	with ,, ,, ,,
1902	Smith, Ellison & Co. (Lincoln)	with Union Bank of London.
	Smith, Payne & Smith (London)	with ,, ,, ,,
	Samuel Smith & Co. (Derby), (Newark), (Nottingham)	with ,, ,, ,,

Year.	Names of Banks Amalgamating.	
	Sam Smith Bros. & Co. (Hull)	with Union Bank of London.
	becoming Union of London & Smiths Bank.	
1903	Prescott, Dimsdale, Cave, Tugwell & Co.	became Prescott's Bank.
1903	Prescott's Bank	with Union of London & Smiths Bank.
1903	Wigan, Mercer, Tasker & Co. (Maidstone)	with ,, ,, ,,
1903	London & Yorkshire Bank	with ,, ,, ,,
1903	Knaresborough & Claro Bank	with National Provincial Bank.
1904	Bradford Commercial Bank	with Bradford District Bank.
1914	Robarts, Lubbock & Co.	with Coutts & Co.
1918	Union of London & Smiths Bank	with National Provincial Bank,
	becoming National Provincial & Union Bank of England.	
1918	Bickerstaffe & Co. (London)	with National Provincial & Union Bank of England.
1919	Sheffield Banking Co.	with ,, ,, ,,
1919	Bradford District Bank	with ,, ,, ,,
1920	Richards & Co. (Llangollen)	with ,, ,, ,,
1920	Coutts & Co.	with ,, ,, ,,
1920	Northamptonshire Union Bank	with ,, ,, ,,
1920	Shilson, Coode & Co. (St. Austell)	with ,, ,, ,,
1922	Dingley & Co. (Launceston)	with ,, ,, ,,
1922	Dingley, Pearse & Co. (Okehampton)	with ,, ,, ,,
1923	Grindlay & Co. (London)	with ,, ,, ,,
1924	National Provincial & Union Bank of England	became National Provincial Bank, Ltd.
1924	Guernsey Bank	with ,, ,, ,,

MIDLAND BANK, LIMITED.

?	Chapman & Co.	with Coventry Union Bank.
?	Sankey & Co.	with North & South Wales Bank.
?	Benson & Co.	with ,, ,, ,,
?	Wakefield & Co.	with Carlisle Banking Co.
1829	Galton & James	to form Birmingham Banking Co.

Year.	Names of Banks Amalgamating.	
1833	Fletcher & Stubbs (Boroughbridge)	with York City & County Bank.
1834	Hordern,Molineux & Co.	to form Dudley & West Bromwich Bank.
1834	Coates & Co.	with Yorkshire District Bank.
1834	Perfects & Co. (Pontefract)	with „ „ „
1835	Miller & Son	with Leicester Banking Co.
1835	Dresser & Co.	with Yorkshire District Bank.
1836	Moss & Co. (Liverpool)	to form North & South Wales Bank.
1836	J. Connell & Co.	to form Carlisle City & District Bank.
1837	Farrer, Williamson & Co. (Ripon)	with York City & County Bank.
1840	Wright & Co.	with London Joint Bank.
1841	Weaver & Co. (Leicester)	with Leicester Banking Co.
1843	Rimington & Co. (Sheffield)	with Sheffield & Retford Joint Stock Bank.
1843	Yorkshire Banking Co.	with Yorkshire District Bank.
1845	Sheffield & Retford Joint Stock Bank	with Sheffield Union Bank.
1845	Frankland, Wilkinson & Co.	with York City & County Bank.
1846	Clark, Richardson & Co.	with „ „ „
1846	Leicester Banking Co.	with Coventry Union Bank.
1848	Chas. Foster & Sons (Walsall)	with Birmingham Banking Co.
1851	Bates & Robins (Stourbridge)	with Birmingham & Midland Bank.
1857	Williams, Davies & Co. (Aberystwyth)	with North & South Wales Bank.
1861	Craddock & Bell	with Coventry Union Bank.
1862	Nicholls, Baker & Crane	with Birmingham & Midland Bank.
1863	Goodricke, Holyoake & Co.	to form Midland Banking Co.
1863	Herefordshire Banking Co.	with „ „
1864	Challis & Son	to form Albion Joint Stock Bank.
1864	London & Northern Bank	with Midland Banking Co.
1865	Woodcock & Co. (Coventry)	with Birmingham Banking Co.
1866	Head & Co.	with Cumberland Union Bank.

Year.	Names of Banks Amalgamating.	
1870	Alliance Bank (South- wark)	with London Joint Stock Bank.
1871	Albion Bank	with ,, ,, ,,
1872	J. Backhouse & Co. (Thirsk)	with York City & County Bank.
1872	Saxton Bros.	with Midland Banking Co.
1873	Robertson, Fraser & Co. (Manchester)	with Manchester Joint Stock Bank.
1873	Wills & Co. (Merioneth- shire)	with North & South Wales Bank.
1877	Bala Bank (failed)	with ,, ,, ,,
1878	Harding & Co. (Bur- lington)	with York City & County Bank.
1880	Stourbridge & Kidder- minster Bank	with Birmingham Banking Co.
1880	Metropolitan Bank	Title changed to Royal Ex- change Bank.
1882	Rochdale Joint Stock Bank	with Oldham Joint Stock Bank.
1883	Union Bank of Birm- ingham	with Birmingham & Midland Bank.
1883	Darlington District Joint Stock Bank	with York City & County Bank.
1888	Swansea Bank	Title changed to South Wales Union Bank.
1889	Staffordshire Joint Stock Bank	with Birmingham Banking Co.
1889	Royal Exchange Bank becoming Metropolitan	with ,, ,, ,, & Birmingham Bank.
1889	Coventry Union Bank	with Birmingham & Midland Bank.
1889	Leamington Priors & Warwickshire Bank	with ,, ,, ,,
1889	Cooper, Purton & Sons (Bridgnorth)	with ,, ,, ,,
1890	Leeds & County Bank	with ,, ,, ,,
1890	Exchange & Discount Bank (Leeds)	with ,, ,, ,,
1890	Derby Commercial Bank	with ,, ,, ,,
1890	Jos. Dickenson (Alston)	with Carlisle City & District Bank
1891	Pugh Jones & Co. (Pwllheli)	with National Bank of Wales.
1891	Central Bank of London becoming London	with Birmingham & Midland Bank, & Midland Bank.

Year.	Names of Banks Amalgamating.	
1891	Godfray, Major & Godfray (Jersey)	with Channel Islands Bank.
1891	Lacy, Hartland & Co.	with London & Midland Bank.
1892	South Wales Union Bank	with Metropolitan & Birmingham Bank,
	becoming Metropolitan Bank (of England and Wales).	
1892	Manchester Joint Stock Bank	with London & Midland Bank.
1893	Bank of Westmorland	with ,, ,, ,,
1893	Imperial Bank (Lothbury)	with London Joint Stock Bank.
1893	National Bank of Wales	with Metropolitan Bank (of England and Wales).
1894	Hull Banking Co.	with York City & County Bank.
1895	Preston Banking Co.	with London & Midland Bank.
1895	Hardy & Co. (Grantham)	with Leicester Banking Co.
1896	Carlisle City & District Bank	with London & Midland Bank.
1897	Barnsley Banking Co.	with York City & County Bank.
1897	Huddersfield Union Banking Co.	with London & Midland Bank.
1897	Channel Islands Bank	with ,, ,, ,,
1897	North Western Bank	with ,, ,, ,,
1898	Oldham Joint Stock Bank	with ,, ,, ,,
1898	City Bank	with ,, ,, ,,
	becoming London City & Midland Bank.	
1899	City of Birmingham Bank	with London City & Midland Bank.
1900	Leicester Banking Co.	with ,, ,, ,,
1901	Leyland & Bullins (Liverpool)	with North & South Wales Bank.
1901	Cumberland Union Bank	with York City & County Bank.
1901	Yorkshire Banking Co.	with London City & Midland Bank.
1901	Sheffield Union Bank	with ,, ,, ,,
1905	Nottingham Joint Stock Bank	with ,, ,, ,,
1908	North & South Wales Bank	with ,, ,, ,,
1909	York City & County Bank	with London Joint Stock Bank.
1910	Davies, Banks & Co. (Kington)	with Metropolitan Bank (of England and Wales).
1910	Bradford Banking Co.	with London City & Midland Bank.

Year.	Names of Banks Amalgamating.	
1913	Lincoln & Lindsey Bank	with London City & Midland Bank
1913	Sheffield & Hallamshire Bank	with „ „ „
1914	Metropolitan Bank (of England and Wales)	with „ „ „
1917	Belfast Banking Co. (affiliated)	with „ „ „
1918	London Joint Stock Bank	with „ „ „
	becoming London Joint City & Midland Bank.	
1920	Clydesdale Bank (affiliated)	with London Joint City & Midland Bank.
1923	North of Scotland Bank (affiliated)	with „ „ „
1924	London Joint City & Midland Bank.	became Midland Bank.

WESTMINSTER BANK, LIMITED.

Year		
1826	Ricketts, Thorne & Wait (Bristol)	with Stuckey's Bank.
1826	Stuckey's Private Bank	converted into Stuckey's Joint Stock Bank.
1829	Sparks & Co. (Crewkerne)	with „ „ „
1831	Payne & Co.	with „ „ „
1835	Reeves & Porch (Wells)	with „ „ „
1836	Pare's Banking Co. (Leicester)	to form Pare's Joint Stock Bank.
1838	Phelps & Co. (Crewkerne)	with Stuckey's Bank.
1838	Kingslake & Co. (Taunton)	with „ „
1838	London & Middlesex Bank	with London & Westminster Bank.
1841	Woodland & Co. (Bridgwater)	with Stuckey's Bank.
1841	Whitmarsh & White (Yeovil)	with „ „
1841	Walters, Waldron, Timbrell & Barton (Frome)	with „ „
1841	Tufnell, Falkner & Falkner (Bath)	with „ „
1842?	J. & T. Chapman	with London & County Bank.
1842?	Wilmshurst & Co.	with „ „ „
1842?	Jeffreys & Hill	with „ „ „

Year.	Names of Banks Amalgamating.	
1842	Hector & Co.	with London & County Bank.
1842	Emmerson & Co.	with ,, ,, ,,
1843	Davenport, Walker & Co. (Oxford)	with ,, ,, ,,
1849	Trapp, Halfhead & Co.	with ,, ,, ,,
1851	Berkshire Union Banking Co.	with ,, ,, ,,
1851	Denison, Heywood & Co.	became Heywood, Kennard & Co.
1856	Strahan, Paul & Co.	business taken by London & Westminster Bank.
1859	Western Bank of London	business taken by London & County Bank.
1859	Fuller & Co.	with Sapte, Muspratt, Banbury & Co.
1861	Commercial Bank of London	business taken by London & Westminster Bank.
1863	Hankey & Co. (London)	with Consolidated Bank.
1863	Bank of London	with ,, ,,
1864	Jones, Loyd & Co.	with London & Westminster Bank.
1865	Thos. Firth & Co.	with Parrs Bank.
1867	Metropolitan & Provincial Bank of Macclesfield	with ,, ,,
1868	Cooke & Co. (Doncaster)	with Beckett & Co.
1870	F. W. Jennings (Leek)	with Parrs Bank.
1870	Nunn & Co. (Manningtree)	with London & County Bank.
1870	Unity Joint Stock Bank	with London & Westminster Bank.
1871	Alliance Bank (Liverpool business)	with National Bank of Liverpool.
1873	Badcock & Co. (Taunton)	with Stuckey's Bank.
1874	T. Woodcock & Sons, & Eckersley (Wigan)	with Parrs Bank.
1875	Bower & Co. (York)	with Beckett & Co.
1877	Crompton, Newton & Co. (Derby)	with Crompton & Evans.
1877	W. S. Evans & Co. (Derby)	with ,, ,,
1878	Chesterfield & North Derbyshire Joint Stock Bank	with ,, ,,
1878	Dixon & Co. (Chester)	with Parrs Bank.

Year.	Names of Banks Amalgamating.	
1879	J. Taylor & Sons (Bakewell)	with Crompton & Evans.
1879	Swann & Clough (York)	with Beckett & Co.
1883	Dunsford & Co. (Tiverton)	with Stuckey's Bank.
1883	National Bank of Liverpool	with Parrs Bank.
1891	Fuller, Banbury & Nix	with ,, ,,
1891	Hove Banking Co.	with London & County Bank.
1892	Alliance Bank	with Parrs Bank,
	becoming Parrs & Alliance Bank.	
1894	Shrubsole & Co. (Kingston-on-Thames)	with ,, ,,
1894	Croxon, Jones & Co. (Oswestry)	with ,, ,,
1894	Sir Samuel Scott, Bart., & Co. (London)	with ,, ,,
1896	Consolidated Bank (London)	with ,, ,,
1898	Derby & Derbyshire Bank	with Parrs Bank.
	Old name re-adopted.	
1900	Ashton, Hyde, Stalybridge & Glossop Bank	with Parrs Bank.
1902	Pare's (Leicester) Bank	with ,, ,,
1907	F. Burt & Co. (London)	with London & County Bank.
1908	Robin Bros. (Jersey)	with Parrs Bank.
1908	Whitehaven Joint Stock Bank	with ,, ,,
1909	Stuckey's Bank	with ,, ,,
1909	London & County Bank	with London & Westminster Bank
	becoming London County & Westminster Bank.	
1914	Crompton, Evans & Co.	with Parrs Bank.
1915	Thos. Barnard & Co.	with ,, ,,
1917	Ulster Bank (affiliated)	with London County & Westminster Bank.
1918	Parrs Bank	with ,, ,, ,,
	becoming London County Westminster & Parrs Bank.	
1919	Nottingham & Notts Bank	with London County Westminster & Parrs Bank.
1921	Beckett & Co. (Leeds & York)	with ,, ,, ,,
1923	Stilwell & Sons (London)	with ,, ,, ,,
1924	Guernsey Commercial Bank	with ,, ,, ,,
1924	Name altered to Westminster Bank.	

LLOYDS BANK, LIMITED.

Year.	Names of Banks Amalgamating.	
?	Watkins & Co.	with Northampton Union Bank.
?	Moule & Co.	with North Wilts Bank.
?	Robins & Co.	with Wilts & Dorset Bank.
1826	Nicholson & Co.	with Devon & Cornwall Bank.
1826	Eaton & Co.	with Glamorgan Banking Co.
1826	Rowland & Co.	with „ „
1826	Hingston & Prideaux	with Devon & Cornwall Bank.
1829	Sparkes & Co.	with „ „ „
1831	John West	with Wilts & Dorset Bank.
1834	Bartlett & Co.	with Bucks & Oxon Union Bank.
1834	English & Jersey Union Banking Co.	with Hampshire Banking Co.
1834	Atkins & Sons (Portsmouth)	with „ „ „
1835	Coates, Woolley & Gordon	with Moilliet, Smith & Pearson.
1836	Beck & Prime	with Coventry & Warwickshire Banking Co.
1836	Bunney & Co.	with „ „ „
1836	Tomes & Co.	with Warwick & Leamington Banking Co.
1836	Moore & Robinson (Notts)	to form Moore & Robinson's Nottinghamshire Banking Co.
1836	Rawson & Co.	to form Halifax & Huddersfield Union Bank.
1836	Darby & Co. ⎫ Hordern & Co. ⎪ Biddle & Co. ⎬ Reynolds & Co. ⎭	to form Shropshire Banking Co.
1836	Russell & Co.	with Gloucester Banking Co.
1836	Hartland & Co.	with „ „ „
1836	Pitt, Bowley, Croome & Wood	to form City & County of Gloucester Banking Co.
1836	County of Gloucester Bank	with „ „ „
1840	Southern District Banking Co.	with Hampshire Banking Co.
1842	T. & R. Strange	with City & County of Gloucester Bank.
1843	Vizard & Co.	with „ „ „
1849	Tice & Welch	with Wilts & Dorset Bank.
1854	Wickham & Co. (Winchester)	with Hampshire Banking Co.

Year.	Names of Banks Amalgamating.	
1855	Towgood & Co.	with West of England & South Wales Bank.
1855	Storey, Thomas Banking Co.	with Wilts & Dorset Bank.
1856	Cheltenham & Gloucester Bank	with City & County of Gloucester Bank.
1860	Everett, Ravenhill & Co. (Warminster)	with North Wiltshire Banking Co.
1861	Heath & Co. (Andover)	with Hampshire Banking Co.
1863	Atkins & Sons (Portsmouth)	with „ „ „
1864	Seymour & Co. (Basingstoke)	with „ „ „
1864	Barnett, Hoare & Co.	with Hanbury Lloyd & Co.
1865	Moilliet & Sons	with Lloyds & Co., to form Lloyds Bank.
	P. & H. Williams	with Lloyds Bank.
1866	Ward, Merriman & Co. (Andover)	with North Wiltshire Banking Co.
1866	Warwick & Leamington Banking Co.	with Lloyds Bank.
1866	Stevenson Salt & Co. (Stafford)	with „ „
1866	Gill, Morshead & Co. (Tavistock)	with Fox, Fowler & Co.
1867	Stevenson, Salt & Sons (London)	with Bosanquet & Co.
1868	A. Butlin & Son	with Lloyds Bank.
1872	R. & W. Fryer (Wolverhampton)	with „ „
1873	W. Footner & Sons	with Wilts & Dorset Bank.
1874	Shropshire Banking Co.	with Lloyds Bank.
1875	Sealey & Co.	with Wilts & Dorset Bank.
1875	Arkwright & Co.	with Moore & Robinson's Nottinghamshire Bank.
1877	North Wiltshire Bank to form Capital	with Hampshire Banking Co., & Counties Bank.
1878	Harwood & Harwood (Clevedon)	with West of England & Bristol Bank.
1878	Willis, Percival & Co. (London)	with Capital & Counties Bank.
1879	Tweedy, Williams & Co.	with Cornish Bank.
1880	Coventry & Warwickshire Banking Co.	with Lloyds Bank.
1880	Beck & Co. (Shrewsbury)	with „ „

Year.	Names of Banks Amalgamating.	
1882	Whitchurch & Ellesmere Bank (failed)	with Lloyds Bank.
1883	Webb & Co. (Ledbury)	with Gloucester Bank.
1883	Locke, Tugwell & Co. (Devizes)	with Capital & Counties Bank.
1883	Haydon & Co. (Guildford)	with Capital & Counties Bank.
1884	Rocke, Eyton & Co.	with Burton Lloyd & Co.
1884	Ludlow & Tenbury Bank	with Worcester City & County Bank.
1884	Bosanquet, Salt & Co. (London)	with Lloyds Bank.
1884	Barnett, Hoare & Co. (London)	with ,, ,,
1885	Clymo, Treffry, Hawke, West & Co.	became Western Counties Bank.
1886	J. Knight & Son (Farnham)	with Capital & Counties Bank.
1886	Gloucester Bank	with ,, ,, ,,
1887	Moxon & Percival (Towcester)	with Northampton Union Bank.
1888	Grant, Gillman & Long (Portsmouth)	with Grant & Maddison's Bank,
	forming Grant & Maddison's Union Bank.	
1888	Pritchard, Gordon & Co. (Broseley)	with Lloyds Bank.
1889	Worcester City and County Banking Co.	with ,, ,,
1889	Birmingham Joint Stock Bank	with ,, ,,
1890	Hancock & Son	with Wilts & Dorset Bank.
1890	Western Counties Bank	with Capital & Counties Bank.
1890	Northampton Union Bank	with ,, ,, ,,
1890	Three Towns Bank	with Devon & Cornwall Bank.
1890	Wilkins & Co.	with Lloyds Bank.
1890	Beechings & Co.	with ,, ,,
1891	Commercial Bank of Cornwall	with Cornish Bank.
1891	Garfit, Claypon & Co.	with Capital & Counties Bank.
1891	Whatts, Whidborne & Co.	with ,, ,, ,,
1891	Cobb & Co. (Margate)	with Lloyds Bank.
1891	Praeds & Co.	with ,, ,,
1891	Hart, Fellows & Co.	with ,, ,,
1892	R. Twining & Co. (London)	with ,, ,,

Year.	Names of Banks Amalgamating.	
1892	Bristol & West of England Bank	with Lloyds Bank.
1893	Cox, Cobbold & Co. (Harwich)	with Bacon, Cobbold & Tollemache & Co.
1893	Mellersh & Co. (Godalming)	with Capital & Counties Bank.
1893	Herries, Farquhar & Co.	with Lloyds Bank.
1893	Curteis, Pomfret & Co.	with ,, ,,
1894	Bromage & Co. (Monmouth)	with ,, ,,
1894	Wells, Hogge & Lindsell	with Capital & Counties Bank.
1895	Slocock, Matthews, Southby & Slocock.	with ,, ,, ,,
1895	Paget & Co. (Leicester)	with Lloyds Bank.
1896	Wheeler, Thomas & Co. (High Wycombe)	with Capital & Counties Bank.
1896	Henty & Co. (Worthing)	with ,, ,, ,,
1896	St. Barbe & Daniell (Lymington)	with ,, ,, ,,
1897	Williams & Co. (Chester)	with Lloyds Bank.
1897	County of Gloucester Bank	with ,, ,,
1897	Pinckney Bros.	with Wilts & Dorset Bank.
1897	R. & R. Williams & Co.	with ,, ,, ,,
1898	Glamorgan Banking Co.	with Capital & Counties Bank.
1898	I. & C. Wright (Nottingham)	with ,, ,, ,,
1898	Jenner & Co.	with ,, ,, ,,
1899	Stephens, Bland & Co.	with Lloyds Bank.
1899	Burton Union Bank	with ,, ,,
1900	Oakes, Bevan, Tollemache & Co.	with Capital & Counties Bank.
1900	Vivian, Kitson & Co.	with Lloyds Bank.
1900	Liverpool Union Bank	with ,, ,,
1900	Brooks & Co.	with ,, ,,
1900	Brown, Janson & Co. (London)	with ,, ,,
1900	Williams, Brown & Co. (Leeds)	with ,, ,,
1901	Lacons, Youell & Kemp	with Capital & Counties Bank
1901	Moore & Robinson's Nottinghamshire Bank.	with ,, ,, ,,
1902	Cobb, Bartlett & Co.	with Bucks & Oxon Union Bank
1902	Bucks & Oxon Union Bank	with Lloyds Bank.
1902	Pomfret, Burra & Co.	with ,, ,,

Year.	Names of Banks Amalgamating.	
1903	Foster & Co.	with Lloyds Bank.
1903	Cornish Bank	with ,, ,,
1903	Hodgkin,Barnett,Pease, Spence & Co.	with ,, ,,
1903	Grant & Maddison's Union Bank	with Lloyds Bank.
1903	Hammond, Plumpton, Hilton & Co.	with Capital & Counties Bank.
1905	Bacon, Cobbold & Co.	with ,, ,, ,,
1905	Hedges, Wells & Co.	with Lloyds Bank.
1906	Devon & Cornwall Bank	with ,, ,,
1906	Berwick, Letchmere & Co.	with Capital & Counties Bank.
1907	Eyton, Burton, Lloyd & Co.	with ,, ,, ,,
1908	Lambton & Co.	with Lloyds Bank.
1909	D. Jones & Co. (Llandovery)	with ,, ,,
1910	Halifax & Huddersfield Union Bank	with Halifax Joint Stock Bank,
1911	becoming West Yorkshire Bank.	
1911	Hill & Sons	with Lloyds Bank.
1912	Peacock, Wilson & Co.	with ,, ,,
1914	Wilts & Dorset Bank	with ,, ,,
1918	Capital & Counties Bank	with ,, ,,
1919	West Yorkshire Bank	with ,, ,,
1919	London & River Plate Bank (affiliation)	with ,, ,,
1919	National Bank of Scotland (affiliation)	with ,, ,,
1921	Fox, Fowler & Co.	with ,, ,,
1923	London & Brazilian Bank (affiliation)	with ,, ,,
1923	Cox & Co. and H. S. King	with ,, ,,

BANK OF LIVERPOOL & MARTINS, LIMITED.

1836	Rawdon, Briggs & Co.	to form Halifax Commercial Bank.
1870?	Chippendale, Netherwood & Carr	with Birkbeck, Robinson & Co.
1870	J. & C. Robinson	with ,, ,, ,,
1875	Alnwick & County Bank	with North Eastern Bank.
1880	Birkbeck, Robinson & Co. (Settle)	became Craven Bank.

Year.	Names of Banks Amalgamating.	
1882	Mackie, Davidson & Co. (Carlisle)	with Carlisle & Cumberland Bank.
1883	A. Heywood & Sons (Liverpool)	with Bank of Liverpool.
1884	Grice & Co. (Bootle)	with Wakefield, Crewdson & Co.
1886	Codd & Co.	with Cocks, Biddulph & Co.
1888	Valance & Payne (Sittingbourne)	with Martin & Co.
1889	Liverpool Commercial Bank	with Bank of Liverpool.
1892	Dale, Young, Nelson & Co.	with North Eastern Bank.
1893	Wakefield, Crewdson & Co. (Kendal)	with Bank of Liverpool.
1906	Craven Bank (Skipton)	with ,, ,,
1911	Carlisle & Cumberland Bank	with ,, ,,
1914	North Eastern Bank	with ,, ,,
1918	Martin & Co.	with ,, ,,
	becoming Bank of Liverpool & Martins.	
1919	Halifax Commercial Bank	with Bank of Liverpool & Martins.
1919	Cocks, Biddulph & Co.	with ,, ,, ,,
1919	Palatine Bank	with ,, ,, ,,

LANCASHIRE & YORKSHIRE BANK, LIMITED.

1832	B. Wilson & Sons (Mirfield)	became Mirfield & Huddersfield Banking Co.
1836	Hagues, Cook, & Wormald (Dewsbury)	with ,, ,, ,,
	becoming West Riding Union Bank.	
1836	Grundy & Wood (Bury)	became Bury Banking Co.
1872	Alliance Bank (Branch)	with Lancashire & Yorkshire Bank.
1882	Preston Union Bank	with Union Bank of Preston.
1888	Bury Banking Co.	with Lancashire & Yorkshire Bank.
1894	London & Lancashire Bank	with Mercantile Bank of Lancashire.
1894	Preston Union Bank	with Lancashire & Yorkshire Bank.
1899	Adelphi Bank	with ,, ,, ,,
1900	Manx Bank	with Mercantile Bank of Lancashire

Year.	Names of Banks Amalgamating.	
1902	West Riding Union Bank	with Lancashire & Yorkshire Bank.
1904	Mercantile Bank of Lancashire	with ,, ,, ,,

WILLIAMS DEACONS BANK, LIMITED.

1836	Walker, Eyre, Stanley & Co.	formed Sheffield and Rotherham Joint Stock Bank.
1874	Heywood Bros. & Co. (Manchester)	with Manchester & Salford Bank.
1881	C. Royds & Co. (Rochdale)	with ,, ,,
1890	Manchester & Salford Bank	with Williams, Deacons Bank.
1906	Sheffield & Rotherham Bank	with ,, ,, ,,

DISTRICT BANK, LIMITED.

1829	Christy, Lloyd & Co.	formed Manchester & Liverpool District Banking Co.
1836	Skinner & Co. (part firm only)	with ,, ,, ,,
1837	Hartley & Co.	with Bank of Whitehaven.
1845	Nantwich & South Cheshire Bank	with Manchester & Liverpool District Banking Co.
1863	Loyd, Entwistle, Bury & Jarvis (Manchester)	,, ,, ,,
1865	Alcock & Co. (Burslem)	with ,, ,, ,,
1884	Southport & West Lancashire Bank	with ,, ,, ,,
1891	W. J. & T. Brocklehurst (Macclesfield)	with ,, ,, ,,
1907	Lancaster Banking Co.	with ,, ,, ,,
1915	Bank of Whitehaven	with ,, ,, ,,
1924	Name changed to District Bank.	

MANCHESTER & COUNTY BANK, LIMITED.

1826	Buckley & Co.	formed Saddleworth Banking Co.
1866	Saddleworth Banking Co.	with Manchester & County Bank.
1871	Bank of Stockport	with ,, ,, ,,
1897	Bank of Bolton	with ,, ,, ,,

MISCELLANEOUS.

Year.	Names of Banks Amalgamating.	
?	Towgood & Co.	with Monmouth & Glamorgan Bank.
?	Jones and Davis	with ,, ,, ,,
?	Carne & Co.	with Western District Bank.
1835	G. Smith & Co.	with Leeds & West Riding Bank.
1836?	Boase & Co.	with Western District Bank.
1836	Backhouse & Co.	to form Northumberland & Durham Bank.
1836	Aspinall & Co.	to form Liverpool Central Bank.
1836	Bywater & Co.	to form Leeds Commercial Bank.
1836	Chapman & Co.	with Sir W. Chaytor, Frankland & Co.,

forming Newcastle Union Bank.

1836	Hope & Co.	to form Liverpool Borough Bank.
1836	Magor & Co.	with Western District Bank.
1836	Norfolk & Norwich Bank	with East of England Bank.
1839	Ridley & Co. (Newcastle)	with Northumberland and Dur-Bank.
1839	Mansfield & Co. (Leicester)	with Clark & Philips (Leicester).
1842	Dorriens & Co.	with Currie & Co.
1842	Ladbroke & Co.	with Glyn & Co.
1843	Heming & Needham	to form Leicester & Warwickshire Bank.
1855	Towgood & Co. (Cardiff)	with West of England & South Wales District Bank.
1859	Newcastle Union Bank	with Woods, Parker & Co.
1860	Egham & Co.	with Mangles Bros. (Guildford).
1862	Kingsbridge Joint Stock Bank	with West of England & South Wales District Bank.
1863	Alloway & McDougall (Ross)	with ,, ,, ,,
1864	Mangles Bros.	became South Eastern Banking Co.,

and amalgamated with

	Burgess & Co. (Ramsgate)	then became English Joint Stock Bank.
1866	Rogers, Olding & Co.	with ,, ,, ,,
1898	Leeds Joint Stock Bank	with London & Northern Joint Stock Bank
1902	Melville Fickus & Co.	with F. Huth & Co.
1924	Royal Bank of Scotland	with Drummond & Co.
1924	Child & Co.	with Glyn & Co.

APPENDIX III

REPORT OF THE TREASURY COMMITTEE ON BANK AMALGAMATIONS.

TREASURY MINUTE DATED 11TH MARCH, 1918.

The Chancellor of the Exchequer states to the Board that he has appointed a Committee consisting of the following :—

Lord Colwyn (Chairman),
Lord Cunliffe, G.B.E.,
Hon. Rupert Beckett,
Hon. Herbert Gibbs,
Sir Arthur Haworth, Bt.,
Sir Richard V. Vassar-Smith, Bt.,
Sir John Purcell, K.C.B.,
Captain H. Keswick, M.P.,
Mr. E. Manville,
Mr. H. McGowan,
Mr. John Rae,
Mr. Douglas Vickers,

to consider and report to what extent, if at all, amalgamations between banks may affect prejudicially the interests of the industrial and mercantile community, and whether it is desirable that legislation should be introduced to prohibit such amalgamations or to provide safeguards under which they might continue to be permitted.

The Permanent Secretaries recommend to the Board that Mr. C. L. Stocks be appointed to act as Secretary to the Committee. My Lords concur.

REPORT.

TO THE LORDS COMMISSIONERS OF HIS MAJESTY'S TREASURY.

1. We, the undersigned Committee, appointed by Treasury Minute of the 11th March last, beg to submit our report to Your Lordships.

2. We have held eight meetings, and have examined the following witnesses, viz. :—

Sir E. Holden, Bart., Chairman and Managing Director of the London City and Midland Bank,

Professor H. S. Foxwell, Professor of Political Economy in the University of London,

Mr. O. C. Quekett, Chairman of the Stock Exchange Committee,

Mr. Henry Bell, Director and General Manager of Lloyds Bank,

Mr. Gaspard Farrer, of Baring Bros. & Co., Ltd.,

Mr. Harold Snagge, of Messrs. E. Boustead & Co.,

Mr. J. F. Darling, General Manager of the London Joint Stock Bank,

Mr. Beaumont Pease, Deputy Chairman of Lloyds Bank,

Mr. Oswald Stoll,

Mr. Thomas Goodwin, Manager of the Co-operative Wholesale Society's Bank,

Mr. Sidney Webb,

Mr. A. W. Flux, of the Board of Trade,

Sir Charles Addis, of the Hong-Kong and Shanghai Banking Corporation, Ltd.,

Sir Herbert Hambling, Chairman of the London and South Western Bank,

Mr. Christopher Nugent, of the Union Discount Company of London, Ltd.,

Viscount Cowdray,

Mr. Gordon Selfridge,

Sir James Hope Simpson, General Manager of the Bank of Liverpool, Ltd.,

Mr. T. B. Johnston, of Messrs. Pountney & Co., Ltd., Bristol,

Lord Inchcape, Director of the National Provincial and Union Bank of England, Ltd.,

Mr. Walter Leaf, Chairman of the London County, Westminster and Parrs Bank, Ltd., and

Mr. D. Drummond Fraser, Joint Managing Director of the Manchester and Liverpool District Banking Co., Ltd.

We have also received a number of communications in writing from gentlemen in various parts of the country, in response to a notice which we inserted in the Press inviting representations from the public generally. Unfortunately, time did not permit of our taking oral evidence from more than a limited number of witnesses.

3. Bank absorptions and amalgamations are, of course, no new phenomenon in this country. About 300 instances have occurred in the past, more than half of which have taken place in the last 50 years. In one or two cases arrangements made

provisionally for amalgamations have been defeated by the opposition of local customers of the bank which it was proposed to absorb ; but, on the whole, banking policy has gradually but steadily pursued the path of consolidation and absorption, and, until recently, the amalgamations effected have, generally speaking, been carried through without stirring up serious opposition or arousing public interest. As a result, the number of private banks has fallen from 37 to 6 since 1891, and the number of English joint stock banks from 106 to 34 during the same period.

4. Several recent amalgamations, however, have undoubtedly provoked an unusual amount of interest, and have been seriously criticised in certain quarters. This change in public opinion appears to be due mainly to the fact that amalgamations have changed their type and consist no longer in the absorption of a local bank by a larger and more widely spread joint stock bank, but in the union of two joint stock banks, both already possessing large funds and branches spread over a wide area. These two types of amalgamation differ very materially from one another, and arguments used to justify the former type do not necessarily apply to the latter.

THE OLD TYPE OF AMALGAMATION—ABSORPTION OF LOCAL BANKS BY A LARGER AND MORE WIDELY-SPREAD JOINT STOCK BANK.

5. As modern amalgamations are mainly of the new type, it is unnecessary for us to elaborate the various arguments used in connection with amalgamations of the older type. Very briefly, what the arguments amount to is that both the local (or more or less local) bank and the larger widely-spread bank secure to their customers certain advantages of a different kind, but that, like other institutions, each has also the defects of its qualities. Some districts—notably Lancashire and Yorkshire—have clung to their local banks. But in most instances amalgamation schemes have been carried out without serious difficulty, and if material hardship had resulted to the trade generally in the districts affected, there would no doubt have been greater local opposition to subsequent absorption schemes, and new local banks would even have been opened.

The New Type of Amalgamation—Union of one Large Joint Stock Bank with another similar Bank.

6. As regards the new type of amalgamation, the main arguments laid before us in support of the policy of amalgamation are as follows :—

(a) *The convenience and gain to Trade secured by an extension of Bank areas.*—Just as the large banks of the past secured certain advantages to trade by collecting deposits from parts of the country where they were not required, and placing them at the disposal of other parts which stood in need of advances, so it is claimed that this process can be carried still further with advantage by amalgamating large banks with one another.

This is no doubt true, though, of course, the degree to which an extension of area is in fact secured by amalgamating banks differs considerably in each case. The following table is an analysis of two recent amalgamations and one proposed amalga-amtion in this respect :—

TABLE I.
NUMBERS IN 1918 (IN ROUND FIGURES).

	London Branches.	Provincial Branches (excluding Sub-Branches and including only one Branch in each Place).	Foreign Agencies held
(a) { National Provincial	26	251	31
(a) { Union of London and Smiths	31	78	150
(b) { London County and Westminster	110	180	400
(b) { Parrs	35	160	35
(c) { London City and Midland . .	107	419	850
(c) { London Joint Stock	41	109	70

Note.—In London an amalgamation can secure no material extension of area, and usually means a net reduction in the number of competing banks in the City, as all other important competitors are already represented there and cannot therefore, as is sometimes the case in other districts, add a new element of competition to counterbalance the amalgamation. Should no such new element arise, there will be a similar net reduction in the number of competing banks in nearly all the most important towns outside London at which the second of the two banks was represented in cases (a) and (c) above, as the first bank in each case was established at most of them already. As regards the provinces generally, excluding sub-branches and sub-agencies, in the above cases the first bank in each case secured the following number of new places out of the total number taken over, viz., (a) 51 (out of 78), (b) 152 (out of 160), (c) 54 (out of 109). In cases (a) and (c) very few of the new places secured were in towns of importance. The 55 overlapping places in case (c) include such towns as Barnsley, Barrow, Darlington, Doncaster, Gateshead, Grimsby, Hull, Leeds, Middlesbrough, Newcastle, Portsmouth, Sheffield, West Hartlepool and York ; and in case (a) the 27 overlapping places included Bath, Birmingham, Bournemouth, Bradford, Brighton, Bristol, Derby, Doncaster, Exeter, Grimsby, Huddersfield, Hull, Leeds, Lincoln, Nottingham, Plymouth, Sheffield, Southampton and York.

It should be added that, in case (c), in addition to the branches shown above, the Joint Stock Bank have 106 sub-branches in small places where they have no branch, and that in only about nine of those places are the City and Midland represented. Similarly, the Union of London and Smiths had a number of sub-branches in small places, at most of which the National Provincial were not represented.

There must come a point when the policy of substituting one large bank for two will usually mean a very small extension of area, if any, and some reduction of competition. That point has already been reached in London, and is being approached in a few of the largest towns where most of the important competing banks are already established.

It should be added that if both the amalgamating units have, before amalgamation, lent up to their full resources, home trade *as a whole* cannot gain any increase in accommodation as a result of the amalgamation. Except at the expense of smaller traders, large trade combines could not obtain larger advances in all from the combined resources of the amalgamation than they obtained from the separate banks before.

(b) *The argument from size.*—Numerous representations have reached us to the effect that large banks are better for traders, and particularly for large traders, than small banks because, with their larger resources, they can safely make individual advances on a more generous scale. And it is argued that banks must grow now to keep pace with the growth in size of business houses generally, and to enable them to deal with the demands of after-the-war trade both at home and abroad.

TABLE II.

PAID-UP CAPITAL, RESERVE AND DEPOSITS OF THE FOLLOWING BANKS AS SHOWN IN THEIR BALANCE SHEETS OF 31ST DECEMBER, 1913, AND 31ST DECEMBER, 1917.

	31st December, 1913.	31st December, 1917.
	£	£
London City and Midland . . .	101,882,230	230,083,434
London County and Westminster .	} 143,000,000	228,000,000
Parrs		
National Provincial	} 118,864,590	185,223,173
Union of London and Smiths . .		
Lloyds	98,720,663	183,076,718
	June, 1914.	
Barclays	66,940,267	135,675,971
	31st December, 1913.	
London Joint Stock	41,678,237	62,274,280

This is an important point. Various Government Committees have drawn special attention to the question of banking facilities after the war, and it is very desirable that all possible steps should be taken to adapt the banking interest to the new position which will then arise. The point, however, with regard to the size of banks is one of degree only, and it is a question whether the continued practice on the part of exceptionally large firms of resorting to two or more banks, instead of one, for advances would not suffice to meet all their needs, and whether the existing large banks are not in fact large enough to meet the requirements of the immediate future, at any rate if supplemented, as far as may be necessary, by combinations for special purposes on the lines of German " Konsortiums " or otherwise. We have received no conclusive evidence on this point. But the table on page 222 shows, at any rate, that the resources of our leading banks were very substantial even before the recent amalgamations.

The above argument with regard to post-war trade can of course only be used with some caution as regards foreign trade, in view of the special dependence of English banks on deposits withdrawable at call or on short notice. This is especially the case as regards long-term advances for such trade, to which special reference is sometimes made. The following figures, taken from the *Economist*, show how comparatively small are the capital and reserves of English joint stock banks :—

TABLE III.

	Paid-up Capital and Reserves.	Deposits.	Ratio.
	Million £	Million £	Per cent.
1890	68	369	18
1895	69	456	15
1900	79	587	13
1905	82	628	13
1910	81	721	11
1915	82	993	8
1917	84	1,365	6

7. We have endeavoured to review impartially the arguments which have been put forward as justifying the necessity in the public interest—quite apart from questions of profit to shareholders—of bringing about the new type of bank amalgamation. There is undoubtedly much weight in these arguments as far as they go. And even if the absolute *necessity* of large new amalgamations is not clearly proved, yet the absence of proof of the public necessity for business re-organisations is not, in itself, any reason for objecting to them, and it is a serious step at any time to interfere with the natural developments of trade. Before, therefore, considering any restrictive proposals, we endeavoured to ascertain what is the real basis of the fears—often vaguely felt, and vaguely expressed — which have undoubtedly been aroused by recent amalgamation schemes. The main grounds for objecting to further amalgamations appear to be as follows :—

(a) *Writing down of Bank Capital.*—The proportion of capital to deposits is now so small in the case of English joint stock

banks, even excluding the temporary war increase in the amount
of deposits, that any further shrinkage of bank capital is clearly
undesirable, in the interest of depositors, if it can be avoided.
Attention has been drawn to the fact that amalgamation schemes
usually mean a reduction in the total paid-up capital and uncalled
liability of the two pre-amalgamation units. This has frequently
been the case in the past, and it has also been a feature of recent
amalgamations and proposed amalgamations. The amalgamation of the National Provincial Bank of England, Ltd., with the
Union of London and Smiths Bank, Ltd., resulted in a reduction
of over £1,000,000, or 16 per cent., in the total paid-up capital,
and of over £9,000,000, or over 48 per cent., in the uncalled
liability of the Union shareholders. The amalgamation of Parrs
Bank, Ltd., with the London County and Westminster Bank,
Ltd., while it resulted in an addition of £243,000 to the total
paid-up capital, brought about a reduction of nearly £1,770,000,
or 17 per cent., in the uncalled liability of Parrs shareholders.
The proposed amalgamation of the London City and Midland
Bank, Ltd., with the London Joint Stock Bank, Ltd., would
effect a reduction of nearly £1,000,000 in the total paid-up
capital, and of over £9,000,000, or over 50 per cent., in the uncalled
liability of the Joint Stock Bank shareholders.   In each of these
three cases, therefore, substantial benefits to shareholders are
purchased at the expense of some of the security of the depositors.
But the reduction of capital (as opposed to the reduction of uncalled liability) resulting in two of the cases appears to be only
nominal, the sum written off, or some sum approximating to it,
being added to the inner reserves, at any rate at present.

(b) *Dangers of reduced Competition.*—Although, in the past, we
believe that amalgamations have not, in most instances, led to
a reduction of bank competition, yet, as we have pointed out
in paragraph 6 (a) above, in London (and possibly before long
in certain large towns) amalgamations between large joint stock
banks must now usually mean a net reduction in the number of
competing banks.   It is true that this reduction is only slight in
each case, and that there still remain at present a fair number
of competing banks.   But we have received representations from
certain municipal corporations to the effect that banks vary very
much in their willingness to allow reasonable overdraft facilities
to corporations, and that sufficient money, and cheap enough
money, has only been obtained hitherto by resorting to different
banks, the number of which is now falling steadily.   On this
ground a number of resolutions have been forwarded to us by
corporations protesting against further amalgamations, and sug-
gesting that it is not in the national interest that large funds
belonging to the public should be in the hands of a few companies.

Strong representations have, on similar grounds, been made to us on behalf of the Stock Exchange and the Money Market. It is claimed that the world-wide fame of the London Market before the war was due to the freedom with which London bills could be negotiated, owing to the ease with which Discount Houses obtained ample funds from a wide number of banks, and that the fewer the lending constituents in the Discount Market, the less flexible is the market and the less fine the rates. It is added that the number of members in the Clearing House is already becoming very small, and that any further decrease in the number of its constituent members, or any greatly preponderant power on the part of particular members, might impair confidence in its smooth working and raise apprehensions in the market. Moreover, it is pointed out that a reduction in the number of important banks must mean, and has already meant, a reduction in the number of first-class acceptors of bills, and that if this reduction proceeded very far, it would become a question whether the Bank of England would not have to place a limit on the amount of acceptances which they would take from any particular bank doing a large accepting business, and whether Continental buyers would not limit the number of bills taken by them.

(c) *The Danger of Monopoly.*—It has been represented to us that there is a real danger lest one bank, by the gradual extension of its connections, may obtain such a position that it can attract an altogether preponderant amount of banking business ; or, alternatively, lest two banks may approach such a position independently, and then achieve it by amalgamation.

Any approach to a banking combine or Money Trust, by this or any other means, would undoubtedly cause great apprehension to all classes of the community and give rise to a demand for nationalising the banking trade. Such a combine would mean that the financial safety of the country, and the interest of individual depositors and traders, would be placed in the hands of a few individuals, who would naturally operate mainly in the interests of the shareholders. Moreover, the position of the Bank of England—which would, it may be assumed, stand outside any such Trust—would be seriously undermined by so overwhelming a combination, and the Bank might find it extremely difficult to carry out its very important duties as supporter and regulator of the Money Market. Any such result would, in our opinion, be a grave menace to the public interest.

Further, it has been represented to us that the Government of the day might not find it easy to adopt a course of which the combine, for its own reasons, disapproved.

While we believe that there is at present no idea of a Money Trust, it appears to us not altogether impossible that circumstances might produce something approaching to it at a comparatively early date. Experience shows that, in order to preserve an approximate equality of resources and of competitive power, the larger English banks consider it necessary to meet each important amalgamation, sooner or later, by another. If, therefore, the argument from size, referred to in paragraph 6 (*b*) above, is to prevail, it can only lead, and fairly rapidly, to the creation of a very few preponderant combinations ; and if those combinations amalgamated, or entered into a joint agreement as to rates and policy, etc., the Money Trust would immediately spring to birth.

8. Such are the main arguments laid before us against further amalgamations. Undoubtedly some of the dangers feared are somewhat problematical and remote, and we should very much have preferred to avoid the necessity for any interference by Government with the administration of banking. But on a careful review of all the above considerations, we are forced to the conclusion that the possible dangers resulting from further large amalgamations are material enough to outweigh the arguments against Government interference, and that, in view of the exceptional extent to which the interests of the whole community depend on banking arrangements, some measure of Government control is essential. Our conclusions on this point were confirmed by the resolution passed at the recent annual meeting of the Association of Chambers of Commerce, in which it was proposed that steps should be taken to guard against amalgamations, etc., shown to be injurious to commercial interests.

We therefore recommend that legislation be passed requiring that the prior approval of the Government must be obtained before any amalgamations are announced or carried into effect. And, in order that such legislation may not merely have the effect of producing hidden amalgamations instead, we recommend that all proposals for interlocking directorates, or for agreements which in effect would alter the status of a bank as regards its separate entity and control, or for purchase by one bank of the shares of another bank, be also submitted for the prior approval of the Government before they are carried out.

As general principles to be acted upon at present by the Government at its discretion, we would suggest that a scheme for amalgamating or absorbing a small local bank, or any scheme of amalgamation designed to secure important new facilities for the public or a really considerable and material extension of area or sphere of activity for the larger of the two banks affected, should normally be considered favourably, but that if an amalgamation scheme involves an appreciable overlap of area without securing such advantages, or would result in undue predominance on the part of the larger bank, it should be refused. Consideration should also, in our opinion, be given to the question of the clerical labour—usually very large—involved by amalgamations during the war, and to the undesirability of permitting an unusual aggregation of deposits without fully adequate capital and reserves.

9. It only remains to make a suggestion as to which Government department or departments should be charged with the responsibility of approving or disapproving amalgamation schemes, etc., under our proposal above. On the whole, we think that the approval both of the Treasury and of the Board of Trade should be obtained and that legislation should be passed requiring the two departments to set up a special Statutory Committee to advise them, the members of which should be nominated by the departments from time to time, for such period as may seem desirable, and should consist of one commercial representative and one financial representative, with power to appoint an arbitrator, should they disagree.

10. We desire to place on record our deep sense of the obligations which we are under to our Secretary, Mr. C. L. Stocks, for the very valuable assistance he has rendered to us in our deliberations and in the preparation of our report.

> COLWYN.
> CUNLIFFE.
> R. E. BECKETT.
> HERBERT C. GIBBS.
> ARTHUR A. HAWORTH.
> R. V. VASSAR-SMITH.
> J. S. PURCELL.
> HENRY KESWICK.
> H. McGOWAN.
> E. MANVILLE.
> JOHN RAE.
> DOUGLAS VICKERS.

C. L. STOCKS,
  Secretary,
   1st May, 1918.

INDEX

Printed in Great Britain by Butler & Tanner Ltd., Frome and London